1991

William James,
Public Philosopher

William James,

PUBLIC PHILOSOPHER

George Cotkin

The Johns Hopkins University Press
BALTIMORE AND LONDON

New Studies in American Intellectual and Cultural History
Thomas Bender, *Editor*

Frontispiece photograph by Pach. By permission of the Houghton Library,
Harvard University.

The Johns Hopkins University Press
701 West 40th Street
Baltimore, MD 21211
The Johns Hopkins Press Ltd., London

The paper used in this publication meets the minimum requirements
of American National Standard for Information Sciences—Permanence
of Paper for Printed Library Materials, ANSI Z39.48–1984.

Library of Congress Cataloging-in-Publication Data
Cotkin, George, 1950–
William James, public philosopher / George Cotkin.
p. cm.—(New studies in American intellectual and cultural history)
Bibliography: p.
Includes index.
ISBN 0-8018-3878-9 (alk. paper)
1. James, William, 1842–1910.   I. Title.   II. Series.
B945.J24C65   1989
191—dc20   89-33036   CIP

for my parents, Estelle and Morris Cotkin,
and Marta Peluso

If philosophy is more a matter of passionate vision than of logic—and I believe it is, logic only finding reasons for the vision afterwards—must not such thinness come either from the vision being defective in the disciples, or from their passion, matched with Fechner's or with Hegel's own passion, being as moonlight unto sunlight or as water unto wine?
—WILLIAM JAMES, *A Pluralistic Universe*

For a man is never an individual; it would be more fitting to call him a *universal singular*. Summed up and for this reason universalized by his epoch, he in turn resumes it by reproducing himself in it as singularity. Universal by the singular universality of human history, singular by the universalizing singularity of his projects, he requires simultaneous examination from both ends.
—JEAN-PAUL SARTRE, *The Family Idiot*

Contents

Acknowledgments

One of the more joyful moments attendant upon the completion of a book manuscript is the opportunity to thank many individuals for their support. My initial introduction to William James as a research subject came during a National Endowment for the Humanities/American Studies Association summer seminar on the Newtonian and Darwinian revolutions in American thought, which was organized by Murray Murphey and Bruce Kuklick. Although other projects intervened before I could pursue work on James, that seminar proved fruitful in terms of ideas and friends. Bruce Kuklick, David Hollinger, and Fred Matthews were all teachers at Haverford that summer, and their advice and example have sustained me over the years. The insight, support, and friendship of two other participants, James Hoopes and Robert Rydell, have proven the most precious returns of that summer sojourn.

Many scholars have commented on portions of the manuscript, discussed James with me, or offered helpful suggestions. Strongest thanks to Ann Schofield, Craig Harlan, Sarah Elbert, and Robert Rydell. Others—some scholars, some prone to more normal occupations—have sustained me throughout this project or offered suggestions and deserve my appreciation: Warren Van Tine, Nantawan and Jonathan McLeod, Debbie Forczek, Diane Michelfelder, Bob Wolf, Robert Burton, Jon Ericson, Bill Preston, Quintard Taylor, Ed Mayo, Max Riedlsperger, Nelson Lichtenstein, Eileen Boris, Henry May, John McDermott, Lewis Perry, and Ralph Leck. Thomas Bender, editor of the series of which this book is a part, has been supportive and insightful. I also wish to thank Henry Y. K. Tom of the Johns Hopkins University Press for seeing this work through publication. Finally, Jane Warth has been a careful and concerned editor; her trained eye saved me from many errors.

No scholar can function or survive without the expertise and friendly assistance of librarians. I especially want to thank Jean Gordon, Pamela

Williams, Janice Stone, and Neil Anderson, all of California Polytechnic
State University's Interlibrary Loan, for receiving my multitude requests
with humor and alacrity. The entire staff of Cal Poly's Kennedy Library
has been helpful to this project. The staffs at the Houghton Library at
Harvard University, in particular, and at Stanford University Library and
the Bancroft Library at the University of California, Berkeley, are also to
be commended for their professionalism and good spirit.

Two grants from Cal Poly helped to finance a research trip to Cambridge, as did a Travel to Collections grant from the National Endow-
ment for the Humanities. Permission to quote from previously published
material has been generously granted by the *Historian* for "Ralph Waldo
Emerson and William James as Public Philosophers" 49 (November
1986); *San Jose Studies* for "William James and the 'Weightless' Nature of
Modern Existence" 12 (Spring 1986); and *ETC.: A Review of General
Semantics* for "William James and the Cash-Value Metaphor: The Cash
Value of a Metaphor" 42 (Spring 1985). Permission to use materials in the
James Family Papers has been gracefully granted by Mr. Alexander R.
James and the Houghton Library.

Although their names are mentioned above, a few people deserve further thanks. David Hollinger, through a blend of critical and supportive
comments, as well as by his example, has been an inspiration for my work
in American intellectual history. Warren Van Tine of Ohio State University has been a longtime friend and onetime adviser whose strictures and
admonitions were always tinged with practicality and caring. Robert
Burton, formerly head of Cal Poly's History Department, has always, in
both his official and unofficial capacities, done all he could to support me
and to further this project.

This book is dedicated to my parents, Estelle and Murray Cotkin, and
to my wife, Marta Peluso. My parents have never wavered, despite all
sorts of provocations on my part, in their support of me and my work. For
their faith and love, I dedicate this book to them. Marta Peluso, artist,
spirit of generosity and vision, has lovingly forced me to focus my energies upon this project and life.

William James, Public Philosopher

CHAPTER ONE

Introduction:
The Varieties of Context

While the once-familiar names and massive tomes of many nineteenth-century philosophers gather their expected amounts of neglect and dust, the personality and ideas of William James (1842–1910) continue to compel our attention. We are drawn to James because he forcefully confronted the essential problems of modernity—the metaphysics of the abyss, the bewildering plurality of a world growing at the edges, the nightmare of reason, and the numbing freedom of subjectivity. His responses to these signposts of the modern world were exuberant but tentative, personal yet philosophical, invariably couched in his familiar dichotomies and mediations: neither an optimist nor a pessimist, James preferred to call himself a "meliorist"; a defender of the variety and efficacy of religious faith, he never abandoned the stance of science. His strictures upon the strenuous and heroic life of action remain a valiant, if shaky, attempt to steer between the twin horrors of the *fin-de-siècle* attitude captured by Théophile Gautier as the choice of either boredom or barbarism.[1] James's wrestling matches with the inner demons of his life history (depression, illness, doubt) and with the pressing philosophical issues of his day (the nature of truth, the structure of experience, the psychology of consciousness) are made more enticing because of his jaunty expressiveness. The literary genes of the James family worked to perfection in this philosopher; who else would have had the audacity, or the élan, to balance the language for his conception of truth upon the precarious but delicious metaphor of "cash-value," or to ask us, in contemplating our relationship to the universe, to imagine ourselves as a cat in a library, surrounded by books but not understanding the knowledge in them or even capable of comprehending what they might represent? James further impresses us with a contagious openness that granted a fair and extended hearing to psychics, mystics, and partisans for the "Anaesthetic Revelation." Finally, who else could achieve all of these things while composing an impressive and enduring body of philosophical and psychological analysis?

Given the varied appeal of James and his work, it is not surprising that the cultural and philosophical arbiters of our day increasingly turn to James for inspiration, direction, or justification. For some he is the exemplar of the modern spirit, for others he is the postmodernist *in abstentia*.[2] Some take a "stroll" with James while others invoke him for political or poetic projects.[3] The danger in treating him quite so gingerly is that, in claiming him as one of our own, we often wrench him from his own historicity. We reduce, in the process, this historically grounded and complex figure into a document to be quoted and thereby contained for our purposes. We do to James exactly what he condemned as the rationalist fiction of subsuming the plurality of experience into a block universe of explanation. The validity, and perhaps even the epistemological necessity, of employing James for our current needs is not denigrated here. But what we gain for our present purposes on the one side, we perhaps lose on the other in terms of fully comprehending James as a historical figure.

The impetus behind this book, in addition to seeking to bathe itself and its reader in the warm light of James's personality and ideas, is to return James to the context of his life and time: not in order to imprison him in the cell of a useless past, but to release him from the chains of present-day amnesia about his past. James is great because he is *ours,* but he was also *theirs,* someone who belonged to an earlier era in America's history. His continuing relevance is the mark of his release from the past. It also serves as a reminder of how some of our present realities were initially forged from the crucible of the last half of the nineteenth century. To recapture James's historical context, then, is to understand both him and ourselves better.

I

This book is an avowedly contextualist reading of James and his philosophy. It is predicated upon the assumption that the personal, philosophical, and historical are emphatically connected. This is not to suggest that approaches which emphasize the purely philosophical or essentially biographical are without value. It is my assumption, however, that an analysis combining all three perspectives promises more in terms of general understanding than any single viewpoint. All too often analysts of philosophy—and certainly students of James may be included in this indictment—are guilty of failing to place philosopher and philosophy within the historical moment.[4] This results, writes Alasdair MacIntyre, in "an abstraction of these writers from the cultural and social milieus in which they lived and thought and so the history of their thought acquires a false independence from the rest of the culture."[5]

Debate over the epistemological validity and pragmatic utility of a contextualist reading of any individual or text currently rages within the historical profession. There are those who follow Jacques Derrida in eschewing any context as a category useful for situating either the thinker or the work. Deconstructionists prefer to ground the text within its own boundaries, though such boundaries are expanded regularly to include other texts and, of course, the context of language.[6] Another view calls for the reading of great texts mainly with regard to their implications for our current intellectual needs and controversies.[7] Other theorists, most notably Quentin Skinner and John Dunn, continue to hold to the validity of a contextualist reading, while requiring that the historian pay close attention to the linguistic conventions that surround any textual expression. By so doing, they submit, the historian can understand the critical but often hidden questions to which a particular philosophical or political text was originally addressed.[8]

However we draw the line of interpretation around an individual philosopher and his or her text, be it with an eye toward intentionality, social interaction, or cultural placement, there remains the charge, raised most uncompromisingly for historians by Dominick LaCapra, that one will never find "*the* context."[9] Complex texts have too many contexts, all highly controversial, that conspire to undermine historians in their quest to render the work of philosophy or literature comfortable within a particular and meaningful interpretation. Indeed, as another intellectual historian, John P. Diggins, has phrased it, contextualists are faced with the disconcerting hypothesis that "the genesis of an idea may defy the immediate context of time and space."[10] With the demise of context, one might claim, the practice of history falls by the wayside, to be replaced with literary criticism.

The "intractability of the text" argument can be engaged, and perhaps even rebutted, on pragmatic principles. The value of a theory, James was fond of saying, is less a matter of its abstracted truth value than of its "cash-value." This categorization in terms of theory means that the validity of a contextualist positioning of the philosopher and philosophy within the crucible of society, culture, and politics must reside in how well this perspective leads us forward by bringing forth new insight and understanding. In the end, it matters less whether each of these designations is logically coherent or even if it is a reified entity. What does matter is the degree to which our contextualization impels us toward interesting, instructive, or just plain useful interpretations. Thus the contextualist interpretation within this book asks to be evaluated according to how well the reader can "ride" its conclusions toward a fuller appreciation of James, his philosophy, and his public context.[11]

My contextualization will examine the cultural, social, and political realities that surrounded James. These contexts are historical in nature, subject to change, and particularly important for the era in which James lived and wrote. To be sure, the designation of a historical context, as I define it, is limited by nature: its definition is a function of how one proposes the task. We may, quite correctly, designate as historically contextual the reading that situates James within the flow of the history of philosophy. This approach, which casts an eye toward James in relation to previous and subsequent philosophers, is especially valuable. Its import grows out of the powerful fact that James was first and foremost a philosopher and psychologist, someone whose reputation ultimately depends upon the strength and influence of his ideas. I have no unrelenting quarrel with the results or methodology of the philosophical or history-of-ideas approach to James. But I do think that another perspective on James might be profitably offered.

Perhaps it will be excusable in the name of clarity to give a quick description of the thesis and findings that arise out of my contextualist methodology. I argue that James's life and thought may be fully comprehended, and the grand contours of this great thinker heartily embraced, by demonstrating the centrality of his role as public philosopher. To be a public philosopher meant accepting responsibility for addressing public problems and for applying insights gained from one's technical work to public issues; James did this during his years of greatest success and acclaim, from 1890 until his death in 1910. The direction of this philosophical engagement was not a simple trickle down from technical to public, professional to popular. As is demonstrated in the final chapter of this book, popular concerns and public issues also rose up to influence and to inscribe themselves within the texts of James's most enduring professional philosophy. The lines between professional and public philosophy are usefully blurred, excitingly interactive. Moreover, James's public posture, expressed in both his popular and professional philosophy, is in many ways exemplary of the engage intellectual who many find regrettably absent from the scene of present-day academic and public life. When viewed through the interpretive glass of public philosophy, James's life and thought demonstrate that one can effectively balance the demands for philosophical depth with the needs of a public presence.[12]

When we proceed from this angle of vision, a new view of James begins to emerge: not James as the philosopher forever alone in his study struggling with Immanuel Kant or Josiah Royce's Absolute, or James as the artist whose *sui generis* genius transformed everything he touched.[13] Instead, we see a James of yet another story, a philosopher whose life was intimately linked with public concerns and who directed much of his writing toward issues of cultural moment. The results of such a perspective, the fruits of my interpretive tree are: (1) a new comprehension of the central import of the popular lectures and writings to James's life and thought, as well as a recognition of how the public dimension echoes within his more technical works of philosophy; (2) an emphasis upon the critical role played by a discourse of heroism in James's life and philosophy; (3) an explication of the depth and significance of James's work as a public philosopher; (4) a new recognition of the crucial interplay in James's early years between individual and social problems mediated through philosophical rumination; (5) an awareness of the philosophical importance and challenge that America's march into imperialism presented to James's philosophy of heroism; and (6) an explanation of how the text of *Pragmatism* (1907) is not only philosophically redolent but also representative of James's deepest reckoning with the problems of *tedium vitae* and imperial will, which were critical to his cultural milieu.

I choose to pursue a more external interpretation of James than has been attempted by other scholars. I examine James's more popular writings and philosophical masterworks less for their inherent brilliance or approximation of philosophical truth than as expressions of and interventions into the life and culture of the period from 1880 to 1910. James and his work are case studies of the interactive dialogue between individual and culture, ideas and public problems. This book chronicles the sustained attempt of an inspired, yet not unrepresentative, intellectual to grapple with cultural, social, and political forces. It attempts to see in this confrontation the dialectically mutual influence of culture acting upon the individual and of the individual acting upon the culture. James is returned to the incubus of his culture and society but not because I think that these abstract formulations will explain everything about him. But I do hope that my mode of external contextualization will serve as a useful and suggestive companion to the abundant examples that internally analyze James and his philosophy.

II

This book alternates between the public and the private James, between his ideas and their social expression. I attempt to locate James and his philosophy within the social, political, and cultural realms. But the focus of attention within this imperative shifts between chapters two and three and the chapters that follow them. The former engage the public and social aspects of James's private life. Chapters four and five place James within the general contours of the long-term cultural problems that dominated the American scene from 1880 until his death. This contexualization serves to develop the general foundation for chapters six and seven, which consider James's confrontation with the rise of American imperialism and his philosophical intercessions against it. Thus the initial emphasis is upon joining the social and the private; the subsequent desire is to situate the private and philosophical within the context of society.

The familiar, yet crucial, terrain of James's early years is the starting point for my inquiry. This is hardly new territory for analysts of James. Howard M. Feinstein, Cushing Strout, and R.W.B. Lewis, to name only a few, have demonstrated the importance of the intimate relationship between James's early life history and his later philosophical expression.[14] The basic elements of this connection between biography and philosophy form around James's vocational dispute with his father; William wanted to follow the artistic calling only to find his hopes crushed by the "benign tyranny" of a father who desired that his son become a scientist. The father's victory, according to most interpreters, was achieved at great cost to the son. With the demise of art as vocation, William soon found himself caught in a web of depression, debility, and doubt.[15] The final resolution of these problems, while perhaps largely a function of a psychological restructuring of James's life, eventually found expression in his mature philosophical formulations of the will to believe, the strenuous life, and pragmatism. Although interpretations differ over the exact genesis of James's difficulties and their resolution, all scholars essentially respect the important nexus between youthful problems and mature philosophical doctrines.[16]

I wish to neither demur from the important insights that these scholars have furnished to students of James nor question the crucial connection between James's personal history and his particular philosophical doctrines. Where I differ is in my placement of the problem. Most analysts of James intensively direct their emphasis toward the family situation. There are compelling reasons, to be sure, for this precise and excited attention. The internal dynamics of the family, the mercurial, omnipresent father, Henry James, Sr., the brilliant siblings, Alice and Henry, and the fascinating expressions of illness and neurosis all combine to make the Jameses, with the possible exception of the Adamses, into the leading family of American intellectual life in the nineteenth century. No historian can fare too badly by snuggling close to the intellectual and emotional fire of William James's family context.

However, we must remember that James's problems—inability to decide upon vocation, difficulties with decision-making, metaphysical uncertainty, and nagging physical ailments—were common to many young men of James's social, intellectual, and economic class. Of course, the particular expressions of James's difficulties were to a significant degree defined by the always peculiar circumstances of the James family. These problems, however, were not unusual. Building upon Feinstein's excellent research, chapters two and three of this book therefore reexamine the private quandaries of William James from a different perspective.[17] In these chapters James's personal life is fitted into the fabric of his society and culture to discern exactly how his problems were common to his generational cohort. If this tends to lessen the singularity of James's difficulties, it neither denies them nor negates their importance to the development of his philosophical program.

A new comprehension of James's early years emerges through emphasizing the social parameters of his crisis. The Civil War becomes, quite as much as his celebrated vocational dispute with his father, a significant factor in James's crisis of confidence. Nonparticipation in that conflict looms as a missed experience. James is placed within the category, first described by his friend Oliver Wendell Holmes, Jr., of being one "judged not to have lived," of being condemned for not participating in the crucial defining event of their generation.[18] When James's nonparticipation in the war is compared with the experiences of his friends who did fight, his continuing problems with doubt and debility become more understandable, though no less central. The Civil War alleviated the vocational indecision, as well as the physical and emotional maladies, common to many of James's friends. In essence, the horror and thrill of combat strangely allowed participants in the war to shake off their youthful doubts and debilities. For those young men who did not participate, emotional and vocational uncertainty continued to fester. Even after James emerged from his depressive years in the mid-1870s, the consuming fact of his nonparticipation in battle remained a troubling concern. This sense of having been "judged not to have lived" eventually exercised itself within James's mature philosophy, in the ideas of the strenuous life and of the moral equivalent of war, and within his general moral and religious philosophy. The context of the Civil War, then, helps to expand our understanding of the private nature of James's vocational angst and concomitant depression, while serving as an additional explanation for the central aspects and concerns of his mature philosophical expression.

The stigmata of James's depressive years—the divided self, intense and numbing doubt, philosophical and physical invalidism—anticipated attitudes that would come to dominate the form and content of certain segments of late nineteenth-century American culture.[19] The problems of the individual, first experienced by James in the early 1860s, were propelled by the social and personal predicaments he had encountered in the denial of his art career and failure to serve in the Civil War. Both were further complicated by the prolonged and often-repressed conflict of wills with his father. In this sense, the private and the public combined to mold the identity of young William James. James's socially inscribed and privately experienced identity problems became philosophically useful and publicly engaging when they assumed public symbolism; they eventually were viewed as a social expression of the plight of modern men and women.[20]

The precise genesis of the crisis of individual autonomy which gripped Americans in the late nineteenth century is difficult to pinpoint; it appears as a constellation of ideas, emotions, and suspicions that something was amiss with traditional views of the individual and with the arena in which the individual was expected to perform. A case can be made, and applied to James's particular doubts, for granting priority to scientism as the causal agent in the crisis of the individual. In this view, the implications of mechanistic science and the impact of Darwinism plunged many thoughtful Americans into a state of intellectual somnambulance. They suffered because science as a cultural icon or normative concept seemed to have dangerously undermined many cherished assumptions of American religion and individualism.[21] Natural theology, no less than natural-rights theory, fell into benign neglect, if not disrepute, as scientific ideas gained cultural hegemony. Although many intellectuals proved inventive and effective in combining the new assumptions of science with previously favored religious ideals, the effective weight of this revolution in science was to raise more questions than it answered. Consequently, doubt appeared as a defining and characteristic stance for many intellectuals.[22] For those intellectuals who still preached a doctrine of confident progress, their nostrums increasingly seemed shallow, vain attempts to convince themselves that science meant no harm to traditional systems of thought.

Also severely wounded by the implications of a mechanistic science were assumptions that supported freedom of will, individual possibility, and autonomy.[23] James both experienced and captured this intellectual and emotional predicament caused by mechanistic science when he complained, in 1869, that "we are wholly conditioned, that not a wiggle of our will happens save as the result of physical laws."[24] What would later serve as the agenda he addressed in the famous essay "The Dilemma of Determinism" (1884) was thus already recognized by the young James as the essential philosophical bugaboo to be dispelled if freedom—even when defined as a useful fiction—would have any play within the world. James eventually resolved this dilemma by retaining his faith in science as method while continuing to champion the causes of the individual will and of religious belief. In developing this solution, James responded to both narrow concerns within the history of philosophy and to general cultural problematics centered around this widely perceived and experienced crisis of the individual will. James's problems, in essence, replicated the general intellectual difficulties that afflicted his cultural milieu.[25]

James confronted the crisis of the individual will for reasons other than the dilemma of determinism or as a result of the presumed inroads upon

the mind made by mechanistic and materialistic science. While his famous and prolonged depression was largely a result of his despair over
personal problems and the philosophical implications of a determinist
view of the world, James's concerns in this period focused upon another
ghost, the terrifying possibility that the universe confronting modern men
and women was not determined but absolutely without order; it was a
void or an abyss. The figure of Hamlet, taken from Shakespeare's play,
which was especially popular in late-nineteenth-century America, came
to represent the plight of an individual facing an uncertain and chaotic
world. Thus chapter three explains James's fear of determinism as only
one side of the coin of his depression, the other side being the legal tender
of what Nietzsche called the certitude of the abyss—the metaphysical
suspicion, or perhaps the certainty, that the universe was without unity
and was indeterminate rather than determined.[26] To a young man such as
James, without a firm and confident ego structure, terror accompanied
the thought that the world might essentially be nothing more than an
"abyss of horrors" or a mere illusion. This recognition was more than
sufficient to plunge James deeper into his depression and debility.[27] The
forgotten but significant "old mole" of metaphysical fear about an indeterminate universe helps to explain the personal and philosophical problems that James ruminated over in the mid-1860s and early 1870s.

It is striking how the imagery of the abyss anticipates and reverses the
vision that would come to form the happy core of James's later metaphysics. In his mature philosophy, the notion of a universe described by
James in *Pragmatism* as essentially "tramp and vagrant," as well as "unfinished, growing in all sorts of places," would become the credo for
voluntarism and choice; plurality and movement would be celebrated as
the linchpins of freedom in the modern world.[28] Freedom and possibility
in an open universe, however, were hardly the tokens of security that
James found himself capable of cashing in during his depressive years.

This dilemma of depression, the fearsome result of envisioning the
universe as either solely deterministic or purely indeterminate, was eventually resolved by James through a mélange of external factors (college
teaching position, marriage), psychological ploys (emphasis upon the
cultivation of habits that would lead to proper beliefs), and philosophical
promptings (his adoption of the attitude of free will, suggested by his
reading of Charles Renouvier). James combined all of these methods into
his philosophical and personal program of renewal. What transformed
James's private problems and solutions into issues of great moment and
public priority was that the problem of the individual—the problem that
James had confronted in the years immediately following the Civil War—
became the common social and economic, as well as intellectual, property of *fin-de-siècle* Americans.

The crisis of individual autonomy that James's mature philosophy addressed was only partly an outgrowth of the implications of Darwinism and various forms of scientism. It also resulted from a host of social, cultural, and economic forces. While it must be emphasized that the crisis of individual autonomy palsied the will of the upper classes most fully, the problem variously afflicted the lives of Americans from diverse backgrounds. In brief, for some upper-class Americans—those whom James addressed most directly in his public pronouncements—the presumed death of free will was concomitant not only to scientific ideas and the rise of religious doubts but also represented an expression of social and cultural difficulties. These Americans felt hemmed into a world of increasing bureaucracy and ease; they confronted what James would designate as the *tedium vitae* of modern life. Existing in a manufactured, incorporated world of decorum and kitsch, the individual wills of some in the upper class became trapped in sentimentality and certain progress. In this view, America seemed a land without zest, and life creaked under the burden of too much comfort, as well as too many respectable prescriptions for the conduct of life.

In response to this perception and reality of tedium, there arose a culturally expressed longing for a life of "intense experience" through which the comfortable elites might recapture some of the intensity associated with an earlier and hardier American experience.[29] But this desire for intensity of experience competed with the equally strong wish for peaceful unity and progress. While constrained by sentimentality, leisured Americans felt comforted by such constraint. As Henry Adams well understood, when one was faced by the world as chaos or dynamo, the appeal of a doctrine of unity and order could not be ignored.[30] This drift between a longing for intense experience and a desire for peaceful order formed the borders of experience for many from James's social world as America approached the turn of the century. James would replicate this dualism and drift in his famous emphases upon the world as one and many, his mediation between science and belief, and his dual notions of a "gospel of relaxation" and "the strenuous life" as the presumed palliatives for the problems of Americans.

For those born into an America of less luxurious circumstances, another crisis of the individual presented itself. Few in the working classes had the time or inclination to bemoan the loss of the frontier of intense experience or to posit order or unity to the world. They were too busy trying, in strenuous fashion, to survive the economic and social rollercoaster ride that defined their era. If workers did hold to any generalized ideology, it was to the constellation of views called the Republican Ethos. Republican views were predicated upon a belief in individual autonomy and possibility. Yet in this period those assumptions threatened to be exposed as a sham. Social theorists such as Henry George and Edward Bellamy spent much print pointing out the contradiction between an ethos that stressed the possibility of individual initiative and hard work resulting in success and the oppressive reality of economic concentration of wealth in the hands of the few, as well as increasing poverty and decreasing opportunities. The prevalence of class tensions and labor strife only seemed proof positive that the era of the mass had replaced that of the individual.[31]

James engaged these issues of cultural, social, and political moment in his professional and popular philosophy. The interventions he developed surfaced out of his own earlier intense wrestling with the problem of the individual will. The familiar Jamesian imperatives of the will to believe, the strenuous life, and the pragmatic attitude became the anodynes that he prescribed to the next generation of neurasthenic and disgruntled Americans.[32] James's passionate vision and espousal of life *in extremis* formed a counterweight to the bureaucratic logic celebrated by those of his generational cohort who had fought in the Civil War. To James's ears, calls for organization and bureaucratic discipline sounded strangely hollow, expressions of the very poison that debilitated the American body politic in the late-nineteenth century.[33] In an interesting turnabout, James, the young man who had not fought, came to formulate a popular philosophical program, a discourse of heroism, that proved a pertinent, powerful, and, ultimately, problematic response to the crisis of the individual will.

III

As noted earlier, the theme that redounds throughout much of this book emphasizes how fully, if unevenly, James addressed the public issues of his day. In this engagement, James accepted and exemplified the role of "public philosopher"; his philosophical doctrines were public statements, or "social expressions," of interest and concern to an audience broader than that of professional philosophers. In addition, his popular writings were not greatly distanced from the technical work. Common concerns and implications flowed out of the work of popular and professional philosophy. Throughout all of his published work, James attempted to maintain the moral imagination of philosophical discourse in the face of inroads made by imaginative literature in the nineteenth century. Philosophy as a vehicle for self-examination and social reflection became a central tenet of James's public philosophy. Public philosophy interrogated social problems and proposed solutions to cultural difficulties.[34]

James communicated his ideas to a wide audience of Americans. Soon after publication of the abridged version of his two-volume *Principles of*

Psychology in 1892, James was much in demand as a speaker on a variety of topics, ranging from "exceptional mental states" and pedagogy to morality and metaphysics. As David A. Hollinger reminds us, many of James's lectures were directed to middle- and upper-class, college-educated men and women who not only shared his prosopographical characteristics but also his concerns about the state of religion and culture in America.[35] The audiences assembled at the universities where James delivered many of his lectures—Harvard, Yale, Brown, Bryn Mawr, Radcliffe, Columbia, Berkeley, and Stanford—were clearly composed of America's ruling elite, or at least those with pretensions of entering into that group. A similar class of auditors were no doubt present when James offered public lectures before the American Philosophical Association, American Psychological Association, Society for Psychical Research, Unitarian Minister's Institute, and even philosopher Thomas Davidson's Catskill Mountain Summer School. And the journals in which many of James's lectures were converted into essays—*Mind,* the *Nation, North American Review*— were hardly subscribed to by masses of Americans. Thus there is certainly strong evidence to support Bruce Kuklick's contention that James's discourse comfortably fell within the bounds of the "acceptable beliefs" of "the articulate public of nineteenth-century New England."[36]

Nevertheless, James also delivered lectures to large crowds of "[g]reat hulking rustics from prairie farms, with their thick hands" and to adoring Chautauqua visitors who celebrated American middle-class proprieties.[37] The published versions of James's lectures on religion, morality, and educational theory did sell widely and probably penetrated into an even more diverse audience. For example, two of his most popular and important lectures—"On a Certain Blindness in Human Beings" and "What Makes a Life Significant"—were culled from their original source, *Talks to Teachers on Psychology* (1899), and published separately as a slim volume entitled *On Some of Life's Ideals* (1900).[38] The best attempt to gauge the wide appeal of James's public philosophy was a rudimentary, but nonetheless interesting, survey conducted by the St. Louis Public Library from 1931 to 1934. This survey, begun twenty-one years after James's death, found that his books were being read by a diverse audience composed of "a trunk maker, machinist, stenographer, retired farmer, clerk, three wives, two physicians, a salesman, and a post office worker," as well as two ministers (one black, one white). Even the more purely professional works, *Pragmatism, A Pluralistic Universe,* and *Some Problems of Philosophy,* were borrowed, and presumably read, by a probation officer, a laundry worker, and several salesmen. These impressionistic samplings do little, of course, to demonstrate conclusively the dispersion of James's public philosophy during his lifetime.[39]

Perhaps the strongest contemporary evaluation of James's popularity in America, and of his intense identification with the aspirations of Americans from a variety of circumstances, was formulated by colleagues and philosophical antagonists. Royce, for example, called James a representative American thinker, someone who expressed "the spiritual life of his own people." George Santayana further noted that James "had a prophetic sympathy with the dawning sentiments of the age, with the moods of the dumb majority. His scattered words caught fire in many parts of the world." The ability to accomplish this end, and in the process to raise questions and to propose solutions to the pressing cultural issues of his day, helps to account for James's popularity and success as a public philosopher; it forms the essential focus of this book.[40]

IV

Following in Ralph Waldo Emerson's footsteps, James was one of the greatest and last of those who assumed the role of public philosopher.[41] Santayana once remarked that public philosophers associated with Harvard in the nineteenth century were "clergymen without a church . . . at once genuine philosophers and popular professors."[42] To Santayana, the institution of public philosophy denigrated the status of the philosopher by forcing him to bow to the tastes and preconceived notions of his auditors. Other problems faced the thinker, such as James, who might aspire to the station of public philosopher. The impetus to simplify and compose philosophy in accessible fashion at times prevented James's discourse from climbing to a summit of high exactitude, sustained exposition, and logical force. Moreover, the time expended in preparing and presenting popular addresses drained limited reserves of energy and postponed completion of the "arch" of James's philosophical system. Public philosophy forced James to both narrow and expand his focus. The flights of analytic philosophy demanded by the professional tribe were grounded in exchange for an accessible confrontation with public issues. This undermined, as James acknowledged in response to his critics, any attempt to develop a systematic philosophy. The public aspects of James's philosophizing also contributed to significant problems in expression. James's repeated attempts to demonstrate the subtlety of pragmatic ideas were often undermined by the jarring rhythms of his metaphors and analogies.[43] But James's chances of ever completing a systematic philosophy in a rigorously technical style of expression, even without his popular presentations, remains debatable; systematization and technical presentation were not James's favored modes of philosophical exposition.

The requirement of public philosophy to make ideas accessible to a general public proved demanding and difficult. It was not impossible, as James demonstrated. Indeed, the corpus of James's philosophy and psychology is marked by the centrality of its popular form of presentation. With the exception of the essays gathered into the posthumously published collection *Essays in Radical Empiricism* (1912), almost all of James's work was directed toward a general audience, rather than a philosophically erudite one. His first book, *The Principles of Psychology* (1890), essentially functioned as a textbook designed to define the field of physiological psychology. That it did more is a testament to James's ability to work within a particular genre while expanding its boundaries. The volume he was working on at the time of his death, *Some Problems of Philosophy* (1911), was also intended as both textbook and summation of his philosophical system. Sandwiched between these two works was a body of popular presentations in which James developed almost all of his significant ideas.

The composition and presentation of public philosophy was not without substantial appeal. It allowed the philosopher to have a public influence and significance that extended well beyond the confining walls of the academy. Presenting himself and his philosophy before the public, James admitted, actually allowed him to keep "more in tune with one's fellow countrymen."[44] In its most buoyant moments, public philosophy furnished the philosopher with an audience and a cause; it permitted him to manufacture a world view that combined personal experiences and philosophical expressions with an eye toward the era's social and cultural issues. In such a manner, the public philosopher occupied the cultural station of the minister without necessarily surrendering his philosophical concerns and conclusions. Philosophy functioned within a public as well as a technical locale; it responded to perennial philosophical problems while lending prestige and presence to historically and culturally specific concerns.

The public philosopher engaged philosophy as an act of edification and education rather than one of systematization and abstraction. Drawing upon some of the distinctions developed by Richard Rorty's *Philosophy and the Mirror of Nature,* the notion of edification suggests that philosophers such as John Dewey, Friedrich Nietzsche, Martin Heidegger, and certainly William James wanted philosophy to be a conversation, a playful yet serious and enlightening confrontation with philosophical and cultural issues.[45] Truth with a capital *T* was not the concern of the edifying philosopher; self-knowledge, playful probing, and fuller intercourse with the world were his imperatives. In setting up familiar divisions between the tough- and tender-minded, or the one and the many, James sought, in the style of philosophy as edification, to mediate and question. His resolutions to philosophical and cultural problems were at times more passionate than precise, more methodological than systematic. To a degree, philosophy as edification was also philosophy as therapy and jeremiad. For James, the philosophical statement, even when presented in its most technical form, responded both to perennial philosophical conundrums and to deeply held private tensions and public concerns. The genesis of James's brand of public philosophy developed from the private predicament of his early encounters with doubt and debility, and it continued by responding to social issues of his mature years.

At the same moment that he wore the hat of public philosopher, James also confronted a series of post-Kantian questions on the nature of truth, the relationship between science and religion, and other pressing philosophical dilemmas. Through his public philosophy James codified his revolt—and enlisted himself among those who practiced philosophy as edification—against the pretensions of professional philosophy. James found the "*technical* writing, on *philosophical* subjects" of his generation of professional philosophers to be "a crime against the human race." The "oozy" style of academic philosophy had no place within the confines of public philosophy. The Jamesian spirit was a combative response to the "abstract rigmarole" of those professional academics who threatened in their writings to "obscure the truth."[46] James wanted energetic questioning, movement, and new ways to conceive and approach old problems; he wanted his philosophy to be "passionate vision," as well as an intelligent, compelling, and complex response to purely philosophical problematics.[47]

While public philosophy provided James with a forum and focus for his philosophical expression, it also demanded, as Santayana well understood, a particular mode of presentation. To maintain credibility, the public philosopher often had to transform controversial problems, either personal or social, into perennial philosophical issues. To engage these issues in partisan language was to tempt alienating one's audience.[48] Even when in a strongly political and partisan mood, in opposition to American imperialism at the turn of the century, James presented his most effective arguments against imperialism and the imperial temper in the abstract language of pluralism, his philosophical reckoning with the issue of the one and the many. Hiding the message within the text limited James's political interventions by obliterating the possibility of a well-conceived and directed theory of politics and society. Public philosophy also brought to his sketchy social and political philosophy a welcome air of timeless engagement rather than one of dated argumentation. Thus his essay "On a Certain Blindness in Human Beings" (c. 1898) meditates on the seemingly unrelated problems of feeling fully alive and judging other individuals, while serving as a sustained argument against the imperialistic spirit then coming to dominate American foreign policy. Jamesian public philosophy demonstrates how deeply imbricated his philosophical positions were within the social, cultural, and political context of his life and times.[49]

James's writings in the category of public philosophy are not without additional problems. Arising as they do out of the incubus of his stormy personal life history and his perception of the era's social problems, they necessarily reveal themselves as limited and contradictory. Much as James preached a doctrine of empathy, of openness to the inner realities of others, he could never escape the strictures of his social and class background. Nor could he ever quite resolve the pragmatic contradictions inherent in the application of his doctrines of the strenuous life and openness within the social realm.[50] Chapter five shows how James's doctrine of the strenuous life was centrally drawn within his philosophical and religious views. Strenuosity, passion, and heroism were all strong responses to the metaphysical problems of his earlier years; they also served as a jeremiad and solution to the social lethargy, to the numbing *tedium vitae* that James believed afflicted many Americans in the late-nineteenth century.

The implications of the strenuous life and the drive for heroism would eventually haunt James. For him, echoes of the strenuous and heroic life assumed a frightening form of expression in the political popularity of Theodore Roosevelt's jingoism, the call to arms against Spain in 1898, and the imperialistic temper that predominated in the new century. James, who abhorred these developments, felt compelled to reevaluate the implications of his doctrines of the strenuous and heroic life; in the process, he sought to expand various aspects of his philosophical position which might serve to mitigate the imperial logic that the discourse of heroism seemed to have created. In chapter six, James's engagement with these problems is shown to result in his dual solution to the dilemma of the culture of the crowd and the imperial temper. Here James's doctrines of openness and the moral equivalent of war are examined in detail, for their promise and problems, as well as part of his critical discourse on heroism.

The final chapter of this book evaluates how Jamesian pragmatism's public text responded to the problems of imperialism and passivity. The "extra philosophical" aspects of pragmatism take center stage. From this vantage point, the Jamesian emphasis upon action—which perplexed and troubled many of his contemporaries—is understood as both a response to social problems and as a function of the conventions of public philosophy. Rather than denigrating the philosophical import of *Pragmatism*, such an analysis expands the space of that classic book by showing how it was a cultural and social document of historical specificity.[51] In *Pragmatism* James grapples with the problem of American imperialism, with his fear that imperialism's activity and vitality might be confused with the more subtle imperatives of pragmatic doctrine. The "truth" of imperialism, James attempts to demonstrate in pragmatic terms, was false because the utility of such vitalism did not meet necessary standards for truth. James argues that imperialism violated at least three pragmatic tests: it did not respect the experiential reality of others, it failed to comprehend the multiple facts of the world in concrete fashion, and it did violence to the bedrock of American traditions.

The doctrine of pragmatism not only represented James's response to a variety of philosophical issues but also functioned as an intervention into certain turn-of-the-century political concerns generally associated with American progressives and Social Democrats. The doctrine's emphases upon meliorism, voluntarism, and concerted action apparently corresponds with the reform agenda that came to dominate American public life in the first decade of the new century.[52] Yet the anarchistic edge of James's early metaphysics would always prevent him from embracing any easily definable political attitude. He was a progressive but never a Progressive; his flirtation with Fabian Socialism never reached the stage of engagement. James's anarchistic pluralism impelled him to be wary of all governments, be they capitalist or socialist, and of the institutionalization of philosophy and science.

V

This book examines James's private problems as social ones; his philosophical expressions are viewed as possessing social, political, and cultural resonance, as well as brilliance and purity. The absolutely private James is only a reification, a fiction. Likewise the privileging of James's "purely" philosophical texts is the choice of an interpreter to erect a wall between varied but connected forms of philosophical expression and activity. James was a whole man, or at least someone who recognized that each person represents an amalgam of numerous roles. We cannot easily or fruitfully cast off one role and assume another at will. James's private rumblings never cease to be heard in his professional philosophy, and his professional philosophical notions never fail to find expression in his more popular pronouncements.

The Ariadne thread joining the private and the philosophical at many turns is the public realm. Society, culture, and politics are a context, albeit a complex one, for James's private problems and philosophical ideas. This context, quite as much as earlier and current intellectual controversies, demanded attention and expression in James's mature philosophy. James would not have wrenched either his private self or his philosophical texts from the historical specificity of the world he so passionately inhabited. Although James admitted that he often ignored a historical context for thought and action, he did so only hesitantly, noting that "men do think in social situations . . . *I simply assume the social situation.*" In practice, contextualism was essential to James's philosophical position. "The individualized self, which I believe to be the only thing properly called the self," James wrote in his one of his more professionally directed essays, "The Experience of Activity" (1904), "is a part of the content of the world experienced."[53] To re-create James's world is to bring back the context that defined his early years and to return him to the cultural, social, and political milieu in which his mature philosophy functioned.

CHAPTER TWO

"Judged Not to Have Lived"

As a public philosopher, William James addressed, of necessity, issues of general cultural concern. As a professional philosopher, he directed his attention and career to the traditional problems of metaphysics and epistemology. In both enterprises, the lines drawn between the public and the professional were never exact. In each endeavor James's private life helped to shape his philosophical discussion. Therefore, the evaluation of James's thought begins with the realities of his private existence, especially the years of Sturm und Drang, when he tumbled through his long depression (from the early 1860s until well into the 1870s). The importance attributed to these depressive years and their role in the development of James's identity is unusual in our age of pure textuality. But James's personality is indelibly written on every page of his philosophy. Even Ludwig Wittgenstein was unable to divorce James the man from his philosophical text; Wittgenstein believed that James's status as a "real human being" made him a good philosopher.[1] And, of course, James himself often gave temperament equal billing with content in a philosopher's discourse: "The history of philosophy is to a great extent that of a certain clash of human temperaments."[2]

The analysis of James's private self is traditionally drawn around the James family history. William James began this interpretive habit when he noted that his brother Henry was first and foremost "a native of the James family," someone with "no other country" to claim his allegiance and no other land with which to identify.[3] Brilliant and eccentric, the James family often constituted a world unto itself. Henry James, Sr.—a philosopher of independent mind and means—was never the absent father; his benign patriarchy orchestrated the movements of the family's existence. His intervention into the educational process of his children translated itself into a frenetic chase after the proper pedagogical situation on the European continent. The quest for education resulted in much dislocation for the children but also in the acquisition of foreign languages and a cosmopolitan consciousness that few American children of the era could match.[4]

William James's *Bildung* is so intimately connected with an ongoing family romance that interpretations based solely upon the dynamics of the James family often appear complete and exhaustive. The fascinating world of the James family begins to exist outside the context of culture and society. Howard M. Feinstein's well-received analysis of William James impressively posits that the "primal scene" behind his identity crisis originated in a dispute with his father over vocational choices: Should William follow his heart and become an artist or obey his father and pursue science? The history of this squabble—sometimes hidden, occasionally explicit—meanders into the texture of the James family history, exacerbated by William's tendency toward indecisiveness and his father's proclivity for shifts of opinion. William's failure to break free from his father's benign tyranny, coupled with his own inability to banish his desire for the life of the artist, Feinstein demonstrates, led to James's years of neurosis and illness, crisis and doubt.[5]

Other interesting aspects of James's life might also be explained by understanding the umbilical cord linking him with his singular family. One can recognize in William James's fast and feisty style of philosophical writing an uncanny family resemblance with his father's favored mode of argumentation.[6] Likewise, one might find a sibling correspondence between Henry James's narrative stylistics, multiple perspectivism, and narrational ambulation, and William's philosophical doctrines of pragmatism and pluralism.[7] Clearly the James family figures as the mother lode for mining the genesis and expression of William James's mature philosophy.

Has this rich vein been tapped once too often? This chapter does not seek to slight the very significant insights that placement of William James within the family circle offers; indeed, it profits greatly from such analyses. It does attempt to demonstrate, however, how the private self, as James later pointed out in his *Principles of Psychology,* is also a social self. While the social self James presented there was composed of various identities adapted to particular situations, he remained cognizant that factors external to the family situation played a critical role in shaping the individual's sense of personal identity.[8] Although it should be obvious that the specifics of James's identity crisis and its expression and development were drawn from the internal dynamics of the family, the general contours of this crisis were the common property of his generational cohort. A problematic relation between fathers and sons, grave uncertainties over vocational direction, and neurasthenic disabilities were the shared inheritance of James's generation—at least among those members from his social and class background.

This chapter focuses upon the social and cultural contexts that confronted and molded James and his generational cohort. Individual and group were largely defined as a generation by two factors: a shared vocational crisis during the years immediately preceding the Civil War and the resolution of that crisis through participation in that conflict. In any event, in two significant ways the cannons of the Civil War wounded even those young men who did not serve. First, it hurt them with a sense of nonparticipation in the crucial, defining event of their time: a sense of failure, a nagging suspicion that they lacked a will or were guilty of cowardice. Second, the problem of vocation loomed larger. The memory of their pained inability to fight in the Civil War haunted them and expressed itself in the postwar years as an incapacity to arrive at a satisfactory vocational decision.

William James will be present but not highly visible in the initial pages of this chapter, because the concerns and problems of his generation must first be sketched. Then the particularities of the James family romance will be seen as both private and public, individual and cultural. This is not to reduce the singularity of the James family into an expression of social or cultural trends; the specifics of the James family did help to define the severity of William James's problems. The public and private meld in acute fashion in James's life. The confluence of the public and private not only defined much of the early years of his life but also, most importantly, would become a subtext within his philosophy. James's blending of the public echoes of his early experiences with memory and identity formation became expressive of the social and political within his philosophy.

James figures as an interesting and engaged social and political thinker not only because of his ability to universalize the events of his private life into public symbols and parables, but also because his private domain was from the very beginning culturally and socially shared with other Americans in the last half of the nineteenth century. James's experiencing of his own version of what came to be called the crisis of the individual in the 1860s would serve as the basis for his understanding and empathy for the crisis of belief, will, and individualism which became a predominant concern among certain sectors of American society in the generation which followed that of James. William James's philosophy, then, expressed something more than his private life history rendered or translated into philosophical doctrine. What largely made James a successful public figure—someone to whom Americans turned to for guidance and inspiration in many matters—was his ability to universalize his private universe into public discourse, as well as the reality that his private turmoil was the common cultural property of other Americans. In the process of participating in his private monologue, James inevitably entered into a public dialogue. Thus James developed into a "national philosopher," as Josiah Royce phrased it, someone who "must know us better than we know ourselves, and this is what indeed James has done for our American moral consciousness."[9]

I

"The generation of 1840," observed one of its most illustrious members, Oliver Wendell Holmes, Jr., had "been set aside by its experience" in the Civil War.[10] But the process of generational formation, the development of a collective sense of self—at least for those young men of the same patrician economic and social class as Holmes and James—was well underway before the guns of April 1861 sounded at Fort Sumter. Labeled by Ralph Waldo Emerson, in one of his less generous moments, as part of the generation of "sloth and ease," these young men had led highly sheltered and privileged lives as the favored sons of wealthy and generally beneficent patriarchs.[11] Circumstances allowed this generational cohort to enjoy a prolonged period of adolescence. Adolescence, Erik Erikson tells us, is a time when vocational confusion is paramount. "In general," he writes, "it is the inability to settle on an occupational identity which most disturbs young people."[12] This generation's moratorium from the difficulty of choosing a vocation did not prove helpful. Although granting precious time for career considerations, it also plunged them into nervousness and nagging doubts about themselves. Left to its own devices, the generation of 1840 might have long continued in a state of vocational drift.

Members of James's generational and personal cohort—Henry Lee Higginson, Charles Russell Lowell, Henry and Charles Francis Adams, Steele Mackaye, and John LaFarge, to name only a few—hesitated before the momentous question raised by one of their generation: "What shall I be?"[13] Tied to this query were others equally troubling: How shall I be useful? Need I travel a vocational path leading in only one direction? The young men of the generation of 1840 faced these "tremendous" questions with the handicap of a "divided self." They were agonizingly torn between their intense desire to continue their lives of leisure, wherein the cultivation of youthful interests reigned supreme, and the counterdemand of their parents and society that they settle down and pursue a career in a serious and directed fashion.[14]

The anxiety level of the generation of 1840 intensified because it was born of deep ambivalence. These young men were not self-conscious rebels; they espoused little of a bohemian negative identity and expressed only minuscule amounts of overt disdain for social etiquette and parental expectations. In large part they shared the parental and social consensus that one should pursue a useful, respectable calling. Yet they feared that to settle upon a calling too hastily would result in a form of imprisonment, confinement to a career that might prove personally unfulfilling. Moreover, it is quite possible that their hesitancies were also caught up in Oedipal rivalries and tensions marked by premonitions of failure in the hardy competition of life, in which some of their fathers had already proven themselves beyond doubt. If not sufficiently complicated by all of these factors, this particular adolescent crisis was further rendered problematic by its historical positioning. The generation of 1840 confronted a multitude of heady career options, especially when compared with earlier generational cohorts. Surrounded by adolescent uncertainties and paternal examples, these young men were overwhelmed by a free and wide-ranging choice of occupations.

Earlier generations of American males did not have to face a bewilderingly varied set of career options. Although the pursuit of a calling had always been an event of great moment in a young man's life, its horrors were assuaged by tradition, social hierarchy, and scarcity of alternative careers. In Puritan times, for example, the young man pursued the calling that his father chose for him, though the process was eased somewhat of its patriarchal dominance by paternal concern not to deny his son's natural or God-given aptitude.[15] Generations later, when Emerson faced the world of work and career as a recent Harvard graduate in the 1820s, his fate was confined to the socially acceptable and predictable realms of the ministry or teaching. How poorly these genteel and prescribed callings suited Emerson is well known. He only escaped from their "corpse cold" embrace by embarking upon a career of his own creation, one devoted to man thinking and lecturing. This middle-ground choice was a compromise for Emerson, a gently curved line that connected the best aspects of Unitarian self-culture with the explosive potentialities of self-creation outside of any established institutional framework. But, as Emerson recognized, choices had been limited for his generation.[16]

America, for the generation coming of age in the late 1840s, suddenly offered its youth an entirely new and expanded set of vocational opportunities. The "economic revolution" of the Jacksonian era had transformed the basis of wealth and status; in Massachusetts, as well as in other states, the revolution had resulted in a shift of population and capital into industrial manufacturing.[17] Tied to this industrial relocation of resources was a momentous change in political and social realities which loosened the grip on society of entrenched wealth and privilege. This joint process, however uneven and in the end uncertain, brought forth what historian Robert Wiebe has called a "Revolution in Choices." The 1830s witnessed a tremendous multiplication of career opportunities, many a direct outgrowth of the dazzling industrial development. The Jacksonian revolution played a role in this process as well, with the longtime elite professions of law and medicine, for instance, becoming democratized as they expanded to meet the burgeoning needs of a growing and increasingly mobile nation. The Republican Ethos of upward mobility as a function of individual initiative and ability brought into the legal profession many Americans for whom the practice of law would have been pure fantasy, an unattainable goal, a generation or two earlier.

The impulsive nature of this mobility and expansion would not continue unabated. By the 1850s a process of retraction had begun; the "learned professions" sought to professionalize and thus regain control from the democratic masses. With this process of retrenchment, these professions reclaimed a large degree of their previous dignity and status, at least in the mind of the elite classes. What makes all of this of interest for the generational cohort of 1840 is that its members came of age at the moment when occupational opportunities were most expansive and when, as a result of the counterrevolution against the perceived excesses of democracy, these "learned professions" were once again turned into respectable career options.[18]

The attempt to find the right career in a period of varied options proved a lengthy and debilitating process; it began with naïve hopes and ended with perplexity and trauma. The occupational biographies of the generation of 1840 are a testament to the uncertainty of direction and the multiplicity of possibility. Henry Adams (1838–1914), perhaps the most celebrated member of that generation, admitted that "the choice of career was more difficult than the education which had proved impracticable."[19] Born with the impeccable credentials of the Boston mercantile and intellectual elite, Charles Russell Lowell (1835–1864) recognized the valor of work while retreating from its drawbacks. In Emersonian fashion, circling back upon the doubleness of work, Lowell noted in his Harvard Commencement Address that "fruitful labor" in the Puritan sense of the term was a reward insufficient for the young men of his own generation who burned with "zeal and vigor." How to bring into the world, through sustained labor, "fresher and purer ideals?" Where to alight the fires of these ideals? These questions plagued Lowell as he flitted about from commercial bookkeeping to being a "common workman." Within six years of his Harvard graduation, Lowell had toiled in earnest in iron manufacturing, "bronze founding," and railroad and farm enterprises.[20]

Lowell and most of his generational cohort—with the ringing exception of Henry Adams, who later complained that he was "for sale, in the open market"—expressed little dissatisfaction with or deep understanding of the marketplace. Perhaps because they came from privileged backgrounds and were in need of vocation rather than employment as such, they were able, unlike many of the writers of the American renaissance, to avoid the ordinary limitation and stigma of having to earn a living. Lowell was gripped by vocational, rather than financial, uncertainty; his dilemma was existential rather than economic. No vocation seemed capable of satisfying his ideal yearnings. He acknowledged as much in a letter to his mother, in which he admitted that he simply did not know "how to choose" a vocation.[21]

Lowell was not alone in facing the problem of bewildering vocational choices or in experiencing difficulties finding satisfactory work. William James obviously was haunted by this specter of vocational drift and uncertainty. Others in this generational and social cohort replicated the same concerns. Henry Lee Higginson (1834–1919), reared in a wealthy and influential New England merchant family, was stymied by the conundrum of vocational choices, the frustratingly endless possibilities available to him. In 1853, in an exasperated state, he wrote a twenty-four-page letter to his father, listing and by turns evaluating the professions open to him at that particular moment; his list reads like an ode to the correctness of Wiebe's designation of this period as one marked by a "Revolution in Choices." Lawyer, physician, clergyman, merchant, engineer, surveyor, musician, and chemist all fell under Henry Lee Higginson's sober glance only to be ultimately dismissed from consideration for one compelling reason or another.[22]

This multiplicity of vocational directions confused but also furnished young men such as Higginson with a perfected excuse for avoiding final career decisions. Thus such young men were allowed welcomed additional time for the pursuit of deeply felt yet socially less-than-acceptable desires. Higginson most wanted to be a musician; his love of music was intense and his lengthy sojourns in Europe were a record of cultural tastes satisfied and vocational decisions delayed. Similarly, the artist John LaFarge (1835–1915), a close boyhood friend of William James, was defined by "the slow and even unpremeditated fashion in which" he "drifted into his vocation." LaFarge's final entry into his vocation of painter was marked by an attitude "indifferent and uncertain before the gate."[23] A slowness to mature and an inability to find the correct vocation for one's energies and proclivities were the generation's common complaints. Charles Francis Adams (1835–1915) considered his early years wasted in the pursuit of incorrect vocational goals. Thus, more than once in his autobiography, he came to describe himself as "a round peg in a square hole" during those years.[24] And, of course, the failure of his brother Henry's "education" has been inscribed as a commonplace in American intellectual history.

The star of the father was never fully absent from this galaxy of vocational possibility, illuminating the sons' extended adolescent avoidance tactics. In some cases, the anger and resentment against the parent might be overtly expressed, as when Steele Mackaye (1842–1894) revolted against his father's wish that he attend a military academy by affecting a daring and dangerous escape from its confines.[25] Charles Francis Adams maintained a longtime grudge against his father's coldness and lack of help. Reflecting back upon his years of adolescent turmoil and career indecision, Adams wrote that "as I look back on his course towards me, well as he meant it and thoroughly conscientious as he was, I should now respect myself more if I had then rebelled and run away from home, to sea or the Devil."[26]

Irony was an indirect, albeit effective, method fathers employed to steer the career choices of their sons in a preferred direction. Oliver Wendell Holmes, Sr., who had dabbled with the law as a young man, dismissed his son's desire for legal study: "A lawyer can't be a great man."[27] The resort to irony, however powerfully it might work in its own subtle fashion, actually indicated the breakdown of patriarchal influence; it was at best an indirect avenue of control. The image of the benevolent father appears to have been, at least among the parents of those in the generational cohort discussed here, the preferred mode of child-rearing; it certainly captures the style of Henry James, Sr. By the late-eighteenth and early-nineteenth centuries, a significant shift had occurred in child-rearing patterns, which would indirectly affect vocational issues. The role model of the father as stern and omnipotent patriarch was being replaced by the image, and increasingly by the reality, of the father as benign nurturer. The child was to be unshackled, freed from overt and harsh parental guidance, tradition, and punishment. The pursuit of one's inalienable rights thus became not simply the motto for the national ethos but also the model for child-rearing and nurturing.[28]

Paternal support and youthful freedom, however, were never absolute in practice. The fathers of the generation of 1840 were men of standing and influence; not surprisingly, they possessed strong personalities and secure opinions. While forced by social convention to covertly inhibit or guide their sons' choices in vocational matters, they nonetheless succeeded in this endeavor through a mixture of benevolence, financial power, and the inducement of guilt. The wounds of a policy of "vague benevolence" or subtle dictation, when tied to the guilt felt by a child who opposes paternal wishes, did little to ease the entrance of young men into a career. In that elongated letter in which Higginson presented his litany of career choices, he had, in effect, hoped to build a case for the continuance of his meandering pursuit of musical pleasures in Europe. As a dutiful son, dependent upon paternal approval and financial support,

Henry left the final decision of continuance in Europe or return to America in his father's kindly hands. He did so, however, only after making it clear that he preferred or thought it best that he remain in Europe. Ever the benevolent and concerned father, George Higginson wavered for months before finally, and agonizingly, deciding that it was best that Henry return to America and place himself "under the influence of Cambridge worthies."[29]

The problems involved in vocational choice and the dynamics of father-and-son relationships received ironic resolution in the prevalence of neurasthenic maladies among the generation of 1840. William James was not alone in this combination of vocational uncertainty and neurasthenic complications.[30] The lives of Charles Russell Lowell, Henry Lee Higginson, Steele Mackaye, and John LaFarge were regularly terrorized by this dual reality of vocational doubts and neurasthenic complaints. Various imprecise explanations for this outburst of illness among Americans were commonly offered in this period. George M. Beard, the first chronicler of neurasthenia and one of its initial therapists, found its symptoms peculiar to the more advanced civilizations, common among those races caught up in the hubbub of a quickened pace of life. Modernity, with its emphasis upon change and choice, seemed the culprit. Beard thought that the rage for neurasthenia offered a means of escape from the demands of modernity.[31]

More recent analyses of the disease stress the origins of neurasthenia within the powerful antinomies of the American work ethic. In this argument, the frustrations of the ideal of work for work's sake, of methodical labor without end, and of the concomitant inability of the individual to find satisfaction, rest, or salvation through work forced many American males, from various classes, toward an inability to function, a paradoxical incapacity for work.[32]

For young men dissatisfied with their anticipated careers or frustrated by their failure to choose a calling, neurasthenia provided an agreeable moratorium, an excuse for inactivity on account of physical or mental infirmity. Higginson was typical in his medley of complaints. Eye problems prevented him, as he insistently reminded his father, from entering Harvard and methodically pursuing a career. Interestingly, these ocular difficulties did not inhibit his travels and study of music in Europe. A "strange and inopportune" arm ailment followed the eye problems and prevented him from practicing music as a profession at the moment when Henry was guilt-ridden about his responsibility to return home to aid his father during the trying years of the financial panic of 1857. Henry later suffered from a badly sprained ankle, which prevented him from working in a merchant's office.[33] Similarly, Charles Russell Lowell's stint as an iron manufacturer was stopped by a "serious hemorrhage from his lungs," a malady that would linger when convenient to allow him to meet his vocational imperatives half-heartedly, always wary of "over-exertion."[34] Steele Mackaye, whose escape from the military academy had proven insufficient grounds to deter his father's wishes that he be a military officer, finally avoided army life when he suddenly and conveniently contracted a case of "brain fever."[35] Many in James's generation found the pre-Civil War years dominated by vocational doubt, neurasthenic disability, and a general sense of vocational drift. Relief was in the offing, but it would exact a terrible cost upon them and the nation.

II

To a large extent, the problems of vocation and conflict with fathers were solved, or at least mitigated, by the onset of the Civil War. The physical debilities that had dogged the sons and rendered pursuit of a career impossible largely vanished with the call to arms. "Chaos breeds life," Henry Adams recounted, "when order breeds habit. The Civil War bred life. The army bred courage."[36] Lowell, who would not survive the conflict, described the effects of the war simply: he entered the fight without any thirst for blood or certitude of final victory, but rather out of the belief that the war "will do us all much real good in the end."[37]

Higginson's vocational doubts and indecision in the prewar years evidenced themselves in his typical stance of uncertainty about whether he should involve himself in the war effort. The "general enthusiasm for the war," as well as a chance to put to rest those carpers who had posited his generation's "degeneracy for years and years," finally decided the issue for Higginson. Gone were the eye, arm, and leg ailments; Higginson valiantly assumed his duties as a first lieutenant in the Second Massachusetts Regiment. Even a case of typhoid fever was shrugged off, as Higginson reported himself now "hearty as a bull."[38] Mackaye, whose "brain fever" had earlier exempted him from a military vocation, served as a second lieutenant of black troops, a chore that, as he proudly noted, required "energy, address, courage and quick perceptions."[39] Charles Francis Adams wavered at first about joining the Union army. Not wanting to be considered a "prig," he enlisted. Hesitation gave way to resolution and then to relief as Adams later considered his decision to serve as a "moment of inspiration—the time when I resolved to burst the bonds and strike out into the light from the depths of the darkness. No wiser determination did I ever reach."[40]

Not only were these neurasthenics able to serve in the war effort but they also resolutely credited the Civil War with curing them of their previous problems of vocational indecision and physical complaints. Higginson seconded this thesis in no uncertain terms when he wrote in

1863 that the war represented a chance for both him and the nation to gain "salvation." The war was an educational experience unlike any he had encountered. It did not nullify his musical and cultural inclinations; in fact, he later founded the Boston Symphony. The war allowed Higginson to face life directly and to become a "useful citizen." Although his postwar ventures varied, he approached them as necessary preludes to a secure career as an investment banker.[41] Similarly, Charles Francis Adams believed that his military experience had given to him "that robust, virile stimulus to be derived only from a close contact with Nature and a roughing it among men." The Civil War was a crucial stage in this generation's process of self-education and identity formation. Indeed, historian George Fredrickson contends that those who served in the Civil War translated skills learned in the conflagration into the bureaucratic and administrative imperatives that increasingly came to dominate postwar American business and society.[42]

No one expressed more fully and with greater self-consciousness the effect of the Civil War upon the generation of 1840 than Oliver Wendell Holmes, Jr. His generation had been "touched with fire" and thus was "permitted to scorn nothing but indifference." The war had resolved its chronic inability to choose, and its doubting mania, by giving to youth the necessary doses of duty, discipline, and direction. As Holmes made clear in "The Soldier's Faith," his famous address of 1895, the Civil War's "vicissitudes of terror and triumph" had armed his generation with the ability to overcome "individualist negations" and to face modern life—a life of business, vocation, and change—with courage and heroism. Holmes's message would have been seconded by many of his generation who had begun with trembling over vocational possibilities and their inability to decide upon a course of action but had arisen, phoenixlike, out of the ashes of the Civil War, to become useful and confident members of society. But what of those young men of Holmes's generation who he "judged not to have lived" by dint of their failure to fight in the Civil War? How would they deal with their haunting "individualist negations?"[43]

III

William James did not serve in the Civil War; he faced the peril and embarrassment of "being judged not to have lived." James had approached the great conflict with difficulties quite similar to those that plagued his friends. He was hounded by the dilemma of making a vocational decision, one further complicated by the "benevolent" opposition of his father. William longed to be a painter, and in that regard he had begun study at William Morris Hunt's studio in Newport, Rhode Island.

Henry James, Sr., made it clear, through various means, apparently including hints of suicide, that a dutiful son should forget about painting and honor a father's wishes by pursuing a career in science.[44] Many of James's friends encountered similar difficulties over career choices with their fathers, but their problems were alleviated by service in the Civil War. The war allowed them to break the familial bond of dependency by giving them a new-found sense of confidence and independence. This new and perhaps heartier view of life allowed them to enter into fruitful and successful careers without experiencing uncertainty, which had confounded them in the prewar years. Unfortunately for William James, the Civil War did not provide him with a greater sense of confidence: his lack of activity in the conflict only exacerbated and prolonged his vocational problems; it fed into a repast of physical debility and philosophical doubt, eventuating in the failure of will that marked his years of depression. These problems confronted William James for the next ten years of his life, years that would see him begin various avenues of study only to find his journey halted by poor health and indecision. Not until the early 1870s, after finally accepting Charles W. Eliot's offer of a faculty position at Harvard, would James finally begin to function successfully in the public world.

There is no reason to doubt the centrality of the Civil War to William James's intellectual and personal development. Unfortunately, precious little information from either James's pen or from his family's letters during this period or later exists to illuminate the war's role in the psychic development of William James. This is especially unfortunate, because the onset of the war in spring 1861 occurred in close proximity to such crucial and influential events in James's life as his decision to forsake art in order to enter the Lawrence Scientific School at Harvard, and with the beginnings of the nagging physical and emotional debilities that would come to define in somber terms much of his remaining life. Fredrickson has imaginatively posited a nexus between James's failure to serve in the Civil War and the later development of his philosophy of the heroic; Marian C. and Edward H. Madden have suggested that James's wartime bench-sitting contributed to his physical and mental duress.[45] Yet most analysts have followed Leon Edel's advice that "it is impossible to judge what role the Civil War played" in the life of either William or Henry James.[46] Unfortunately, there is an attendant danger here. Although we should not believe that James's life was shaped primarily by the war, rather than by other watershed events or realities, such as his vocational conflict of wills with his father, we must not gravitate to the other extreme and ignore or avoid the impact of the Civil War—this "grim intermission" as Henry James later called it—upon William James's personal and intellectual development.[47] For, after all, as Holmes never hesitated to make apparent, the Civil War was his generation's distinguishing event and its signature.

Three reasons have been tendered to explain William James's failure to serve in the Union army. Ralph Barton Perry, Gay Wilson Allen, and Gerald E. Myers, all important biographers of James, posit that William and his brother Henry were either not "rugged enough" or prevented due to "physical frailty," previous injury, or excessive inwardness from service in the conflict.[48] One difficulty with this explanation is that many who did serve—including Higginson, Mackaye, and Lowell—would easily, given their impressive array of ailments before the commencement of the war, belong to the category of the insufficiently rugged or psychically frail. Moreover, evidence indicates that William James's physical health was reasonably good at least until the family's return from Europe to Newport in late 1860. His poor health, then, was not of long duration when the war began.[49]

Some argue that William could not serve in the Civil War because of a severe character flaw, a congenital defect in his decision-making process, exacerbated by the complicated infrastructure of the James family. In the most forceful presentation of this thesis, Marian C. and Edward H. Madden contend that James's enlistment in the war "would have required the kind of commitment—and an unpleasant one at that—that James was habitually unable to make."[50] In this view, James was stymied with the philosophical Hamletism that would define his later years of doubt and depression. The rejoinder to this hypothesis is the same as to the argument of poor health: many Brahmins exhibited a similarly severe doubt, both on vocational grounds and over the initial decision to enlist. Yet, in the end, they were able to make the commitment. Unlike Hamlet, they were able to kill the king of debility by serving in the war.

Finally, and perhaps most importantly, there is the role of Henry James, Sr., in this matter. He boasted of his personal intervention in keeping his two eldest sons out of the conflict: "I have had a firm grasp upon the coat tails of my Willy and Henry, who both vituperate me beyond measure because I won't let them go." Although Henry James, Sr., was a vociferous and impassioned advocate of the Union cause, he rationalized his decision to keep William and Henry above or outside the fray by explaining: "first, that no existing government, is worth an honest human life and a clean one like theirs. . . . Secondly, I tell them that no young American should put himself in the way of death, until he has realized something of the good life; until he has found some charming conjugal Elizabeth or other to whisper his devotion to, and assume the task, if be, of keeping his memory green."[51]

Why these arguments were applied only to the elder sons and not to the younger—Robertson and Wilky both joined the army at young ages without parental opposition—is a question that cannot be adequately answered.[52] The important point here is that Henry James, Sr., successfully prevented William from entering the Union army. This was accomplished, one may suppose, by a combination of all the aforementioned explanations: parental opposition combined with William's declining or uncertain health, and a life history of difficulties in making any commitment. In any case, no set of reasons, no matter how logical or necessary it appears in retrospect, could exempt young William James from the psychic turmoil consequent with not having served in the Civil War.

Nonparticipation in the Civil War caused problems for James, though one cannot with certainty draw a causal connection between his wartime passivity and the inauguration of his physical and mental debilities. But the confusion, suffering and anxiety initiated by the war must have been immense. After all, James's friends and family were staunch advocates of the Northern cause; two of his brothers, as well as his cousins Gus Barker and William Temple, served with distinction.[53] The severe wounds these young men suffered in battle—fatal in the cases of the cousins—probably increased William's sense of unreality and his alienation from the crucial event of his generation. However, little exists to document this supposed angst and alienation. One account does remember William as too embarrassed to speak with his friend Charles Russell Lowell during a review of the latter's regiment. James was looking on from the sidelines while Lowell, in a pose that one observer thought regal, was center stage, proudly astride his horse.[54] A couple of years later, in commenting upon the bravery of, as well as the horrible wounds suffered by, his brother Wilky in the battle of Fort Wagner, William could only describe himself as feeling in comparison "small and shabby."[55] Brother Henry replicated such a sense of smallness on the periphery of events years later in his novel *The Bostonians* (1886). One of his characters, Olive Chancellor, expresses a clawing envy for her distant cousin Basil Ransom, whom she despises because "he had fought and offered his own life" during the Civil War. Like many others of her sex, Olive had missed out on the opportunity for glory.[56]

Such a record of regret or envy also surfaces occasionally in William James's later writings and speeches. The sense of having been "judged not to have lived" with his generation in their moment of greatest trial never escaped him. Perhaps he was speaking of himself when he ended his lecture "Is Life Worth Living?" (1895) by warning his audience not to allow doubt to prevent them from entering the worthy battles of life. Who, the mature William James once inquired of his audience, would have liked to have been in Crillon's shoes when faced with Henry IV's postvictory remonstrance to "Hang yourself, brave Crillon! We fought at Arques, and you were not there."[57]

Alexander Agassiz, a reluctant nonparticipant in the Civil War because of filial devotion to his father, Louis Agassiz, registered a similar plaint. Staying at home made Alexander feel "ashamed."[58] This sense of alienation and self-denigration must have been exacerbated by the reactions of his friends. Oliver Wendell Holmes, Jr., later recalled feeling remorse because he had, for much of the war, harshly rejected his close friend William Everett, who had chosen not to participate in the conflict and went to England to study.[59] How might William James have reacted to the poem "Voluntaries" by family friend Emerson?

> In an age of fops and toys
> Wanting wisdom, void of right
> Who shall nerve heroic boys
> To hazard all in Freedom's fight,—
> Break sharply off their jolly games,
> Forsake their comrades gay
> And quit proud homes and youthful dames
> For proud famine, toil and fray?
> Yet on the nimble air benign
> Speed nimbler messages,
> That waft the breath of grace divine
> To hearts in sloth and ease.
> So nigh is the grandeur to our dust,
> So near is God to man,
> When Duty whispers low, *Thou must,*
> The youth replies, *I can.*[60]

William James was unable to reply, *"I can,"* though his feelings of inadequacy and guilt did impel him and his brother Henry to contemplate in 1863 a futile attempt to become involved in the war effort through a project whereby they would labor alongside recently freed slaves.[61] James's heading for his notebook in that year is revealing in this regard; he writes "Son of man! Stand upon thy feet and I will speak unto thee."[62] Of course, the problem was that William could not stand or decide to stand upon his own two feet. His hesitations seemed to transform him into his era's version of Hamlet; both Hamlet and William were aware of the need to act and of the goal to be achieved but was incapable of acting. Thus, throughout the Civil War, William not only had to deal with the questioning stares—real or imagined—from friends who served or supported the cause but also from the conflicting signals about the war that fired forth in a blazing stream of rhetoric from his own father. That Henry James, Sr., was like quicksilver in his opinions and not a man prone to consistency is well established: indeed, Feinstein places many of William James's vocational and emotional problems at the door of the father's shifting perceptions regarding the value of the artist's role in society.[63] Imagine the son's consternation at being kept out of the war when hearing his own father, in the famous 4 July 1861 oration "The Social Significance of Our Institutions," directly contradict the reasons he had confidently given his sons about why they should not serve in the Civil War.[64]

The argument that no cause or institution of government was worth the blood of young men occupied no place of honor in James's 4 July oration at Newport. It is unrecorded whether William attended his father's speech, but one must assume that he was cognizant of its sentiments. Henry James, Sr., began the oration typically, in his favored realm of the abstract, with a discussion of America's mission, of its national soul and attendant problems in realizing its magnificent destiny. Following a lengthy comparison of the meaning of America with the exhausted significance of Europe, James assigned social sentiments and responsibilities a priority over personal selfishness and inwardness. This commonly expressed view of James's developed into a sustained harangue in favor of the Northern struggle to defeat the South and to scourge the land of the sin of slavery. According to the senior James, it was only a question of the "transition from youth to manhood, from appearance to reality, from passing shadow to deathless substance."

The conflict's demands represented both a national trial and a personal enterprise. No man should allow his trivial problems to interfere with the higher call to duty: "And we must not hesitate for a moment to fight it manfully out to its smiling end." One had the choice, quite simply put, of rising to the heights of "all beautiful human proportions, into all celestial vigor and beatitude" or "of descending into the inevitable torments which alone discipline such uncleanness."[65] What answer might young William James have offered to his father's exclamations that one should "manfully fight it out" other than to enter into his long torment of neurasthenic debility?

For those who did not participate in the war, feelings of being "small and shabby" were ubiquitous and consequently necessitated various strategies of retreat into fantasy or transference. Although not precisely of the generation of 1840, philosopher Chauncey Wright was thirty-one when hostilities broke out. There was little chance that Wright, who was never blessed with physical exuberance or moderate habits, would participate in the conflict. Instead, he remained in Cambridge, where he practiced philosophy and supported himself by his occasionally frantic calculations for the *Nautical Almanac,* while his younger brother, Frederick, served as a lieutenant of the Union army. Chauncey expressed what might have well been the common refrain for those who supported the cause but who, for whatever reasons, did not participate in it when he wrote to his brother Frederick: "To be a mere looker on. *[sic]* leading a very dull life . . . is a condition of passive uncertainty in which it is very hard to be cheerful."[66]

Feelings of "passive uncertainty" soon led to psychological acts of transference as a way of resuscitating a weakened sense of self-esteem. In spring 1863, Chauncey "bruised the instep of his right foot." This injury somehow developed, according to his physician, into a severe fever marked by intense pain and suffering. Although eventually checked, the injury required Chauncey to hobble around on crutches for almost five months. Incapacity rendered any thought of participation in the Civil War impossible; it also drew forth a strained but significant identification between him and his fighting brother. In this equation, not only was Frederick's contraband black servant now enlisted to attend to the needs of the incapacitated stay-at-home brother, but Chauncey could report that "I have all the external appearance of a veteran soldier, with my wound, my crutch, and my contraband." When, on 5 June 1864, Chauncey learned that his brother had been wounded—a blow at first thought not serious but one that would in three weeks' time claim Frederick's life—Chauncey offered his brother advice on how to recover: "Hope is good medicine but don't let it stimulate you to impatience." The essential incongruity of their situations did not wholly escape Chauncey's sharp mind, but its dimensions were diminished when he referred back to his own leg injury of the previous year, noting that he "had also to exercise the courage of patience . . . with my inglorious wound."[67]

Despite all of the ailments that began to define his life in 1861, William James never quite compared any of his "inglorious wounds" with the horrible suffering he had witnessed when his brother Wilky lay painfully at the family home. While Wilky slowly recovered from a leg wound suffered during the ill-fated charge of Colonel Robert Shaw and his black troops upon Fort Wagner, William, then studying science at Harvard, was immersed in strenuous battles over his vocational future. Should William follow a course leading to "material comfort" at the cost of "a kind of selling of one's soul," or should he opt for one leading to "mental dignity and independence; combined, however, with physical penury"? Business and science were the acceptable, but separate, options; his choice was complicated by his desire to pursue a career that would allow him to settle down and marry. As was his wont, William admitted, "I confess that I hesitate."[68] Like Chauncey Wright, William transferred his hesitations and trepidations over his vocational and physical problems into an identification with his heroically suffering and performing brothers. William James must have realized that the heroism of real life and the valor of war—themes that would be redolent within his later philosophy— threatened to evade him. He would seek to replicate the experiences common to his generation and his brothers by another path, through participation in the Thayer expedition of 1865, organized by Louis Agassiz to explore and collect scientific objects and data in the Amazonian wilderness of Brazil.

IV

William James was one of a handful of similarly privileged young men who served as assistants to naturalist Louis Agassiz on a scientific fact-finding trip to the Amazon region.[69] For Agassiz, the expedition represented a welcome escape, a chance to regain his faltering health, an opportunity to collect specimens that might help him to stem the tide of Darwinism, and a needed respite from the acrimony of the Civil War.[70] James's reasons for going appear, at least according to one of his biographers, to have issued from a desire for adventure.[71] A more recent analyst of James suggests, on a metaphorical level if not a concrete one, that the Amazonian expedition typified James's errand into the wilderness, his exile in the desert, his descent into hell, all of which acted as the prelude to his process—conceived in terms of the Puritan conversion narrative—of spiritual reclamation.[72] If so, the project marked only a beginning of the journey, for James did not return spiritually rejuvenated.

The Brazilian enterprise was certainly, at first, a welcome relief from vocational uncertainty for James. It offered him escape from the tedium of the Lawrence Scientific School, to which he had been shuttled off by his father. If Feinstein's thesis is on target, and William was during this period pining after his recently forsaken art career, then the trip to the Amazon afforded him—under the acceptable mantle of a scientific quest—a chance at the picturesque and exciting. William's letters home, as lush in their imagery as the Brazilian landscape, are evidence that his painter's eye and disposition were operative during this trip.[73] For James, the journey also served as an experience analogous, at least in theory, to the rigors his friends and brothers were then encountering in the Civil War. All the elements of drama, adventure, and danger were present on the Thayer expedition: exotic natives, unchartered regions, duty, and discipline.

Half in jest, half in seriousness, James translated Agassiz's persona as a scientist into the heroic figure of a military leader. Waiting on board ship in New York harbor for the voyage to Brazil, James described Agassiz as a Civil War general. The scientist's manner of poring over maps and his grandiose plans for the expedition suggested the figure of General William Sherman commanding his troops. James realized that Agassiz had no army, but only ten novices at his disposal. Nonetheless, he carefully placed himself in the guise of the noble foot soldier ready to do his duty and to sacrifice for his demanding executive officer.[74]

The rigors of the sea venture, the rough waters, and assorted illnesses—including a bout with varioloid that incapacitated and blinded James for a short period—contributed to James's belief in the validity of the analogy between his experiences and those of his generational cohort during the Civil War. Just as Holmes remembered an epiphany while he lay close to death on the battlefield, so too did James record, once again in his characteristic mocking and serious manner, that "no one has a right to write about the 'nature of evil' . . . who has not been at sea." What exactly the wisdom to be gained from the "awful slough of despond" remained unclear to James at this point, but he was certain that he could not help but profit from so "profound an experience." Moreover, as he admitted to his parents, the trip and his rough experiences and "isolated circumstances" had awakened within him a keener sympathy with his brothers who had fought in the war. It was only now, early into his Brazilian adventure, that William indicated that he could communicate with them as equals, as men who had shared a journey through hell and lived to tell of their experiences.[75]

William James's "season in hell," of course, was hardly so horrific as a stint in the Civil War but it did, at least in the initial weeks of the expedition, furnish him with a welcome sense of positive identity. However, doubts and problems would not be assuaged easily or for long. The Brazilian expedition was not on a par with service in the war, and James knew this. His valor soon began to tarnish as adversity struck, dissipating whatever benefits he might have gathered from the enterprise.

James's diary and letters home after his bout with varioloid reveal the stammering uncertainty that would plague him for the next ten years. Should he stay with the expedition or return to the comforts of home? Was he equal to the tasks required or lacking in the requisite "grit and energy?" In June 1865, convinced of his shortcomings, James described himself as reconciled to the reality of being "one of the very lightest featherweights," someone fit only for mental activities.[76] The energetic example of Agassiz, combined with the embarrassing lethargy of the Brazilian natives, proved sufficient foils for James to press on with the expedition's activities.[77] Although he stayed through until the end of the expedition, he quickly transformed his experiences into a memory, a picture postcard lacking any sense of reality or educational value, in much the fashion that Henry Adams, another nonparticipant in the Civil War, would later use to describe his life experiences.[78] The Amazonian journey had been a sojourn; it had not been enough to give William the fortitude of will, discipline, and reserves of energy that the Civil War had apparently bestowed upon those of the generation of 1840 who had fought and suffered in a cause. He returned home bereft of the trappings of heroism, which he desperately needed to face his vocational uncertainties and his problems with his father. With a sense of necessity rather than excitement, William quickly settled back into the stultifying, to his mind at least, routine of an internship at Massachusetts General Hospital, soon followed by study at the Harvard Medical School.[79]

V

The nagging sense of having been "judged not to have lived" haunted James for the remainder of his life. Consigned to the recesses of his unconscious, the realization extruded regularly within his philosophical text, especially in the spirit underlining the essays in *The Will to Believe* (1897). Occasional outcroppings also proved revelatory. In 1905 he deeply regretted that he could know nothing about the inner realities of the Russo-Japanese War, because he lacked "concrete experience of war." Without such experience, the philosopher of radical empiricism concluded, one must forever remain on the sidelines, able to watch but incapable of fully understanding the emotions and inner realities of combat. Similar sentiments surfaced in his famous "The Moral Equivalent of War" (1910). Failure to experience war, life *in extremis,* represented a major omission for a man passionately involved in the fight against the Spanish-American War and fiercely interested in the emotional aspects of war fever.[80]

The act of transference, begun with the Amazon expedition, was completed only within the text of his popular philosophy. Here, with great passion and eloquence, James sought through his concepts of the will to believe and the strenuous life to demolish once and for all his inner demons. In the process, he would prove that the practice of philosophy and the demands of everyday life might be heroic in and of themselves. In this stance, James would echo the earlier manifesto of Charles Baudelaire, who found heroism possible in the bourgeois world of counting houses and sentimentality through acts of personal definition and sustained struggle.[81] But the expression of these views would not come to James immediately.

James first had to overcome the depression caused by his inability to pursue an artistic vocation and by his failure to fight in the Civil War. These difficulties were compounded, from the mid-1860s until the early 1870s, by his horror at the culturally commonplace notions that the universe was either coldly mechanical or starkly unformed. In either version of metaphysics, the nightmare implications for the autonomy of the individual proved difficult to dispel. Faced with this horrid vision, James, like many other young men of a generation coming of age after the Civil War, descended into what Henry Adams called "the viscosity of inertia." To escape from this inertia, men "were compelled to waste three-fourths of their energy."[82] Passivity and trembling, as well as doubt and weakness, became the emblems James routinely wore as he faced the metaphysical implications of modern science. The social expression of these issues became known as the crisis of the individual.

The figure of Hamlet would become the cultural symbol most powerfully expressive of the metaphysical problems and the crisis of the individual for William James and others in the late nineteenth century. Through the figure of Hamlet, the despondent and doubting William James addressed the crises of metaphysics and the individual, both within himself and within his culture. His philosophy of the strenuous and his pragmatic ideal would eventually come to serve as his passionate public response to the numbing doubt that had gripped him and that he perceived as responsible for imprisoning the possibilities of his readers and listeners. But before he could preach his message as a public philosopher, James had to grapple with the demons of his depression and debility. In this sense, he required less a "philosophy to save him" than a philosophical understanding of the problem of Hamletism in the modern world.[83] The ghost of Hamlet had to first be confronted; it haunted James and the generation that followed his own.

CHAPTER THREE

From Hamlet to Habit

William James found little cause for celebration as he entered his twenty-fifth year in January 1867. A specter of failure and debilitating illness surrounded him. He had yet to adopt a profession with either sustained ardor or success. The Civil War's strangely salutary effects upon his friends had eluded him, leaving only a sense of regret and shame in their wake. Relations with his father were rocky; a desire for independence competed with a history of dependency and thus caused tension in the James family household. By 1867 life in Cambridge had become unbearable for William. Escape to Europe loomed as the most promising solution to family, health, and vocational difficulties. When James left for Europe in April 1867 he was burdened with the travail of his early years; the expectations he brought to the continent were hesitant, not buoyant. His uncertainties and tensions would prove too hardy for the presumed European cure. From 1867 until 1872, James would descend into what many historians define, without exaggeration, as his years of depression and doubt. James would have agreed with this evaluation. Writing in 1891, James admitted that he "was entirely broken down before [he] was thirty."[1]

This chapter seeks to interpret James's breakdown, accompanying philosophical problems, and eventual recovery through a social and cultural interpretation of his personal problems based upon a sustained metaphor.[2] By the late nineteenth century, the figure of Hamlet had come to serve as a cultural commonplace, a trope expressive of the dangers of the divided self, the individual so consumed by uncertainty that he or she was incapable of sustained or directed activity. Josiah Royce and George Santayana, for example, used the figure of Hamlet to describe this particular and common cultural type; Royce invoked Hamletian inaction as the opposing side to the Jamesian emphasis on the will to believe and the strenuous life.[3] Even as late as 1908 the character of Hamlet as a metaphor continued to retain its cultural power within the discourse of philosophy. In *The Philosophy of Loyalty,* Royce noted that loyalty to a cause, as well as loyalty to the cause of loyalty, "forbids cowardice; it forbids hesitancy . . . it forbids me to play Hamlet's part."[4]

Most importantly, Hamlet had an especially strong resonance within James's own life. James's specific difficulties of doubt and depression and his tendency toward neurasthenic symptoms arose largely out of the destruction of his sense of autonomy. His ego had been shattered by the loss of the desired objects of art as vocation and by lack of participation in the Civil War. In a sense at once metaphorical and empirical, James came to construct and interpret his life along the culturally inscribed lines of Hamlet. Thus Hamlet serves as a useful conduit into James's years of depression, doubt, and debility and as a mode of understanding the personal and cultural psychology behind these problems. Moreover, the trope of Hamlet will aid in examining the form in which James's resolution of these problems was expressed within his public philosophy. Hamlet and James, both armed with their aura of melancholia, doubt, and philosophical uncertainty, will be viewed in this chapter as kindred souls, each of whom expressed the essential contours of the nineteenth century's crisis of the individual.

The suggestion that young William James was textualizing himself into a nineteenth-century Hamlet is not entirely arbitrary. While there are sufficient heuristic reasons for employing Hamlet as a cultural trope useful in comprehending James's depressive years and the general intellectual uncertainty of the period, there are also historically compelling connections between James and the figure of Hamlet. Hamlet was the "old mole" who kept resurfacing in James's reading and thought during these years and who helped to define the contours and conclusions of his sufferings.

The figure of Hamlet was a familiar one to nineteenth-century Americans; performances of *Hamlet* were staples for the theater-going public, and few literate Americans managed to avoid the play or its message. Hamlet came to be viewed in often comical terms, as a person of weak character who was congenitally unable to reach any decision and was incapable of necessary action. The "humor" of Hamlet was only the phenomenal description or the reaction formation to the troubling crisis of the individual will that confronted Americans in this period. Lawrence Levine has explained that in James's era the appeal of Shakespeare's plays, particularly *Hamlet,* over classical Greek tragedies, centered around how Shakespearean characters—even when they were as indecisive as Hamlet—were ultimately held responsible "for their own fate." If they failed, they did so because they lacked sufficient "inner control."[5] Hamlet thus became a useful foil, a person who failed because he lacked the inner resources for action.

In an era when many American increasingly viewed competitive capitalism and bureaucratization as inevitable, *Hamlet* soothed their perceptions. The play confirmed the American belief that one might still retain control; the individual needed to exercise, in proper fashion, power of the will. Americans reasoned that they, unlike Hamlet, could rewrite the text of their lives; they need not be victim to blind forces. Hamlet's inability to kill Claudius and to exact the revenge demanded by the ghost of his father became a puzzle that American audiences solved by inserting their own answers as to how they would have acted under similar circumstances. In the process, American audiences were granting to themselves, and reading into the text of *Hamlet,* a degree of autonomy, confidence, and success that was largely lacking in the texts of their own lives.[6] James interpreted and transformed Hamlet into a figure closer to Greek tragic characters. In this view, Hamlet's inability to act might also be understood as the hesitancy of modern individuals in the face of either a metaphysical abyss or a deterministic universe. In either interpretation, Hamlet's hesitation became fraught with meaning and significance for James and other Americans.

The Hamlet familiar to James's youth and culture appeared as a figure of doubt, indecision, and madness. The lines around this interpretation were largely drawn from analyses by Johann Wolfgang von Goethe and Samuel Taylor Coleridge. Goethe viewed Hamlet as burdened by a task too immense. Hamlet was not only faced with the ghost's imperative that he seek revenge against the usurper Claudius, but also asked to confront his mother's desire for the murderer of her husband and to reform the corruption that defined Denmark within the play. Burdened by responsibilities too broad for his slender shoulders, Hamlet becomes incapacitated; he is reduced to being a man of inaction and indecision.[7] Coleridge also recognized the boundaries of Hamlet's indecision, but he gave to them a more subtle psychological explanation. Coleridge believed that Hamlet had failed to strike the proper balance between the outer and inner, the "real and imaginary," worlds. Dwelling in a universe of ideation and imagination, Hamlet is averse to action; he constitutes himself as a "world within himself." As a deep and preoccupied thinker, Hamlet is capable of recognizing the external situation for what it is; he does, after all, know that things are rotten in Denmark and does decide upon the correct course. But his self-reflection and absorption rob him of the will to act, and his sword of the will is repeatedly blunted by overcontemplation. Thus, within the play's structure, the indecision and self-reflection of Hamlet are countered by the decisiveness and action of Laertes and Fortinbras. Coleridge finds Hamlet self-conscious and failing—"defeated by continually resolving to do, yet doing nothing but resolve."[8] Goethe and Coleridge both sympathized and condemned, in turn, Hamlet's inability to act; his doubt and self-absorption became character flaws, the marks that made this Shakespearean drama a tragedy.

By the closing decades of the nineteenth century, another interpretation of Hamlet—one that would help to define aspects of James's depression—began to gain favor in France. An aesthetic view of Hamlet, one connected to *fin-de-siècle* decadent thought, was developed most fully by Stéphane Mallarmé and also exemplified in the analyses of Hamlet by Jules Laforgue and Paul Valéry. In essence, the French Hamlet was someone whose intense self-absorption was heroic and beautiful, representative of a pure soul faced with a world of deceit and ugliness, murder and manipulation. Hamlet was now presented by the Frenchmen as a searcher after an ideal and absolute world, a world of *l'art pour l'art*. His descent into the conceits of the real world is what draws the lines of this tragedy. Whereas Goethe and Coleridge viewed Hamlet's doubt and inactivity as negative aspects of his persona, the French decadents saw these traits as the proof of the purity of his soul and the essential basis of his appeal.[9]

James encountered *Hamlet* not only through the hermeneutic of previous interpretations but also through direct experience. His closest connection to the play occurred in the late 1860s, the crucial period that marked the onset of his melancholia and severe neurasthenic symptoms. While his recollections of the play and of Hamlet are often impressionistic, the significance of his encounter with Hamlet in these years is apparent. In October 1867, soon after arriving in Germany, James attended a dinner party at the home of Herman Grimm, a celebrated professor of art history and a man of wide learning. The dinner party was especially interesting for James because it is here that he gained his first taste of what he would later consider a peculiar breed, the erudite German *"fach"* professor. To James, however, Grimm did not serve as the archetype for this exalted personage. Wilhelm Dilthey, another dinner guest, gained that honor. That evening, Grimm and Dilthey discussed the problem of Hamlet. Grimm contended that Shakespeare had purposely sought to "mystify the reader and intentionally construct[ed] a riddle."[10] Dilthey, if we may read his later understanding of Shakespeare back into the content of this earlier discussion, probably argued that the character of Hamlet was flawed by self-absorption and was not, in contradistinction to Shakespeare, a man of action. Dilthey believed that Shakespeare had a "dynamic disposition," one directed outward and capable of comprehending characters of a personality quite different from his own. This "empathy" allowed Shakespeare to paint Hamlet as a doubting and indecisive character without any desire to deceive or confound his audience in the process.[11] In his letter home recounting this discussion of the play and of Shakespeare's personality, James did not record what role, if any, he assumed in the discussion. But his initial months in Germany had already been touched by an extensive and philosophically sophisticated discussion of Hamlet's character and of the accompanying philosophic problems raised by the play.

James experienced *Hamlet* during his stay in Germany. In April 1868 he attended a production starring Karl Devrient. James found Devrient's Hamlet to be quite as riveting and convincing as the portrayal by Edwin Booth, which he had seen in Boston.[12] Having attended at least two productions of the play in a short period of time, James once again encountered Hamlet within another text, Goethe's *Wilhelm Meister*, in which the play elicits an impassioned and dizzying response from Wilhelm, a response quite similar to the one that Hamlet had drawn from Claudius in the famous scene where he sought to "capture the conscience of the king."[13]

The play and the figure of Hamlet worked their way into James's consciousness during this period. In a diary entry of 13 April 1868, James confided that he was stunned by the "endless fullness of it *[Hamlet]*. How it bursts and cracks at every slam." Hamlet's way of looking at life was emotionally compelling but James wondered, thinking no doubt of himself, whether such an outlook was only a way station on the road to a more classical, rational, contained view of life. For Hamlet, as for James in his years of depression and debility, "actions of any sort" seemed "inadequate and irrelevant" in the harsh light of "feeling."[14]

On the same day that he recorded this diary entry, William again wrote about Hamlet, and he explicitly reflected upon the closeness between Hamlet and himself. In a letter to his brother Henry, William discussed *Hamlet* and also included an analysis of the validity of the classical conception of the universe as ordered and rational. William closed this epistle by admitting that he feared that his brother might "now be in the same doubt about *my* own sanity as most people are about Hamlet's." Although William next warned his brother to ignore "the bosh which my pen had lately got into the habit of writing," he had, by his own pen and the emerging script of his life, drawn a comparison between himself and the figure of Hamlet.[15] That connection, as a method of understanding the constituent parts of William's depression, needs further explication.

I

William James and Hamlet at first appear distanced from each other by the objects of their desire and by the accompanying nature of their melancholia. Hamlet seems to have an object or end in view at each turn of the play—his promise to kill Claudius and avenge his father is uppermost in his mind. Indeed, Hamlet's obvious vacillation in reaching enactment of this imperative forms the crucial pivot for the entire play, the point from which most interpretations spin. The circle of interpretation about what constitutes Hamlet's object of desire, however, is not so precisely drawn.

In 1897 Sigmund Freud remarked—to his trusted confidant Wilhelm Fleiss in a letter in which he first announced that the Oedipal complex was "a general phenomenon of early childhood"—that Hamlet's indecision about how and when to act was colored by an "obscure memory" within the wellsprings of his own guilt.[16] Hidden within the texture of Hamlet's self-recrimination lay, according to Freud, Oedipal jealousy directed against his father. To strike out against Claudius was to punish himself for desiring the flesh of his mother. Consequently, the very jealousy upon which Claudius acted replicated in content Hamlet's own Oedipal tensions. This interpretation of Hamlet has been revised and expanded by Jacques Lacan, who sees Hamlet as a classic melancholic suffering from the loss of a desired object, what Lacan refers to as "the Other." While Lacan's interpretation revolves around an Oedipal and narcissistic triangle of great complexity, for both Freud and Lacan the presence of Hamlet is marked by a lost object of desire—or at least an object incapable of possession. Moreover, Freud and Lacan likewise find guilt and animosity toward the father and a resultant form of melancholia within the figure of Hamlet.[17]

James's vocational desire was conscious and exact prior to the early 1860s; he directed his resources and talents toward art as a vocation. To achieve that end, he had begun an enthusiastic and promising study of painting at the Newport studio of William Morris Hunt. Thanks to the careful and conclusive analysis of Howard M. Feinstein, it is clear that Henry James, Sr., quashed William's art career through tactics of remonstrance, manipulation, and guilt inducement. With the demise of art as the object of desire, William was forced, without other appealing options, to enter into science as a vocation. While William bowed to his father's wishes, he did so reluctantly and less than successfully at first. William's initial study of physiology was often cursory; his earning of a medical degree from Harvard in 1869 was greater testimony to the program's lax nature than to James's directed study habits.[18]

When James discussed the notion of a "self he murdered" in his essay "Great Men and Their Environment" (1880), he was no doubt reflecting in some way upon his own substitution of science for art. What James meant by the idea of the "self he murdered" was that when a person chooses and becomes *committed* to a career peripheral to one desired more strongly, that individual will probably experience for a period of time a sense of loss. James's desire for art, "the old alternative ego," which was "once so vivid, fades into something less substantial than a dream."[19] Such a sense of loss remained apparent on a conscious level for

James well into the 1870s; in 1872 he could still contemplate his lost object of desire in a letter to his brother Henry. After describing the "soothing and hygienic affects of nature" with a painter's eye for detail, William confided to Henry that "I have been of late so sickened & skeptical of philosophical activity as to regret that I did not stick to painting, and to envy those like you to whom the aesthetic relations of things were the real world."[20]

Being deprived of the possibility for two objects of desire—participation in the Civil War and a career in art—in fairly quick succession by his father weakened James's ego, plunging him into what can best be described as a melancholic state. In essence, as defined by Freud, melancholia occurs to individuals who have lost a loved one or have had an ideal destroyed. What Freud found as the distinguishing mark between common mourning and extreme melancholia—and the distinction is appropriate, when James's life history is considered—is that the melancholiac need not be conscious of the loss of desired objects and experiences a radical diminution of ego strength. With James's objects of desire (conscious and unconscious in the case of art and war) suddenly destroyed by the exercise of paternal prerogatives, his ego structure was greatly diminished. To further complicate the process, William's father operated behind a cloak of "benign tyranny," thus making it more difficult for William to focus his animosity against a new object—that is, the tyrannical father. Throughout William's sojourn in Germany, whose purpose was to escape from his father's influence, his life was marked by deep melancholy, doubt, uncertainty, and a weak ego. Furthermore, as Freud pointed out in terms that might also apply to Hamlet as a cultural icon, the melancholic personality is prone to self-destructive urges, with suicide serving as the perceived solution to problems.[21]

Melancholia raged like a fever within William James as he experienced and repressed his severe disappointment over the lost objects of art as a vocation and service in the Civil War. The role of the father as authority figure dominated such calculations, forcing William to puzzle over what should be "the authority of a Father over his child."[22] This line of thought was not, and never could be, directly or fully pursued; it would have required a psychological mechanism free from guilt and more substantive than the ego structure that William exhibited in this period. A new dialectic of depression developed, one in which the external force of denial, originally and perhaps primally held by the father, was replaced by an internal mechanism of ego denial and self-punishment expressed through illness, doubt, and thoughts of suicide. In this equation, the clinical melancholic rests content with his or her depression; it serves as an excuse for failure and as a punishment for harbored guilt.

Only later did James come to understand fully the structure of melancholy. Writing at the age of forty-eight to his despondent teen-age daughter, James told her that what was worst about the disease of melancholy was how the person suffering from it does not "*want* to get out of it. We hate it, and yet we prefer staying in it."[23] As this internal mechanism of denial and failure, doubt and suffering replaced the older external modes of defeat represented by the father, William's feigned attempts to grasp a new object of desire and to reach a safe haven were sure to be defeated.

Well before his escape to Europe in 1867, young William James had begun to search for another object of desire, one that would not incur the intervention of his father. A logical choice for a genteel young man in his early twenties would have been a young woman of similar age and class background. William's letters from the 1860s, especially those to his sister, Alice, are brimming with evaluations of possible love objects for his attention. Yet for all of their confidence and braggadocio, these letters are also documents of William's worry about defeat in, and lack of fitness for, romance. His failure to decide upon a vocation usually predominates and serves as an excuse to explain why he could not be considered an eligible bachelor. As early as 1863 William confided to his mother that his vocational uncertainties and concomitant financial shakiness would be "hard on Mrs. W.J.," whomever she might be. How, he remarked rhetorically, might he "ask her to share an empty purse and a cold hearth."[24] How, indeed?

James's letters from Germany are a chronicle of love affairs of the imagination and of impossible and implausible objects of desire. He was well aware of the contours of his problem. After telling Alice about how much he had come to value "the domestic affections," he was struck and saddened by the recognition that "temporarily I am debarred from exercising any of them." James perceived that the issue centered around "the absence of any object with which to start up some sympathy and the feeling is real and unpleasant while it lasts." But in both this letter and a subsequent one to his sister, he announced the names of many young women who might become natural objects for his affection.[25] His inability to pursue these objects had been well formed by the time of the European journey. James had already found himself defeated in achieving the object of his amorous desires quite as much as he had been frustrated over art and war. The contrasts that Shakespeare drew between inactive and contemplative Hamlet and decisive and heroic Laertes and Fortinbras are yet another example of how *Hamlet* bears affinities to James's life. For the character of Laertes or Fortinbras, all James needed to do was to insert Oliver Wendell Holmes, Jr.

The tall, gaunt figure of Holmes hovered both appealingly and threatening over James in the years immediately following the Civil War. On the most obvious level, Holmes was an old friend with whom James shared philosophical interests and who was, by all accounts, solicitous about James's failing health and spirits. Yet Holmes was also a competitor and a point of comparison. James's lack of service in the Civil War contrasted poorly with Holmes's heroism. Holmes had emerged from the war confident of his vocation, and he unstintingly applied himself to the study of the law. His father's initial opposition to the vocation of law apparently exercised little inhibiting effect upon the confident Holmes. Envy and jealousy intertwined in James's evaluation of his friend, but what predominated and overwhelmed was the disparity of their lives: Holmes was the hero now on the road to vocational success; James was the bench-sitter during the war and vocationally floundering young man. If this disparity were not sufficient enough to cripple James's ego, then it was magnified by the fact that the two were briefly suitors of the same woman.[26]

In 1866, a year before he left for Germany, William became interested in Fanny Dixwell. He found her "decidedly A1." Lest this object of desire seem too singular, he hedged his desire to "confine" his life to Fanny into a commitment to two other young women, as well as to Holmes, his brother Henry, and to medical school![27] Behind the façade of jocularity lurked desire—if not for Fanny in particular, then for a woman in general. William had stacked the cards to insure failure. After all, Fanny and Wendell were an item, and had been close friends for over eight years. Although Wendell might have been the last to know of Fanny's affection toward him, nearly everyone in Cambridge considered them a pair destined for marriage.[28] Their closeness was apparent, and James was well aware of it. Thus the exclamation "That villain Wendell Holmes has been keeping her all to himself," while true, expressed the impossibility of William's ever winning her.[29]

This focus upon an object of desire to replace earlier lost ones was doomed to futility. In one stroke, James had alleviated his ego's concern that he might win her affection and prove himself unable to accept her, while he gave himself an impossible object of desire; he insured that his failure would not be too painful or unexpected. The pattern had been deeply etched on William's psyche; he would drift about in search of an object for affection yet would be incapable of making a commitment to it. The allure of the "Other" as Woman would only be equalled and perhaps surpassed by the attractiveness of philosophy. But before being able to embrace either a woman or philosophy as an object of desire, William had to work his way out of an increasingly deep cycle of doubt and debility.[30]

II

Between 1867 and 1872, drifting, debility, and depression were the main elements in James's life. Often reduced to invalidism, William complained fully and defensively of a host of ailments—sometimes real and sometimes imagined, but always troublesome. To his brother Henry, William wrote: "I don't know whether you still consider my ailments to be imagination or humbug or not, but I know myself that they are as real as anyone's ailments ever were." The etiology of his problems is not as clear as their pragmatic expressions and consequences. Vision difficulties, as well as dorsal and stomach complaints, all mysterious in origin, gave James an excuse for remaining in Europe.[31] Just as Henry Lee Higginson and other young men of James's social class had used a variety of ailments to prolong their stays in Europe, William James also pleaded at various times with his parents to recognize that the Teplitz baths benefited his aching back or that rest in Berlin was necessary for his health.

When illness as an excuse or implicit demand for parental approval and financial support of his European sojourn sounded hollow, William could take a different approach. Having gone to Europe not only for health reasons but also for educational ones, William began to praise the German university system. He was learning the German language so that he might better audit courses in physiology and general science. When his health permitted, he attended lectures by Rudolf Virchow and Emil DuBois-Raymond in Berlin, or announced plans to go to Heidelberg to listen to the celebrated talks of Hermann Helmholtz and Wilhelm Wundt.[32] But illness also served as an excuse to avoid serious study that might lead to a determinate career. Hopes of studying physiology at Leipzig were thwarted by the realization that "my back will prevent" such an endeavor. All he could look forward to in fall 1867 was "retreat to Vienna where . . . I shall find social relaxation without much expense of strength."[33]

A German university education for James was halting at best, a paltry attempt rather than a sustained exercise. Letters written from Germany during 1867 and 1868 reveal only a young man desperately in search of direction and goal in life; without an object of desire, his consuming activity became fighting off depression. Melancholia and its expression in various physical ailments stemmed from James's failure to pursue art as a vocation and to alleviate such vocational disappointment by participation in the excitement and heroism of the Civil War. The depression was deepened by his sexual longings and frustrations. A sense of shame typical of melancholiacs represented the sum total of these failures and dead ends.

After all, William was the first-born child in the James family; his birth had in a way been anointed by Ralph Waldo Emerson. Henry James, Sr., literally constructed the orbit of the James family around William's star. In Germany it became increasingly evident that William's star was only a nova, a promisingly brilliant star destined to extinguish itself quickly. As

William precipitously fell into melancholia, his shame at earlier failures and lack of a vocational thrust soon overwhelmed him. While his brothers Robertson and Wilky, with their recently freed slaves, struggled against racism and economic hostility to be successful in their Florida plantation, William was, as he expressed it in 1868, marked "without having earned a cent." Compared to his younger brothers, he was a failure and accordingly felt "ashamed" of his status and prospects.[34] The feeling of being "small and shabby," which had come to define his life during the Civil War, also continued in its aftermath. Such emotions still haunted him in Germany, a place supposedly far removed from such concerns. Finally, William viewed himself as a drag on his father's strained financial assets. Because of his own demands upon the family purse for an extended stay in Europe, William was now the person who prevented his brother Henry from effecting a similar escape to Europe, away from the parental nest in Cambridge.[35]

In James's life, shame and debility led to periodic crises, convincing him that he had "touched bottom." In 1870, at about the time he learned of the death of his childhood friend Minny Temple, James suffered what he called "a great dorsal collapse," forcing him to evaluate the current extent of his sunken moral condition.[36] While he was well aware of the need for a life of reasoned action as the only antidote to his melancholy, relief was not to come immediately or easily. Only two years later, James went into another tailspin, which he later recounted under the protective guise of a French correspondent in his *Varieties of Religious Experience*. The details of this "panic fear" as an expression of "the worst kind of melancholy" occupies a secure place within the James literature and its close textual and strategic relation to his father's "vastation" has also been adequately scrutinized. James's "panic fear" was simply another manifestation, albeit a more dramatic one, of the depths of his long-term bout with melancholy and philosophic uncertainty. In its worst aspects, this "panic fear" transformed James; he now "awoke morning after morning with a horrible dread at the pit of my stomach, and with a sense of the insecurity of life that I never knew before, and that I have never felt since."[37]

Crises and panic fears brought James close to suicide, and endowed him with a continuing sympathy for the plight of the suicide. Immediately after arriving in Germany, William's back problems left him severely depressed and in such "low-spirits" that he entertained "thoughts of the pistol, the dagger, and the bowl." In January 1868 James confided to his despondent friend Tom Ward that he had "all last winter" literally been "on the continual verge of suicide." James offered no precise explanation as to what had driven him to contemplate taking his own life, but the structure of the letter indicates that suicidal thoughts were closely connected to his lack of vocational direction and his inability to adhere to an object or end. Both he and Tom Ward—as James began the process of both universalizing and symbolizing his own inner turmoils into attributes shared by others—did not wish to be considered a "mere loafer." James wanted satisfying work that would "allow him to feel that through it he takes hold of the reality of things." James desired, above all else, to escape from his dreamlike and debilitating state of drift—"the dead drifting of my own life," as he once phrased it. His desire was for an object that would motivate and allow him to make a "*nick* . . . in the raw stuff the race has got to shape and so assert my reality."[38]

The assertion of James's reality was a complex problem. Its past history was weighted with dashed hopes and parental intervention. Its present course encountered practical difficulties: What vocation should he pursue and where would he find the resources for that quest? But a philosophical conundrum of no small stature also played havoc in James's mind: What was the nature of reality and what consequences might such a metaphysical reality have upon his chances of pursuing a goal? The solution to his depression and drifting came to have a dual nature, both practical and philosophical. While some commentators may well be correct that James's problems sprang from his vocational dispute with his father, at least as the scene of origin, it will not do to lose sight of the degree to which William consistently symbolized, and in the process expressed and repressed, these disputes into philosophical discourse. The search for a mode of escape from depression became at an early point a philosophical inquiry into the nature of reality. Yet it was greatly aided, in practice, by the intervention of external factors.[39] This interplay between inner resources and philosophical doubt with external realities and demands reminds one of the confluence between the texture of William James's life and the text of *Hamlet*.

III

Notes of Hamletian inaction and philosophical uncertainty ring within James's depressive period; their tune is not quite the same one that analysts traditionally hear in *Hamlet*. Hamlet, according to most accounts, is a young man—in itself a misinterpretation—racked by doubts that propel him into a state of constant inactivity. In contrast to this understanding, the more recent French interpretation of Hamlet views him as someone secure in his philosophical and aesthetic ideals; these ideals separate him from a world of pressing and putrid demands. His life, even when dominated with the demand for revenge, is structured to maintain his purity at all costs. Hamlet constitutes his life as an art form divorced from social requirements and expectations. This stance makes him less a pure

doubter—though there are certainly strong elements of that in Hamlet—
than an aesthetic rebel. What spells Hamlet's doom, and makes the play a
tragedy, is that he is, despite his own desires, forced to play his hand in the
games of the world. In his state of inaction, Hamlet appears as the philosopher ruminating on the nature of man and action, and most fully on
the pressing questions of human autonomy and social determinism. The
intensity of his thought on these issues makes him in the eyes of the play's
other characters all the more prone toward madness. Whether Hamlet's
insanity is a pose—for Lacan the feigning of madness is "the strategy of
the modern hero"—or a philosophical expression of affairs in the rotten
state of Denmark remains a viable issue of debate among interpreters of
the play.[40] The diversity of answers is similar to the interpretive squabbles
and conclusions marking analyses of James's philosophical meanderings
and his flirtation with madness during his depressive period.

Doubt seems, at first glance, to be the defining characteristic of young
William James: doubts about his vocation, doubts about his "manliness,"
doubts about how to act, doubts about the implications of his acts, and
doubt about doubt seem the core of his life between 1867 and 1872.[41]
Some argue that the intensity and inclusiveness of this doubt led to inaction and interminable philosophical rumination. The symptoms of
Jamesian doubt, its metaphysical and psychological structure, have been
imaginatively debated by James scholars whose fine distinctions concerning the nature and timing of James's depression have introduced a new set
of psychological terms into the vocabulary of the debate. William A.
Clebsch presented *acedia* as the correct technical term for James's problems: "Acedia was rather an overscrupulous wondering about what one
ought to do. It prevented one from doing anything."[42] If acedia be at the
heart of James's inaction and depression, then he comes to appear as a
latter-day version of Hamlet the doubter, an individual whose thoughts
and doubts are so immense that they exempt him from the possibility of
action. Sometimes acedia is replaced by *anhedonia* to capture the essentials of James's "pathological depression." The choices of these terms are
not wholly arbitrary, both appear in James's own clinical description of
depression. As James described it in his *Varieties,* anhedonia is marked by
"mere passive joylessness and dreariness, discouragement, dejection, lack
of taste and zest and spring."[43]

Abulia, another clinical term used to describe James's problems, is
borrowed from his *The Principles of Psychology.* James explained, in its
section "The Obstructed Will," that abulia occurs when an individual
has a clear vision as to what must be done (Hamlet's need to avenge his
father's murder would serve as an example), but "the act either fails to
follow or follows in some other way." The will is clear in its choice of
object and even in its desire to act yet is incapable, for various reasons,

from translating wishes into actions. Thus, for some analysts, the psychological problem of how to act, rather than the philosophical question as to why one should act, is the most important issue.[44] It is important to remember that James was caught up, as were many in his cultural and intellectual milieu, in a trembling engagement with metaphysical questions, concerns about the nature of the universe. The implications of these questions, indeed the answers that James initially reached, only served to dampen his spirits and to prevent him from acting. The philosophical aspects, then, of his clinical anhedonia or acedia represent a crucial foundation for understanding James in his depressive years and for comprehending the impassioned social message written into the philosophy in his later years.

IV

During his years of depression and debility, James contemplated the philosophical issues dominating European and American thought in the nineteenth century. The familiar paired opposites of free will or determinism, idealism or materialism, optimism or pessimism demanded resolution or synthesis. In the face of such weighty choices, James and other thinkers at times hesitated, almost preferring to remain lost in their doubts. Mediation or resolution of these dichotomies would not come easily to James; as a young man he already recognized his tendency toward dangerously numbing philosophical speculation. Yet out of these intellectual struggles would evolve the fundamental tenets of Jamesian philosophy, as well as the essentials of its cultural resonance.

The deterministic view held, as James later expressed it, "that those parts of the universe already laid down absolutely appoint and decree what the other parts shall be. The future has no ambiguous possibilities hidden in its womb."[45] Determinism, which clearly compromised and perhaps even destroyed a voluntaristic conception of freedom, stood firm as James's chief philosophical nemesis in the 1860s and 1870s; the dilemma posed by determinism haunted him throughout his life. While he never fooled himself into believing that he might prove beyond suspicion the truth of freedom of the will, he nonetheless held that one should assume the truth of free will and thus begin "acting as if it were true." To this end he would direct many of the essays in *The Will to Believe* (1897).[46]

James's comments on determinism during the period from 1867 to 1872, however, are sketchy; they were more fully developed in "German Pessimism" (1875), "Bain and Renouvier" (1876), and the famous essay "The Dilemma of Determinism" (1884). In the late 1860s, in a series of letters to his friend Tom Ward, James outlined the problem presented to

him by the deterministic position in philosophy: "I feel that we are Nature through and through, that we are wholly conditioned, that not a
wiggle of our will happens save as the result of physical laws."[47] The
serious contemplation of the deterministic viewpoint could, in an ego-
deficient young man such as James, have serious consequences. Why act
when one was little more than a speck of sand in the vast desert of life?
How might a moral stance fit into a world of determined proportions?
James did not want to succumb to the strong logic of determinism—
which was perhaps unassailable on its own terms—especially because its
implications effectively described the reality of his debilitated life. Thus he
continued to maintain, even in his moments of greatest despair, that
reason and action were valid and freely chosen responses capable of
dispelling the fog of determinism.

According to historian Bruce Kuklick, "materialism meant determinism and determinism meant fatalism" for James. Or, as James phrased it
in 1873, "Pessimism must then be fatalism."[48] In this equation, pessimism conspired to deny the acting subject, to delimit human autonomy,
and, in the process, to destroy the possibilities for a strenuous moralism.
For young William James, bereft of the ego structure necessary to act
upon the world, retreat into the sanctuary of depression and debility
seemed the only possible response to the problems of vocation, failure to
serve in the Civil War, denied objects of amorous intent, and a deterministic view of the universe. It is here that James's personal life particularly
colored his philosophical one. James still retained the option of choosing
which slant he might give to philosophical questions. Even if one ac-
knowledges that James viewed determinism as fatalism, there is no reason, especially given the context of nineteenth-century thought, why that
assumption should have been translated into a pessimistic philosophy.
Faced with an increasingly complex and uncertain society, many other
Americans of this period found the deterministic and optimistic vision of
Herbert Spencer and his American followers quite reassuring; Spencerianism transformed uncertainty into certitude, change into progressive necessity.[49]

Cloaked in the culturally normative language of Darwinian science,
Spencerian determinism offered a precise and simple formula that promised to explain how even the most diverse and complex phenomena were
joined into a gloriously ordered evolutionary niche. Spencer's cosmic
philosophy unified the universe, stating that it was moving toward pro-
gressively higher developmental stages. Spencerian ideas were commonly
understood as deterministic paeans to progress. This teleology soothed
the nerves of many Americans: it presented a fatalistic philosophy but
promised happiness; it recognized complexity but offered unity; it championed science but left room for religion. Spencer's American vogue was a

determinism made palatable. And it was, for many American intellectuals of that time, a doctrinal position—whatever its internal inconsistencies or ultimate consequences might have been—that allowed them to accept the ramifications of scientific determinism without surrendering their belief in beneficent progress.

Spencerian optimistic determinism transformed a world that appeared frighteningly complex and chaotic into a calm and ordered universe. It is not surprising that James was initially attracted to Spencerian ideas. Their appeal quickly waned when Chauncey Wright directed his devastating barbs against its scientistic pretensions. Under Wright's tutelage and as his philosophical sophistication grew far beyond the paltry boundaries of Spencerian nostrums, James evolved into one of the more creative and consistent anti-Spencerians. In mock-parody style, James would later "sum-up" the essentials of the Spencerian system: "Evolution is a change from a no-howish, untalkaboutable, all-alikeness to a somehowish and in general talkaboutable not-all-alikeness by continuous stick-to-getherations and something-elsifications."[50] Without the tender, pseudo-scientific appeals of Spencerian evolutionism to fortify him and without the mature confidence of Wright's empirically sustained philosophical view, James was left a solitary figure pondering the frightening nature of the universe. To a young man without self-confidence or vocation, the idea that the universe might be little more than "mere cosmic weather"—one weather system replaced by another in Wright's description—at first proved too much for James to handle, either emotionally or intellectually.[51]

In the 1860s and 1870s, when James surveyed the terrain of metaphysics and science, he increasingly encountered an essentially "restless universe," one marked by disunity, uncertainty, and illusion. As early as the mid-1870s, James had made his peace with this conception of the universe and had actually come to celebrate its varied possibilities. This accommodation became, of course, the defining signature, the expressive paraph, of James's philosophical system. Thus he began erecting the structure for his mature vision of the universe in 1876 when he seconded Charles Renouvier's assertion that "properly speaking, there is no certitude, all there is is men who are certain. . . . Certitude is thus nothing but belief . . . a moral attitude." The individual must, therefore, choose to act with belief in the possibility of freedom. By this time, then, the Jamesian formula that the world of experience was "a blooming, buzzing confusion" prior to conceptualization and attention was securely in place as the emblem of freedom and possibility. James maintained that, even after conceptualization had occurred, the presence of chance—the crucial element in his case against determinism—in the universe kept alive the exercise of freedom. These emerging views forced James to evaluate the pressing and sobering question of responsibility: How to act responsibly and knowledgeably in a dauntingly complex and plural world? James would not fully come to grips with these thorny issues until publication of "The Moral Philosopher and the Moral Life" (1891) and *Pragmatism* in 1907.[52]

However, it is dangerous to assume that possibility instead of horror, and freedom rather than dread, accompanied the notion that the universe was restless, without inherent unity. In his depressive years, during which James lacked the confidence to face the phenomenal world with its vagaries of the moment, the thought of a world indeterminate and open, quite as much as the vision of a world determinate and closed to free will, inspired fear and trembling. This world, which appeared to James at age thirty-one as illusory—described in his diary as a "dream conception" or a "Maya"—initially proved too difficult to accept.[53]

Indeed, the contours of the universe might be even worse than James imagined. He later recounted how a friend had described the open Jamesian universe as "like the sight of the horrible motion of a mass of maggots in their carrion bed."[54] Another friend, philosopher Thomas Davidson, wrote that the Jamesian universe was a too full of "chaotic *maybes* of the formless unknown." Davidson found James's description of existence as presented in "Is Life Worth Living?" (1895) to be a "mere speculation, a mere game of hazard, in which no matter how well you play, you are as likely to lose as to win." Such a conception, Davidson tellingly remarked, "cannot . . . fail to be injurious, especially to reflective young men."[55] Perhaps similar conceptions and fears played in James's mind when he imagined, during his years of debility, that the metaphysical structure of the universe resembled nothing more than an "abyss of horrors."[56] If such a description had any resonance for James during these nightmarish years, then he faced the same unnerving certitude of the abyss that Nietzsche brilliantly described as the legacy of Hamlet and as the cause of Hamlet's madness.

Nietzsche's flashing insight best captures the coloring of Hamlet's madness and also explains the philosophical underpinnings of his separation from and inactivity in the world. In *Ecce Homo* (1888), a work composed when the sound of madness played in his own head, Nietzsche asked the question: "Is Hamlet understood?" People fail to recognize, Nietzsche answered, that Hamlet suffered less from doubt than from *"certainty,"* a certitude born of knowledge rather than of doubt. Nietzsche contended that Hamlet comprehended the nature of existence; he understood the metaphysical structure of the universe. Hamlet encountered only the certainty of an abyss behind the veil of things. A few questions should be asked in the face of such a stark realization: How should one act? How should one come to define and create one's life in a universe bereft of the meaning traditionally bestowed by a conception of God? Answers to these questions were complicated by Nietzsche's belief that "we are all *afraid* of the truth."[57]

Drawing an analogy between Nietzsche's insight into the nature of Hamlet's dilemma and the problems that James confronted presents a new view of his depressive years. The issue for comprehending James is transformed from an explication of simply his doubt and inaction into an evaluation of the nature of his understanding of the truth of the "abyss of horrors," as James confided to his diary, and his concomitant attempts to overcome the implications of this conception of the universe. In 1895 James completely recognized the pressing need to *"not be afraid of life."*[58] While this discussion ensued for James along the lines of the traditional and important philosophical issues of free will versus determinism, and idealism versus materialism, the answer that first troubled James and that forced him deeper into his depression posited the reality of a universe without certitude. It was a "Maya" or an "abyss of horrors." In Nietzschean terms, this illuminating but blinding sense of *"certainty"* forced James toward a psychological method and a philosophical comprehension which might allow him to elevate himself to a higher ground, from where the universe would no longer be painted in such depressing colors.

James would eventually embrace a conception of a universe in which freedom reigned supreme and the individual strenuously and morally accepted responsibility for action. Although certitude of success in such a universe was never assured, at least the individual retained the ability to act. The reality of this imperative alluringly and frighteningly perched almost beyond the reach of a young man who found his self-identity largely destroyed by the removal of his key objects of desire by his benign yet controlling father. William James would eventually succeed in restructuring his interpretation of the implications of this wild universe without the tragedy that befell Hamlet; in the process, James would universalize his solutions into the social expression of an important and sophisticated philosophy that promised to help Americans suffering from a nagging sense of the "weightless," unreal, and unbelieving attitude that all too often seemed to define the modern age.

V

In time, James would formulate his philosophical response to the horror of living in a modern universe of doubt, change, and uncertainty. But, in the late 1860s and early 1870s, James expressed little of the existential confidence, the sober yea-saying to a life of moral struggle, that enthuses the essay "Is Life Worth Living?"[59] The younger William James searched for philosophical assurances and psychological therapeutic to help him face the metaphysics of the abyss. He briefly flirted with classical Greek philosophy, finding solace in the Stoics' dismissal of metaphysical concerns and their accompanying emphasis upon the form of moral activity. Contrary to the outlines of James's Hamletian existence marked by passivity and doubt, the Greeks appeared to reside in a world of action. James remained divided about the intellectual credibility, if not usefulness, of the classical conception of things. On the one hand, the Greeks were impressive because of their understanding of the natural order, the world as "its own justification." This hearty acceptance of the universe allowed them to act without numbing metaphysical rumination. On the other hand, while action-oriented and heroic, the Greeks were also, as James might have phrased it later, guilty of a "once-born" mentality. Not having touched the depths and despair of life, the Greeks, in James's view, had an understanding of the nature of existence that was too smooth around the edges. Although the Greeks were to be admired and emulated as men of action, they stood condemned, in the end, to the sin of "intellectual limitation."[60]

The intellectual limitations connected to such an easy acceptance of the universe and a lack of concern about its inner structure seemed far removed from the questioning attitude of modern men and women, easily prone to get lost in the "maggot" or "Maya" nature of existence. The Greek world view at best served for James as a temporary corrective to Hamlet's vision of existence. Hamlet was confronted by a world without an inner rationale or with a rotten core; reality was marked by deceit and manipulation. As William expressed it in a critically important letter to his brother Henry in 1868, the modern world of flux, indeterminacy, and uncertainty could only be faced by Hamlet with "groans and aches," and the deep "mystery of things" immobilized him. The Hamletian universe must remain "ineffable." Confronted with a universe that was little more than a "Maya," confidence in the power of language to describe and capture reality—and here James alludes brilliantly to the constant punning of Hamlet—had to be "abandoned, one form of words seeming as irrelevant as another." In this universe, much like the one James was then encountering, "crazy conceits and countersenses slip and 'whirl' around the vastness of the subject as if the tongue were mocking itself." In a universe of "Maya"-like mystery, the questions of why to act, of how to act, and of how to arrive at "a moral point of view" seemed immense and insolvable.[61]

VI

The dilemma of Hamlet essentially corresponded to the crisis of the autonomous will that James experienced and that was central to the late-

Victorian era. To face the abyss without a confirmed moral agenda, without a certitude, haunted many thoughtful Americans during a period dominated by massive social change and dislocation. Hamlet had escaped by the route of inactivity. James feared that he would solve this crisis by a descent into madness. He recognized as much by worrying that his brother Henry might actually "be in some doubt about *my* sanity as most people are about Hamlet's."[62]

William James came perilously close to madness during the years when he faced the stark reality of the "abyss of horrors." In S. P. Fullinwider's analysis of James's depression, James actually diagnosed himself as entering into madness. More importantly, according to the period's medical literature, with which James was certainly familiar, in clinical terms he "*was* going insane."[63] Indeed, one historian, Robert J. Richards, asserts that in all probability James was forced to retreat to the McLean Asylum a few years later.[64] The clearest characterization of this descent-into-madness thesis occurs in James's own description of his "panic fear" of 1872. The images and concerns revolving around this particular crisis might equally well describe many of his other crises, which brought him to the verge of suicide and neurasthenic disability, during these years.

The textual expression of James's "panic fear" certainly lends itself to various readings and angles of interpretation. For example, comparisons between William's "panic fear" and the "vastation" crisis endured by his father nearly thirty years earlier are difficult to avoid. This leads Feinstein to suggest that William's "breakdown was more his father's than his own."[65] William's "panic fear" was undoubtedly the culminating expression of his crisis of vocation, and it highlights the battered state of his ego identity after his unsuccessful struggles with his father. But the "panic fear" expressed metaphysical concerns as well, and it may profitably be read as a concrete description of the "abyss of horrors" or the "Maya" world, a symbolic structuring of the dread that James felt in confronting a world unstintingly marked by flux and indeterminacy. In this sense, the well-known phenomenon of late-Victorian doubt appears as only a subterfuge that lessened the frightening certitude that the universe was nothing more than an abyss.

James's recollection of the "panic fear" within *Varieties* commences with him in a Hamletian "state of philosophic pessimism and general depression of spirits about my prospects." Philosophic pessimism, as James understood it during this period, closely related to the apparently contradictory notions that the individual lacked free will and was thus reduced to a type of automaton and yet the world might be without order or progress. Feinstein and others argue that James's trembling concern about "prospects" may well be taken as a veiled reference to his vocational uncertainty. It need not obviate the philosophic undertones inherent in his depressed condition. It seems helpful to quote the full account of "panic fear" before analyzing this important and revelatory expression of James's early life history:

> Whilst in this state of philosophic pessimism and general depression of spirits about my prospects, I went one evening into a dressing-room in the twilight . . . when suddenly there fell upon me without any warning, just as if it came out of the darkness, a horrible fear of my own existence. Simultaneously, there arose in my mind the image of an epileptic patient whom I had seen in the asylum, a black-haired youth with greenish skin, entirely idiotic, who used to sit all day on one of the benches . . . with his knees drawn up against his chin, and the coarse gray undershirt, which was his only garment, drawn over them inclosing his entire figure. He sat there like a sort of sculptured Egyptian cat or Peruvian mummy, moving nothing but his black eyes and looking absolutely non-human. This image and my fear entered into a species of combination with each other. *That shape am I*, I felt, potentially. Nothing that I possess can defend me against that fate, if the hour for it should strike for me as it struck for him. There was such a horror of him, and such a perception of my own merely momentary discrepancy from him, that it was as if something hitherto solid within my breast gave way entirely, and I became a mass of quivering fear. After this the universe was changed for me altogether. I awoke morning after morning with a horrible dread at the pit of my stomach, and with a sense of the insecurity of life that I never knew before, and that I have never felt since.[66]

This description evokes a universe marked by trembling, madness, and chance. Fear issues forth from the indeterminate, arbitrary nature of existence. The Darwinian flavor that James brings to this starkly naturalistic rendering of existence is as predatory in its own fashion as any Victorian nightmare vision of "nature red of tooth and claw." Here, nature is maggotlike in both the mental and physical realms, and the wildernesses of existence and mind lose all distinction. Competition for survival here marks the utter hopeless or useless character of the struggle: the individual is simply the prey of an immense, dark environment. The line that separates the "entirely idiotic" and "non-human" epileptic from the rational, normal James is constantly shifting, if not entirely illusory. The epileptic figure—crouched in the corner and trembling before the naked face of the world—is of the same desperate species as James. Both are mere atoms of existence, fragments of life caught up in a losing battle with the mystery of things. The nature of this fear, illustrated by the "Egyptian cat or Peruvian mummy," makes clear that the individual is only a prisoner of mocking fate or the "abyss of horrors."

Even in his terrible despondency, in the stultifying horror of his "panic fear," James was representative in his perceptions. Royce's "temporary vexations," for example, were sufficient to plunge him into a psychological depression marked by an intense obsessional neurosis and a severe breakdown in the late 1880s.[67] Philosophers were not the sole possessors of panic fears. In the late-nineteenth century, the familiar image of the "madwoman in the attic," as well as the naturalistic fear of a descent into animality and madness in the novels of Frank Norris and other realist or naturalist authors, became cultural commonplaces, testaments to the restructuring of the world by the corrosive force of modernity. Madness became less a pose than a response to various dilemmas and a retreat from commitment.[68] This retreat, James well realized, had its own forms of intense suffering and recrimination. However, a simple question continued to confront him: How to escape from the grasp of fear, doubt, and uncertainty?

James's problems with the will, to act intelligently and firmly, were complicated, for he was a modern, scientific young man. Unlike the Greeks, he could not trust the powers of fate; he did not imagine them as necessarily beneficent. Already a learned student of Darwinian theory, James knew that the Spencerians' mechanistic vision of progressive evolution was substantiated by complacent belief more than by empirical evidence. James walked closer to Darwin's formulation that only change and struggle defined the natural world and that progress was fictive and convenient. James realized that, because of fate in the hands of mechanism or uncertainty, his future could be that of the epileptic; such a recognition was enough to turn him into a "mass of quivering fear." What he would describe, without any especial dread, as the universe's "swarming continuum, devoid of distinction or emphasis" in 1878 was quite capable of immobilizing his conscious will and evoking within him a debilitating "sense of the insecurity of life" in the early 1870s. Certitude and knowledge of the "abyss of horrors" pushed him back into the terrible and familiar world of depression and debility.[69]

VII

A gnawing recognition of the ultimate "insecurity of life" long remained central to James's thought; it prevented the hearty moralism of his later years from sometimes sounding like little more than a philosophic echo of Victorian nostrums regarding the strenuous life. A realization of the universe's metaphysical uncertainty, as well as its endless possibilities, would eventually form the foundation of James's philosophy of freedom and voluntarism. Insecurity continued as a staple of his mature philosophy, but its presence was dwarfed in importance by an emphasis upon melioristic action, the view that individuals could act, and transform the world, in a useful manner. Meliorism promised that the maggotlike world would be transformed from a "blooming, buzzing confusion" into a universe that welcomed Promethean hands.[70] This new world view was more confident and mature; its philosophical development was partly a consequence of James's own transformation from doubter to actor, from a young man without prospects into a mature Harvard professor. Recovery from Hamletian uncertainty and its metaphysical implications marked the first necessary step before James could develop the strength to work out his mature philosophical views. External no less than internal factors, both psychological and philosophical, allowed James to escape from the Hamletian nightmare. As his confidence slowly, painfully increased, so did his suspicion that other individuals might be able to hold their own against, if not conquer, the nightmarish shadings of indeterminacy and uncertainty. This message would become the social expression embedded in James's philosophy. But before its wisdom could be transcribed, James had to discard his Hamletism and enter into the uncertain, phenomenal world of everyday existence.

There is a lively debate among James scholars over how to prioritize the constituent elements in James's slow recovery out of his years of depression and doubt. Some of them stress that James's regeneration only became apparent after certain external factors had come into play. In brief, this view holds that an offer from Charles W. Eliot, President of Harvard, of a position in physiology for the 1872 academic year, followed by the opportunity to teach anatomy and physiology the following year, gave James a goal, an object of desire that allowed him to marshal his reserves of energy and intellect. Armed with a goal, James pushed to the side his tendency toward debilitating philosophizing about the nature of the universe; he began to throw off the ghost of Hamlet. Marriage to Alice Gibbens in 1878 is often cited as the other external factor that saved James from the storm center of his depression. Historians argue that these two external factors, employment and marriage, bequeathed to James a renewed sense of ego strength, solved his thorny problem of vocation, and ended his long period of sexual uncertainty. These external factors, in sum, gave James tangible objects of desire that lifted him out of his depression.[71]

Beginning in the early 1870s, external factors converged and sped James's recovery from depression. In 1872, James accepted the position teaching physiology at Harvard. By settling into the career of university professor, James gained an increased sense of self and place within the world, as well as a standardized schedule that drew him away from his morbid self-preoccupation and speculations about the groaning mystery of existence. Teaching had an efficacious affect upon James. He was pleased to find "the work very interesting and stimulating," to a degree that he "should think it [college teaching] not unpleasant as a permanent thing." Of course, as James had noted in his account of the "panic fear," permanency and certainty were only fictions. Soon after expressing his initial satisfaction with teaching, however, he turned down reappointment at Harvard in favor of another European sojourn in search of health and certitude. Yet, by March 1874, James was sailing home in order to resume teaching the courses "Natural History" and "The Comparative Anatomy and Physiology of Vertebrates." Following the death of Jeffries Wyman, who had been his professor at the school's Lawrence Scientific School, James temporarily assumed direction of the laboratory and Museum of Comparative Anatomy. James, with characteristic shifts and turns over the next twenty years, would move between several departments—from comparative anatomy to physiology to psychology and then, finally, to that of philosophy in 1879. At last he was secure in his object; he was committed, through the largess of circumstance and personal desire, to the career of university professor.[72]

By 1874 James was firmly embarked upon his university career, but his stormy disposition, with its tendency toward depression and debility, required the presumed calming shelter of a wife. Help arrived in the presence of Alice Gibbens. What makes her introduction into James's life so interesting and psychologically instructive is the role that Henry James, Sr., played in this affair. He stood as the negator of his son's desires; through his benign tyranny he had successfully wrenched two objects of desire—the vocation of art and service in the Civil War—from his son's grasp. In the process, the father unwittingly set into motion the forces that would reduce the son into a "low-lived wretch." But what the father could take, he could also restore. Henry James, Sr., first encountered Alice in the late winter of 1876 at a meeting of the Radical Club. From the beginning, he prophesied to himself the likelihood of Alice as his son's future wife. The father, and eventually the son, viewed Alice as the ideal of an intelligent and directed individual, someone who had overcome family adversity with perseverance and unstinting dedication—precisely the qualities needed to deal with William James's often-churlish nature. In essence, Alice came anointed with Henry, Sr.'s blessing, and it appeared that she would be a stable and comforting helpmate for William. Although their courtship may have been as rocky and uncertain as William's first foray into university teaching, their marriage in 1878 inaugurated a life together that would last over thirty years. Demons would continue to haunt James, and his spirits and health would rise and ebb accordingly, but, because of Alice's faithful and steadying presence, he would no longer sink into a "mass of quivering fear." Her power would help to shield him from the "maggots" of the universe while also assuaging the "horror of the abyss" or the mechanistic demands of fate.

When Ralph Barton Perry wrote that James suffered from a "personal

crisis that could be relieved only by a *philosophical* insight," he acknowledged the internal nature and metaphysical roots of James's depression
and suggested the contours that his recovery might assume.[73] James's
problems were deemed ultimately philosophical in essence and hence
solvable by philosophical enlightenment. The assumed source for James's
ascent from depression was the impassioned writings of the French neo-
Kantian Renouvier. Renouvier offered James a doctrine that explicitly
opted for the efficacy of free will. Renouvier allowed free will and conscious desire to have an influence in the universe equal to that of mechanistic interpretations. Renouvier presented this view as an option, one
chosen without certitude but with expectations of satisfaction.[74] The
impact of Renouvier's doctrine of free will and freedom upon James is well
known. In spring 1870, while undergoing one of his periodic crises, James
read the first part of Renouvier's second *Essais*. In his diary, James
breathlessly recalled the profound and therapeutic effect of the *Essais*.
Renouvier's notion of free will as "the sustaining of a thought *because I
choose to* when I might have other thoughts" was soon transformed into
James's motto that "My first act of free will shall be to believe in free
will."[75]

Positing an ideal of freedom—the desire to act without being encumbered with the Hamletian shackles of doubt and neurasthenic disability—unfortunately did not translate into a reality for James. Vague images of the "abyss of horrors," detailed renderings of a deterministic
universe, and the ingrained habit of doubt competed with the ideal of
freely willed actions. Time and outside interests, as well as marriage and
vocation, conspired to draw James slowly away from depression. Psychological insight also played an important role in bringing James into fuller
contact with the energies of life and philosophy. But psychology and,
especially, philosophy were not immediately useful to James. Indeed, in
the 1870s he believed that he must "abstain from mere speculation," the
sine qua non of the philosopher.[76] In 1873 he worried that the necessity of
the philosopher to be someone "who has publicly renounced the privilege
of trusting blindly" threatened to crush his desires to embrace free will.
Thus the "business" of philosophical contemplation, James sadly recognized, "is not normal for most men, and not for me."[77] In time, the
practice of philosophical speculation would become not only normal for
James but also the essence of his life and fame.

VIII

James consistently transformed his personal problems into public issues;
he transcribed his own trying battles with doubt and depression into the
text of his psychology and philosophy. While Freud's reliance upon his

own dreams as the data for analysis in *The Interpretation of Dreams* (1900) far outstrips the centrality of the personal elements that James interjected into his *Principles of Psychology,* elements of his own life history nonetheless strongly enter into it. Who can wonder that the subject of the following impassioned description of a doubt-infested individual in *Principles* is not an evocation of James's own experiences?: "There is no more miserable human being than one in whom nothing is habitual but indecision, and for whom the lighting of every cigar . . . and the beginning of every bit of work, are subjects of express volitional deliberation."[78]

Principles is brilliantly propelled by a series of what Gordon Allport has characterized as "productive paradoxes," or creative riddles. In his work, James creatively engages, without necessarily solving by dint of a system, the psychophysical riddle (mind-body problem), the riddle of positivism (Are the objective techniques of the natural sciences capable of dealing adequately with the subjective aspects of mental life?), the riddle of the self (How can one account for the integration of personality in the face of divergent experiences and diverse impulses?), the well-known problem of free will, and the additional riddles of association (How does the mind connect ideas into more complex entities?) and individuality (What makes our mental states uniquely known to us?).[79] James confronted these "productive paradoxes" with immense erudition. When connected to his willingness to employ the methods of empirical science without slighting the testimony of introspection, these paradoxes make *Principles,* in the strong praise of Jacques Barzun, into "a masterpiece in the classic and total sense."[80]

James also proposed solutions to many of these riddles. *Principles* powerfully asserted that consciousness was teleological, that it was an active instrument bringing order to the flux of reality in accord with the individual's attention and needs. Active rather than passive became the signature of James's description of the psychological reality of the individual. In addition, there is a heroic aspect connected with James's completion of the project. Begun in 1878 while on his honeymoon with Alice, work on the manuscript continued for twelve years. James finally delivered the finished version of his "masterpiece" to Henry Holt, the most patient of publishers, in 1890.[81]

Completion of a project so breathtaking in its scope—in part, to make psychology into a natural science and to posit a teleological function to the mind—would have been unthinkable to the unsteady William James of the late 1860s and early 1870s, the young man who seemed incapable of affirming or acting with free will, or even with sustained effort for any task. In these years, when James sought to follow Renouvier's formula, he found that he first had to vanquish the inhibiting ideas that frustrated his ability to act; in sum, his will to act was stymied by debilitating conceptions of the universe and by the force of bad habits. In the essay "What the Will Effects" (1888)—portions of which were incorporated into the lengthy and crucial chapter "Will" in *Principles* and also in the simpler but telling observations on the will in *Talks to Teachers on Psychology*— James dealt with the mental process involved in the act of willing to believe in free will, or of training oneself in the exercise of free will; the two were not unrelated in James's psychology. As he phrased it in *Principles*, "Freedom's first deed should be to affirm itself" (2:117). But how?

The initial step in any voluntary action, James explained, was to have an idea of the intended deed already etched into the memory: "One cannot will into the void." In this view, all ideas were secondary rather than primary qualities. James illustrated how the individual, through simple accomplishments, might be able to train his or her "voluntary power" to will action. When one moved from simple to increasingly complicated acts, the necessity of having already experienced an idea involuntarily diminished; for example, one need not to have committed a murder in order to murder voluntarily. Complicated initiatives involved the same problem as simple acts of volition; each must have a field free from inhibiting thoughts.[82]

If acting as if one had free will were only an example of ideo-motor activity, as James termed it, then the conception itself would be sufficient to initiate the desired action: "We do not have a sensation or thought, and then have to *add* something dynamic to it to get movement." Thus James warned his readers not to hold to "the common prejudice that voluntary action without 'exertion of will-power' is *Hamlet* with the prince's part left out" (2:1134). Will, or the express feeling of effort and attention, entered into the equation only when other sensations or thoughts conspired to inhibit the original sensation or thought. The desire to act as if one were free might be inhibited by the thought of the absurdity or difficulty of the task in a world too open or closed, or by the momentous implications of the action in a complex universe. In either case, faced with competing sensations or thoughts, the individual enters into a period of "inward unrest known as *indecision*" (2:1136). When indecision becomes chronic and, accordingly, the process of deliberation becomes its own end, then action becomes all but impossible.

James discussed one condition of indecision under the rubric "Unhealthiness of the will." The "obstructed will" described a personality type that closely approximated his own during his years of debility and depression. The individual with an "obstructed will" had a limited attention span and insufficient "focussing power." Lethargy won out over activity: "objects of consciousness fail to touch or break the skin. They are there, but do not reach the level of effectiveness." Such a state of drift occasionally affects all of us; if chronic, it is the mark of the mental disease that James called abulia. Abulia might also define Hamlet's plight. The prince always had a clear vision of his task, but for him "the act either fails to follow or follows in some other way." Thus the world of the abulic individual, like the world of the neurasthenic one, is marked by a feeling of being "distant and unreal" (2:1152–53).

James did not develop or intend to formulate a therapeutic for mental disorders of this or any other type within his *Principles,* yet its numerous suggestions and strategies indicate how to adjudicate the battles between warring conceptions in the mind. The solution was complex; if one idea totally vanquished inhibiting ideas, then reckless action might follow. The individual with an "explosive" type of personality might not consider the action's complexity and moral implications. James encouraged action, but in an effective and responsible manner (2:1144–52).

Attention became the *"essential achievement of the will"* in voluntary action (2:1166). Attention—the ability of consciousness to extract elements from the flux of sensations—brought a difficult object into the central part of one's consciousness and held it firm. Once this is accomplished, there are "immediate consequences." James limited the stage for the act of willing and attention to the realm of the mental: "The strain of attention is the fundamental act of will . . . the whole drama is a mental drama" (2:1168). James admitted that effort of the will "complicates volition." It does so whenever a rarer and more ideal impulse (here we might read into the text the Jamesian desire to act with free will) is called upon to neutralize more instinctive or habitual impulses (here we might think of the James's numbing and habitual doubt) (2:1154). The "very greatness of the resistance itself" determined the amount of attention necessary for one conception to predominate (2:1155). James viewed this as nothing less than a moral endeavor: "To *sustain a representation, to think,* is, in short, the only moral act, for the impulsive and obstructed, for the sane and lunatics alike" (2:1170).

Calls to duty or a plea for action served as Jamesian imperatives. One acted not out of a utilitarian calculus of pleasure and pain, but with heavy feelings of duty tugging at our will power. James did not posit moral actions—those in which attention was forced to rivet itself—as easy or pleasant. Indeed, he suggested that our morals were hereditary, mechanisms selected out for their survival value in the slow process of human evolution.[83] The introduction of efforts of the will allowed attention to lead to action, but it did not exile the validity of counterarguments to the particular course chosen. In this sense, James's efforts of the will were anticipations of the state of mind that he would later celebrate in *Varieties:* the "twice-born" soul. Only after tasks requiring this effort of attention were completed would the individual find the heavy burden relieved, replaced with "pleasure . . . in the joy of being done. . . . Like Hamlet [who makes two appearances in *Principles*,] we say of each successive task,: 'O cursed spite / That ever I was born to set it right' " (2:1162–63).

Sometimes the successful fixation of attention upon a desired goal was less an act of will than a happy circumstance. James used an example drawn from his own memory to nicely illustrate this phenomenon of the falling away of certain conceptions followed by others' concomitant rise to the center of consciousness. By example, James's story of displaced conceptions or sensations might also apply to the possibility of the victory of free-will ideals over competing conceptions of the will. James recounted that we have all felt, while lying awake in a warm bed in a cold room on a frigid morning, the push and pull of conflicting ideas: Should we remain snug under our covers or arise and prepare ourselves for work? Why do we finally choose one alternative over another? Is it because, after our careful deliberation, a feeling of effort results in a decision followed by the requisite action? Sometimes. But in this case James emphasized that the decision was neither deliberate nor strained. The decision to arise from bed instead resulted from a "fortunate lapse of consciousness"— "we forget both the warmth and the cold; we fall into some revery [sic] connected with the day's life, in the course of which the idea flashes across us, 'Hollo! I must lie here no longer.' " Thus we jump out of bed because no contradictory or inhibiting idea is present to our consciousness (2:1132).[84]

James also realized, however, that the overcoming of inhibitions at times also required the cultivation or "education of the will," just as much as lapses of consciousness. By strong and repeated efforts of attention might one's conception of duty undermine opposing thoughts, which consigned the individual to a state of obstruction and doubt. Here James importantly combined his ideas on the will with concepts discussed in his chapter "Habit" in volume one of *Principles*. Indeed, as Gerald E. Myers states, "the chapters on habit and will in *Principles* echo each other."[85]

James's emphasis upon education of the will may be seen as one way of explaining the very existence of free will. James skirted the issue of free will in *Principles*, noting that arguments concerning the presence or absence of free will belonged to the field of philosophy. He did, however, refer readers interested in the question to his fuller exposition in "The Dilemma of Determinism." Nonetheless, he felt compelled to point out in *Principles* that "when scientific and moral postulates war thus with each other and objective truth is not to be had, the only course is voluntary choice, for scepticism itself, if systematic, is also voluntary choice." The key thought then became the need for freedom to "affirm itself" at every opportunity. In sum, freedom became a function of the will or of principles of habit. Through the practice of free will, in effect, the idea itself would translate into an ideo-motor movement, an action without the palsying effects of too much contemplation. Freedom, and with it responsibility, would become habitual (2:1176–77). In a handwritten emendation for the chapter "Habit" in his *Briefer Course* (1892), a shortened version of *Principles,* James wrote: "Sow an action, and you reap a habit; sow a habit and you reap a character; sow a character and you reap a destiny."[86]

Even before consigning these thoughts to *Principles,* James had enunciated them as important considerations for his own existence and recovery from depression and doubt. "Care little for speculation," James had written, "recollect that only when habits of order are formed can we advance to really interesting fields of action." The careful cultivation of habit would help James to submerge thoughts of doubt to conceptions of duty and responsibility. Therefore he must slowly "accumulate grain on grain of willful choice like a very miser; never forgetting how one link dropped undoes an indefinite number."[87]

The issue was more complicated, of course. Throughout his life, James had accumulated numerous habits, including those of depression, doubt, and Hamletian avoidance. Thus the realization that humans beings "are creatures of habit" did little to provide a solution; it only posited the problem's form and the solution's structure. The cultivation of proper habits became James's answer to his persistent problems. Once aware that "morbid manifestations" or bad habits and dispositions were "themselves . . . due to the mere inertia of the nervous organs, when once launched upon a false career," James, or anyone wishing to form new habits, had to begin a regimen whereby, through an initial effort of attention and its repetition, a new, more efficacious habit might become ingrained (1:109–11).

In his emphasis upon the salutary role of habit formation, James was both repeating assumptions of his culture and drawing out implications from his intensive probe into human physiology. For Victorians, the disciplinary function of habit became an anodyne for doubt. While the Victorians, in their mania for certitude, often elevated habitual responses into ends in and of themselves, the emphasis upon habit promised freedom from the inactivity that accompanied intensive contemplation of alternative courses of action. Habit also promised moral benefits; action was not posited simply as a valuable end in and of itself. James maintained that the cultivation of proper habits would result in the development of one's character and destiny. Francis Bowen—James's colleague in the Harvard philosophy department and someone whose overall philosophy is suggestive of an earlier era in American thought—would on the issue of habit have found himself in agreement with James's strictures. Bowen stressed the efficacious nature of habit, as well as the training of the moral will, which was central in Scottish common-sense philosophy and the process of education. In 1885 he wrote that "*Virtue* deserves its name only when, by long practice it has become a *fixed* habit; for then only is it freed from the stains of selfishness."[88]

In *Principles* James presented habit as ideo-motor movements. Habit formation allowed the simplification of the voluntary process by avoiding the presence of intervening thoughts, which might inhibit the desired action. Will, attention, and the feeling of effort—all present in the process of deliberation—need not be present in actions of a habitual type. Proper habits developed through "daily drill and years of discipline" would eventually come to "*make our nervous system our ally instead of our enemy. . . . For this we must make automatic and habitual, as early as possible, as many useful actions as we can*" (1:126). Here, in essence, was James's therapeutic. Each time a conception to act in a valuable fashion arises and is met by insufficient inhibiting ideas, then we must act immediately. Repetition of the act grows easier and more automatic. This is a physiological law, based on the plastic nature of the brain; once a nerve current "has traversed a path, it should traverse it more readily still a second time" (1:113. Drawing upon the work of British psychologist Alexander Bain—whose psychology of habit nicely supplemented Renouvier's emphasis upon free will—James fashioned his role for habit in making action possible.[89] The daily "*gratuitous exercise*" of useful habits promised freedom from the painful inactivity that had plagued James. His first act was not only to believe in free will but also to act as if it were so, despite facts and conceptions to the contrary. By his successful exercise of his will, future demonstrations would grow easier (1:130). Although the willing attitude would not prove freedom of the will, it would alert individuals to their conscious direction of the feeling of effort and would in turn allow them to function more energetically than previously. Through his exercise of will and attention, James would exile Hamlet's ghost. The work of philosophy would no longer plunge James into debilitating speculation. The prince of philosophy would embark upon a royal career.

IX

Through cultivation of his powers of attention and efforts of the will, by dint of his heady philosophical assertion of free will in the face of competing conceptions, and with the aid of his marriage and vocation, James began to emerge from his depressive years armed with a hearty yet sober view of life. His own "twice-born" mentality would be reflected in his many important ruminations on belief, free will, and the nature of experience. In focusing his "feeling of effort" upon philosophical issues, James would engage the issues that would eventually define him as a philosopher and would make his philosophy important and compelling. Numerous metaphysical conceptions would confront him, but never again would any particular philosophical opponent weigh him down with indecision and numbing doubt. James would never cease to wrestle with metaphysical demons, but he pinned them and, in the process, demonstrated both his greatness and appeal as a philosopher.

Although James had by the mid-1870s won his match with the metaphysical and personal enemies contributing to his inability to act in a sustained manner, he recognized that many other Americans during the period from 1870 until well into the new century were greatly troubled by doubt and marked by a concomitant state of abulia or neurasthenia. Hamlets abounded on the American cultural scene. In part, such American Hamlets, drawn from the general confines of the educated and wealthy classes, suffered from what James characterized as the *tedium vitae*.

A therapeutic for modern forms of abulia was, of course, hinted at in *Principles*. James would later direct much of attention in his works of popular philosophy toward the problem of this social ennui, the intellectual and physical drift plaguing many Americans. These problems arose, to a degree, from the fact that "civilized life" had created a situation in which, in James's words, "it has at last become possible for large numbers of people to pass from the cradle to the grave without having had a pang of genuine fear" (2:1034).

In this interpretation of cultural realities, James found that the heroic instincts, no less than the heroic duty, of the individual, seemed to have been undermined by the lack of external goads and stimuli. This dearth of opportunities seemed to have undermined the individual who through *"gratuitous exercises"* might hope to develop an habituallly heroic approach to life. As James phrased it in his *Talks to Teachers on Psychology*, "New habits *can* be launched . . . on condition of there being new stimuli and new excitements." Although he continued to maintain, and sought in his popular philosophy to prove, that "life abounds" in excitements, there is much in his writings from the 1870s until his death that demonstrates his awareness of the coin's other side, which undermined the individual's exercise of the heroic.[90]

In *Principles* James condemned and pitied those individuals trapped in the iron cage of doubt. He recognized that, contrary to traditional, utilitarian pleasure and pain calculations, even numbing pain could have appeal, noting the reality of "the occasional tempting power of badness and unpleasantness as such" (2:1159). Leaving the full analysis of this mental state to the Freudians, he maintained a moral offensive against lives wasted "in a weltering sea of sensibility and emotion," existences spent without "a manly concrete deed." James repeatedly declared his support for the heroic outlook on life. The heroic-minded individual can face objects that "are sinister and dreadful, unwelcome, incompatible with wished-for things." Praise lapsed into a rhapsody for the heroic individual:

> The world thus finds in the heroic man its worthy match and mate; and the effort which he is able to put forth to hold himself erect and keep his heart unshaken is the direct measure of worth and function in the game of human life. He can *stand* this Universe. He can meet it and keep up his faith in it in presence of those same features which lay his weaker brethren low. He can still find a zest in it, not by "ostrich-like forgetfulness" but by pure inward willingness to take the world with those deterrent objects there. And hereby he becomes one of the masters and the lords of life. He must be counted with henceforth; he forms a part of human destiny. (2:1181)

These words are an appropriate description for William James the philosopher. In both his popular philosophy and his technical formulations, James attempted to demonstrate that heroic and moral activity would excise the ghost of Hamlet. James accomplished this by psychological therapeutic and philosophical argument. Part of his task was to analyze rigorously the extent to which Americans had become inured to life's heroic possibilities; this description of the *tedium vitae* served as a necessary prelude for James's greater enterprise—to champion the philosophical possibility for heroic and moral activities in the modern world. Yet in his credo of energy and vitality, sometimes marked by exuberant and misleading metaphors, James never forgot the importance of responsibility and restraint. These ideals forced him to battle the forces that celebrated the will as an end in and of itself. Upon the stage of modern life, the Jamesian pragmatic activist would replace the Hamletian doubter.

CHAPTER FOUR

Tedium Vitae

With his promotion to professor of psychology at Harvard in 1885, and publication of *The Principles of Psychology* in 1890, William James at last appeared to have thrown off the somber cloak of Hamlet. James's nervous energy and doubt had been directed away from the dangerous tides of neurasthenia into the calmer waters of professional advancement and philosophical accomplishment. In the 1870s James evaluated "philosophical activity as a *business* . . . not normal for most men, and not for me," because the true philosopher refuses "the privilege of trusting blindly."[1] In the 1880s James could confidently battle against determinism, develop his voluntarism, attack scientism, and establish the groundwork for radical empiricism. Moreover, he would even contemplate a pragmatic notion of truth in "The Function of Cognition" (1884).[2]

The practice of professional philosophy did not lock James into his study or isolate him in the hallways of the Harvard philosophy department. The expansiveness of James's mind and personality—his "fourteen doors" outward—meant that he would be a keen participant in his era's cultural conversations.[3] Issuance of a shorter version of *Principles* in 1892 increased James's appeal as a lecturer for popular audiences; he now regularly addressed issues of the cultural and philosophical moment.[4] In numerous writings, many of which were published in *The Will to Believe* (1897) and *Talks to Teachers on Psychology* (1899), James presented his analysis of the cultural problems confronting Americans. In the very act of discussing the cultural crisis of his era, James gave philosophical recognition to its contours and, through his philosophy and moralism, helped to develop solutions. Culture did not cause James's philosophy to take the form that it did; culture simply—yet significantly, as Clifford Geertz would have it—provided a context. In this case, cultural problems serve as the context for James's philosophy, both popular and technical.[5]

I

The period from 1880 until James's death in 1910 represents a distinct historical unit or, to use Ferdinand Braudel's term, a *conjoncture*. During these years, the bourgeoisie faced an especially difficult time. The essential lines of this nagging crisis are commonly drawn in the form of contrasts: confidence and doubt, freedom and constraint, liberation and domination.[6] Many note the period's uncertain tension between energy and torpor. Tremendous expenditures and wastes of energy were common; hence Howard Mumford Jones's designation of this period as "The Age of Energy." Yet, even before the *fin-de-siècle* spirit was resplendent, the terms *neurasthenic, hysterical, melancholic, powerless, doubting,* and *Hamletian* were used in this period to describe many from the bourgeois class. The bourgeoisie suffered, as two of their most strident critics phrased it, from "moral sea-sickness" or religious weightlessness.[7] "Middle-class culture," in the words of one recent analyst, "had come to seem stifling, enervating, effeminate, devoid of opportunities for manly heroism."[8] This was, then, an age of contrasts, one captured in its essential push and pull by Henry Adams's famous juxtaposition of the virgin's unity and serenity with the dynamo's multiplicity and energy.[9]

The relationship between energy and inertia was explicitly posited in George M. Beard's *American Nervousness: Its Causes and Consequences* (1881). Here the analysis of the problem was simple, yet daring in its willingness to move from a somatic to an environmental-psychological model of illness. Industrial growth, the birth of a new civilization with dissonant and blaring rhythms, was proving disruptive for many individuals with delicate emotional mechanisms. For such sensitive individuals, excess of modern energy actually served, paradoxically perhaps, to diminish their capacity for action. In this interpretation, Americans living in the "megaphonic" era—James's term for a society marked by an overwhelming cacophony of sensory stimuli—found their energy diminished or totally depleted. Trying to keep up with the energy of modern society proved too much for many Americans to endure. The simplest tasks became impossible. Images of the sickly woman, the nervous intellectual, and the sadly peripatetic businessman became common.[10] James captured the pathos of the latter cultural figure when he described him as "broken-down"; he is marked by "his haggard, hungry mien, unfitted by lifelong habit for taking any pleasure in passive contemplation . . . he tries to cheat the *tedium vitae* by a feverish locomotion, and seems to draw a ghostly comfort from a peevish and foolish criticism of everything he meets."[11]

Even Herbert Spencer, the crown prince of industrial society, was forced to warn American audiences in 1882 that the "high pressure" of

modern life, especially in its conduct of business, caused the bourgeoisie
to experience "feeble health and decreased ability to enjoy life." Twenty
years before James would write about the therapeutic value of relaxation,
Spencer was already counseling a "Gospel of Relaxation" as the cure for
the neurasthenic condition.[12] Henry Adams would later remark that only
recent immigrants seemed able to withstand the psychic tensions of the
modern era of intense and dynamic energy. When faced with this whirl-
igig of activity, Adams preferred to stand on the sidelines. From there,
Adams and others of his class became painfully aware that the historical
moment was passing them by.[13] Bound by neurasthenia, unable to meet
industrial civilization on its own hearty terms, the elite class, in Adams's
dyspeptic vision, became "just jellyfish, and flabby all through . . . as
defunct as the dodo."[14]

The rise of the modern bureaucratic corporation in this period further
contributed to the feeling of ennui that afflicted many in the elite class.
According to this interpretation, the rise of modern business, especially
during the second industrial revolution, brought with it an imperative to
rationalize the form and function of American life. Increasingly, the demands of modern business civilization seemed to undermine the autonomy of the individual, who became little more than a cog in the vast
machinery of ordered, rational business progress. The control and ra-
tionalization exercised by the trust in the period from 1880 to 1910
within the economic sphere of existence came to serve as an analogue to
the psychic economy of the individual: control replaced chaos but also
inhibited excitement and spontaneity. Frederick W. Taylor's ideal of the
individual as machine captured the ideology, if less often the reality, of this
moment in modern civilization: autonomy was sacrificed on the altar of
efficiency.[15]

The neurasthenic condition took root in ground tilled by more than
the changes wrought by industrial growth and urbanization. The tedium
of modern living also played itself out as an event in the life of the mind.
New intellectual currents did much to create and express the cultural
crisis. Darwinian science and the rise of naturalistic models for explaining
human behavior threatened to consign the individual to the "iron cage"
of a determined existence. Well before the naturalistic novels of Frank
Norris, Stephen Crane, and Theodore Dreiser around the turn of the
century had developed the image of the individual as a creature chained to
the fatal force of environment or heredity, the specter of the individual as
without free will had cast its shadow upon the cherished American ideal
of human autonomy.[16]

Thanks to Charles Rosenberg's brilliant exposition of the trial of
Charles Guiteau, who had assassinated President James Garfield in 1881,
we can see how the older, moralistic conception of human volition slowly

began to lose its scientific, if not its cultural, credibility. Some experts held the deranged assassin morally responsible and culpable for his crime, but some physicians maintained that Guiteau was a victim of hereditary circumstances. Hereditary madness had obliterated Guiteau's powers of rational judgment; due to his genetic inheritance, he was unable to control his actions. This thesis had clear and frightening implications for many nineteenth-century Americans. It suggested that the traditional lines connecting morality and responsibility, freedom and understanding, were being erased by the confining power of heredity and environment.[17]

Whereas hereditarian schools of thought promised to reduce human volition to a function of genetic conditions, evolutionary theorists labored to banish human autonomy and will as defining or significant factors in comparison to the power of the environment. Passivity in the face of evolution became the accustomed stance for many intellectuals. William Graham Sumner clearly spelled out the mesmerizing power of the stare of the environment upon human autonomy. For Sumner, human autonomy and individual morality existed only to the degree to which the individual adapted to the environment. While cloaked in the traditional language of Calvinism and of the Republican Ethic, Sumner's philosophy preached acquiescence or passive adaptation to the environment. In "The Absurd Effort to Make the World Over" (1894), Sumner ridiculed would-be reformers who dreamed of effectively changing the course of evolution. Such individuals were blinded by their naïve voluntarism: "Every one of us is a child of his age and cannot get out of it. He is in the stream and is swept along with it. . . . Therefore the tide will not be changed by us. It will swallow up both us and our experiments."[18]

Evolutionary theory in the hands of Spencer or Sumner did, however, promise solace and certitude. These thinkers tried to contain the world's multiplicity and uncertainty within a sustained ode to progress. The individual's role in this march, especially in terms of his or her autonomy, remained less certain. While Spencer presented it as a substitute for traditional religion, his evolutionary doctrine lacked moral imperatives.[19]

Christians of a liberal persuasion were caught between an inability to gravitate toward positivistic science and an unwillingness to proclaim devotion to fundamentalist theologies. In an age of uncertainty, the attempt to place the foundations of religion within a scientific context seemed altogether reasonable. But this act of amalgamation actually weakened the body of traditional religion and individual moral responsibility. In the analysis of James Turner, this *modus vivendi* fatefully compromised the power of religious certitude. In the process, adherents of liberal Christianity found themselves floating in the "weightless" air of unbelief or uncertainty. The oxygen level at this height was insufficient to support the confidence of autonomous individualism.[20]

Evasion represented another, equally passive, response to the delirium of modern existence. As described by T. J. Jackson Lears and Walter Houghton, the flight from reality often meant a descent into tepid sentimentality. The outpouring of sentimental literature, with its images of moral certitude of days past, was a balm to the troubled souls of many Americans. If the world was too harsh for the physical and emotional mechanisms of the elite class, then the minds of its scribes and ministers might revise reality from a still life in garish colors to a tender pastoral where the old values were depicted in their essential purity.[21]

The cultural crisis of the period from 1880 to 1910, then, was defined by its extremely perplexing contours. On the phenomenal level of everyday life, the nation was in a state of upheaval. Change was constant and awesome. Even for those willing to dance to the tune played by modern industrial society, the need to sit out some of its faster numbers became increasingly apparent. For some, however, the only comfortable position to assume was that of wallflowers at the fandango of modernity. Neurasthenics, troubled by the quickness of movement, their emotional gyroscopes upset by changes in the intellectual tempo of their age, were forced to take to the numbing relief of their sickbeds.

This crisis of culture, and the attendant responses to it, riveted James's attention. Indeed its contradictory waters engulfed much of his life: "I am a victim of neurasthenia," James wrote in 1895, "and of the sense of hollowness and unreality that goes with it."[22] James's lifelong sense of neurasthenia was partly a function of intellectual worries concomitant with a decline of religious certitude, as well the legacy of his own problems of vocation, and an expression of a host of philosophical and cultural considerations. By the 1870s James had recovered sufficiently from neurasthenic doubt and debility to lead a productive existence, but he could not help but recognize that many other Americans were troubled by similar problems and doubts. He designed the passion and specifics of his philosophy to battle those who, in philosophical or cultural texts, would forever banish religion and individual autonomy from modern life. In much of his popular philosophy in this period of cultural crisis, James confronted the problems of inertia and *tedium vitae*, as a prelude to the full development of his own discourse of heroism, individual autonomy, and pragmatism. At "the *heart* of his [James's] thought," according to philosopher John E. Smith, was "a consistent voluntarism. Human intentions, purposes, plans, and goals are the dominant powers in his universe."[23]

II

In his analysis of this *tedium vitae*, James assumed the role of public philosopher, addressing issues of both philosophical and cultural concern in a manner that would be accessible to a specific, but not philosophically trained, public. By accepting the position of public philosopher, James was following a philosophical tradition reaching back from the Puritan divines through Emerson, for whom the practice of philosophy and thought was intimately connected to problems of the self and culture. Obvious amounts of sincerity and authenticity made effective James's considerations of the cultural problematics of his era. He had experienced the debility and depression associated with the ennui of modern living and philosophical uncertainty. The debates he undertook in the cultural and philosophical arenas, Ralph Barton Perry had pointed out long ago, were "addressed primarily to himself."[24] In this welding together of private and public concerns, James also situated himself as a modern philosopher. As philosopher Stuart Hampshire remarks admiringly, James "was the first truly modern philosopher, because he hoped to understand the mechanisms by which philosophers, not excluding himself, project their inner conflicts and anxieties upon the universe."[25]

Hampshire errs, however, in positing that James simply projected his own anxieties and conflicts onto the universe. Jamesian anxiety was a cultural commonplace. Indeed, that was what rendered his own particular problems so culturally resonant. James understood this quite well. He directed many of his essays in popular philosophy to a particular audience; he knew their problems intimately, and they shared quite a few of his concerns. When James raised questions about the intellect mired in unsolvable philosophical ruminations, or when he discussed the dangers of the scientific attitude in demeaning the validity of religious or moral belief, he was engaged in a cultural conversation, a dialogue with his era.

The discussions of philosophical and cultural issues in *The Will to Believe,* for example, were intended for an audience of highly reflective men and women, bereft of the religious guidance that might strengthen them for life's moral battles. This was not a generalized social phenomenon: it was largely confined to the bric-a-brac existences of America's intellectual class. Were James to have addressed a group of Salvation Army volunteers, his tone, if not his message, would have been different. These "once-born" true believers needed a corrective blast of "the northeast wind of science" or a healthy dose of skepticism more than anything else. When James counseled religious belief and moral action, he instead directed his words to an audience distant from the assured religiosity of the masses.[26]

James marshalled his considerable powers of evocation, explication, and exhortation to convert those Americans whose "bogey was dessication" *[sic]*—individuals caught in a desert of doubt, unable to think or act in religious and moral terms. The devil of spiritual doubt, in James's analysis, caused a cultural crisis marked by "the abstraction, priggish-

ness, and sawdust" of a particular "vision of 'Science.' "²⁷ James fretted
about the depleted souls of his listeners and readers, people who, like
himself, existed in a passionless world and wondered about science's
assault upon religious precepts. What James hoped to achieve for this
group of Americans, in the words of one of his contemporaries, was "to
kindle the moral ardor of youth."²⁸

James was convinced that the failure of individuals to believe in either
God or their own free will confined them to lives of depression and
debility, doubt and ennui. James wanted to reach the hearts of this class of
thinkers. He analyzed the pragmatic results of the "over-studious lives" of
"reflecting men and women": their intensive intellectualizing had cast
them adrift in a sea of "skepticism and unreality." In such an inhospitable
environment, one that James knew all too well, the doubt-ridden intellectual fell victim to "pessimism and the nightmare or suicidal view of
life."²⁹ James succinctly summarized the nature of his audience and the
contours of its historically specific problems in the preface to *The Will to
Believe:*

> But academic audiences, fed already on science, have a very different need.
> [as opposed to religious believers of the Salvation Army type] Paralysis of
> their native capacity for faith and timorous *abulia* in the religious field are
> their special forms of mental weakness, brought about by the notion, care-
> fully instilled, that there is something called scientific evidence by waiting
> upon which they shall escape all danger of shipwreck in regard to truth.³⁰

III

Composed between 1879 and 1896, the essays in *The Will to Believe*
attempted to expose the pretensions of science, to celebrate the ennobling
powers of religious and moral belief, and to combat the general "moral
sea-sickness" and deterministic philosophies that imprisoned many of
James's contemporaries in debility and disrepair. James also used the
essays as a forum for his emphasis upon voluntarism and heroic individualism in historical and moral change. The essays successfully combined
James's key philosophical concerns with a cultural agenda of wide and
significant appeal.

James stalked the enemy of scientific certitude and determinism
throughout *The Will to Believe*. Because of its cultural power, promise,
and authority, scientism—the most virulent and pompous strain of the
scientific attitude—came to occupy a prominent, though not exclusive,
place in James's anatomy of the factors contributing to the *tedium vitae* of
the era's thinking men and women. It should be remembered, however,
that James in no way intended to reject the empirical, scientific frame of

mind out of which scientism had developed. While stressing passion and intuition, James remained an adherent of the scientific method. Indeed, much of his well-deserved reputation rested upon the terra firma of science. He had, after all, prefaced *Principles* with a plain acknowledgment that its methodology was erected upon a "strictly positivist point of view."[31] Although James may not have been perfectly consistent in his adherence to this ideal, his philosophy was meant to inhabit the same distinguished space as modern science.[32] James would always carefully separate modern experimental science from the pretensions of scientism. The imperial edge of the scientist view of things, the belief that science should insinuate itself through its "conjuring spell" into all areas of life, including the religious and ethical, brought forth a stirring rejoinder from James. As fanatically commended by Thomas Huxley and William Clifford, science hardly seemed to James an appropriate "'creed' for modern life."[33]

In "The Will to Believe" (1896), James defended religious belief and the necessity of individuals taking a moral stand. This belief was in contrast to that of the scientists who counseled a cautious attitude on religious belief and moral action. Science exceeded its boundaries in claiming that an individual who was faced with insufficient or uncertain evidence had an intellectual duty to refrain from choosing. James admitted that the supposed scientific imperative to wait cautiously for more evidence, while perhaps useful in certain abstract or experimental circumstances, might be suicidal, as well as passive in wrestling with moral questions. The subtext of *The Will to Believe* was directed against the Hamletism that the scientistic world view seemed to foster.

In James's pantheon of belief systems, the scientistic and the religious were not always equally valuable or appropriate. When "no forced option" was present, when nothing requiring immediate action presented itself, then science and its promise to save us from deception "ought to be our ideal."[34] When it came to moral situations, James found the scientistic stricture to both know the truth and to avoid error a lopsided choice. In practice, it was the latter that became imperative, at the expense of experiencing the former.[35]

While the scientistic horror of "being duped" certainly bothered James, he refused to consider it the ultimate sin (26). Far greater was his own fear of not following his passional or believing nature. The passive stance of the scientist condemned the individual to watch opportunity pass by. The scientist appeared to recommend that the individual assume the role of Hamlet on the stage of moral life. Science ultimately was judged limiting when confronting questions of a moral moment. James claimed that the desire and need to act often helped to bring about the desired truth. By jettisoning the albatross of scientistic domination, highly contemplative individuals would be freed; action would replace passivity, excitement would push aside ennui. For this individual, able and willing to adopt a "living option" of belief, *"faith in a fact can help create the fact."* To believe otherwise, as the scientists would have it, "would be an insane logic which should say that faith running ahead of scientific evidence is the 'lowest kind of immorality' into which a thinking being can fall." This immorality represented the depths into which the *tedium vitae* of his culture had descended; it expressed scientistic imperialism's dangerous willingness to "regulate our lives!" (29).

The brunt of the will to believe was not a right to deceive, a right to make-believe, or a right to believe in anything one wanted for whatever narrow purposes, as some of James's critics, in his time as well as in ours, have claimed.[36] James intended his doctrine as a corrective to the culturally deadening power of scientific passivity. He thus warned, at the close of his essay, that "*In concreto,* the freedom to believe can only cover living options, which the intellect of the intellectual cannot by itself resolve; and the living options never seem absurdities to him who has them to consider" (32). The cultural impetus behind "The Will to Believe" supported religion against science, individual autonomy against naturalistic passivity; the essay posited forthrightly that the "whole defence of faith hinges upon action" (32).

The potential appeal of strenuous religiosity was muted by certain forms of scientism. The nexus between scientific generalizations and philosophical determinism boded poorly for individual autonomy, for the cultural propriety of science in nineteenth-century American culture reigned unchallenged. Faith in science as the liberator of humanity became, in the words of historian of science Charles Rosenberg, an "increasingly autonomous" belief, one whose assertions came to compose the belief system for most Americans well into the twentieth century.[37] The march of science and of progress thus became connected. James worried where exactly in this equation the individual belonged. As late as 1903, James announced that evolutionary determinism dangerously "denies free-will . . . despises hero-worship . . . and in every way tends to minimize the particular concrete man. Society drags the unit along in its fatal tow."[38]

The cultural hegemony exercised by scientism contributed to the malaise common to modern existence. Scientism and philosophical determinism walked hand in hand with the devil; each, in its own way, obscured the actual practice of science and undermined the exercise of free will. In "The Dilemma of Determinism" (1884), originally delivered as a talk to an audience of Harvard Divinity School students, James sketched the outlines of the deterministic world view, evaluated its implications for human freedom, and proposed his own brand of philosophical voluntarism.

As with many of the essays in *The Will to Believe*, "The Dilemma of Determinism" was composed within a context of religious stagnation which James saw as contributing to the spiritual weightlessness of American culture. He blamed this problem, in part, upon the inroads of Spencerian philosophy. Many of James's contemporaries were moved to a banal ecstasy by Spencer's vision of hope and progress. In summing up the appeal of Spencer for a generation, James singled out the British philosopher's uncanny ability to explain "every conceivable phenomenon, and whose practical outcome is the somewhat vague optimism which is so important a tendency in modern life."[39] Spencerian doctrines were insinuating themselves into the very marrow of the bones of traditional religion, much to its debit.

Religious belief, which had traditionally offered guidance and moral strength, was in recession in the last third of the nineteenth century, at least amongst those of James's class and culture. Traditional religion, which had been based upon a certain and beneficent view of natural law and individual responsibility, had not recovered from the onslaught of Darwinism. Religious leaders as varied in their respective theologies as Henry Ward Beecher and George Frederick Wright had demonstrated how evolutionary doctrines might be appropriated to religious purposes. But the resultant mélange or compromise often negotiated between religion and science, at least in the hands of liberal theologians, perhaps sacrificed too much to the enemy of determinism. Religious liberalism replaced faith with reason, passion with science. The emergent theology of Protestant liberalism might be intellectually satisfying, as well as beautiful, as an abstract system, but it was neither emotionally sustaining nor energizing. James thought that Christianized Spencerianism—in which sentimentalism accompanied progressive evolution's calming reassurances—offered a "white-robed harp-playing heaven . . . and the ladylike tea-table elysium" (130). The doctrinal strength of determinism and scientism in religious circles promised a watered-down form of liberation, one in which the moral striving of the individual was not tolerated.[40]

Hegelians and Spencerians were equally guilty in presenting a deterministic and morally weak vision of the universe. The metaphysics of both their systems promoted a universe whose parts "already laid down absolutely appoint and decree what the other parts shall be" (117). In a predetermined universe, the individual's actions were stripped of their freedom and responsibility, because they merely contributed to a "future [that] has no ambiguous possibilities hidden in its womb" (117). Chance was banished from the determinist universe; individual actions made little difference. While "soft determinism" did, at least in theory, allow the individual a freedom of choice determined by his or her character traits (the free-will argument developed, for instance, by Jonathan Edwards), "hard determinism" boldly proclaimed that because particular action follows closely upon all previous actions, nothing could prove that the action was undetermined. James recognized that the hard, determinist conclusion was philosophically unassailable. Thus he sought to avoid the logic of determinism by asserting a world that was pluralistic and open to chance and change, while demonstrating the dangerous moral implications concomitant with the deterministic argument.[41]

The moral debits that James connected to life-denying determinism centered around its fatalist morality.[42] James illustrated the moral atmosphere created by determinism by relating the story of a horrible murder. According to the determinist perspective, this vicious incident exhibited "a perfect mechanical fit to the rest of the universe." He believed that such a view was the death knell of determinist morality. Determinism was condemned for banishing moral responsibility from the universe by abolishing the responsible possibility of the individual feeling remorse, or even exhibiting regret, over a heinous action (125–27). Determinism reduced human beings to a state of "ethical indifference which infallibly brings dissolution in its train" (132). In a world devoid of ethical activism, "*[t]edium vitae* is the only sentiment" that Spencerian determinism might "awaken in our breasts" (130).

James's solution posited a world of real moral conflicts, a "Rembrandtesque moral chiaroscuro" (130). The value of subjective feeling in deciding that what one sought or ought to do was right became central to James's ethical stance. While James recognized that subjectivism might lead to antinomianism, ethical indifference, or mere sentimentalism, his view of subjective moral responsibility was anchored in the waters of "objective conduct" and he linked such conduct to a strong belief in the moral presence of God (134). In the universe that James drew—one pluralistic, "restless," and open to our actions—possibility always figured; the chance that one's actions would count for something in the course of the universe's development was more than enough to lead James to celebrate "those soul-trying moments when fate's scales seem to quiver. . . . *That* is what gives the palpitating reality to our moral life and makes it tingle" (140). James found no significance, moreover, in a world whose structure made no demands upon the individual's will. Forced to choose between the *"genial will"* and the *"strenuous will,"* James selected the latter, because it alone was ethically sensitive and morally active.[43]

The drama of the world, staged against uncertainty, indicated how far James had traveled from his earlier penchant to hesitate in the face of the abyss. As he noted in the 1880s, those persuaded by the sentimental posturing of Hegelian or Spencerian optimism would find his "restless universe" insufficient and troubling. One critic found James's universe enough to make him "sick, like the sight of the horrible motion of a mass of maggots in their carrion bed" (136). However, the whirl of this maggotlike universe presented James with an opportunity for action. It was roughly analogous to the scene of modern existence, in which change and possibility dominated. Within this universe, James sought to demonstrate, on both the metaphysical and phenomenal level, that individuals were responsible for adding their own passion to the story of the universe. James believed that to be passive in the sea of evolution was to surrender one's volition and to risk drowning in the stormy waters of Hamletian lethargy. But, of course, in order to make the individual's actions less uncertain, James also posited that the world had a sufficient order to allow for our calculations. In addition he posited the presence of a God to support the direction and energy of our actions.[44]

IV

James's assault against determinism focused upon its sociological implications as well as its metaphysics. In either philosophical or sociological expression, the danger of determinism remained anchored within its subtle ability to breed moral acquiescence and personal passivity. From his reading of the popular press in this age of cultural confusion, James was disappointed to find deterministic sociology marching under the banner of Darwinian science. Based upon Spencer's insights into the environment's role in the evolutionary process, deterministic sociology forced James to make an explicit appearance as a social theorist, a role he usually preferred to avoid.[45] But the challenge of determinism necessitated his intervention in two essays, "Great Men and Their Environment" (1880), and its brief sequel, "The Importance of Individuals" (written in 1881 but not published until 1890), both of which appeared in *The Will to Believe*.

James loudly condemned the "philosophy of evolution" for contributing to the *tedium vitae* of modern existence. Especially as developed by Spencer, this "metaphysical creed" spoke for a quiescent attitude toward life; it relegated its followers to a "mood of contemplation" (188). James well remembered this stance of intensive contemplation from his own nightmare years of depression and debility. "My quarrel with Spencer," James wrote to Henry Holt, his editor, "is not that he makes much of the environment, but that he makes *nothing* of the glaring and patent fact of subjective interests which cooperate with the environment in moulding intelligence."[46] What rendered the "philosophy of evolution" all the more dangerous in the hands of Spencer and his epigones was that it gathered additional credibility in American culture by clothing its concepts in " 'scientific' plumes." The emperor of debility might be wearing new clothes, but James's view was that he still acted as the dictator of passivity and resignation—a monarch to be overthrown (188).

A pair of articles by the popular-science writer Grant Allen, a self-professed follower of Spencer, first drew James into the public fray over the relationship between environment, individual, and evolution. In two essays, "Hellas and Civilisation" (1878) and "Nation-Making" (1878), Allen elucidated the "self-evident proposition that nothing whatsoever can differentiate one body of men from another except the physical conditions in which they are set." For Allen, the greatness that was Hellas ultimately resulted from the central influence of its environment and the relationship between Greece and its neighboring areas. Allen contended that national characteristics, "whether in intellect, commerce, art, morals, or general temperament, ultimately depend, not upon any mysterious properties . . . but simply and solely upon the physical circumstances to which they are exposed." This was a strong assertion of physical or environmental determinism. The role of individuals, even superior ones, in the "nation-making" process was constrained by the all-enveloping function of the environment. Physical geography represented destiny.[47]

James proved a formidable opponent of Darwinian sociology when its proponents, such as Allen, emphasized the sanctity of the environment to the exclusion of the individual. In "Great Men and Their Environment," James drew precise and cogent distinctions between the process of Darwinian natural selection and the assumptions behind social evolution. In considering the relationship between individual and environment, James secured for himself a middle ground between those who would valorize the environment and those who would place the individual actor outside the physical environment. Yet James resolutely refused to exclude the exceptional individual's crucial part as an actor in the drama of social and cultural evolution.

Spontaneous variations—those mysterious events within the chain of evolution described by Darwin—alone accounted, as James understood it, for the appearance of geniuses in the train of evolutionary development. But the environment only came into significant use after the genius had already appeared. The social environment, not unlike the natural environment as described by Darwin, selected certain individuals for survival. Environment presented them with conditions to which they had, in effect, to adapt their intellect and abilities; otherwise they must perish or be consigned to anonymity. Nonetheless, the individual left his or her imprint upon the environment. Unfortunately, the general outlines of the evolutionary sociology developed by Allen all too often overlooked the fact that naturalists' knowledge of "how indeterminate the harmonies between a fauna and its environment are." Overdetermination, rather than reductionistic analysis, is the theme James stressed to those who read "Great Men and Their Environment" in *The Atlantic Monthly*. James claimed that Allen had only served to write a parody of the depth and complexity of Darwinism (179).

The deterministic implications apparent in Allen's misunderstanding of Darwinian concepts greatly bothered James. The ideal of social development presented by Allen and Spencer promoted passivity and robbed the individual of autonomy. If James had surrendered on this point, he would have abandoned his hopes of developing his philosophy of voluntarism and his discourse of heroism; he would have rationalized the passivity of his cultural milieu. After all, if the great individual was but a pawn in the environment's previously determined game, then what possible reason would remain to compel an average individual to confront life in a morally energetic fashion? James phrased the question in stirring and historically concrete terms: "Would England have to-day the 'imperial' ideal which she now has, if a certain boy named Bob Clive had shot himself as he tried to do, at Madras? Would she be the drifting raft she is now in European affairs if a Frederic the Great had inherited her throne instead of a Victoria. . . . Leaders give the form" (171).

In *The Will to Believe*, James sought by this example and others to demonstrate his theory that one must grant the "fermentative influence of geniuses . . . as . . . one factor in the changes that constitute social evolution" (172). Great men—Bob Clive, Louis Agassiz, Mahomet, and Benjamin Franklin were among James's choices—establish "a rearrangement, on a large or a small scale, of the pre-existing social relations" (170). As in his argument against closed, deterministic metaphysics, James here, too, constructed a universe where his pluralistic viewpoint might exist alongside the rationalist's tightly drawn picture of the unity of phenomena. Above all else, James's "ethics of optimism" prevented him from accepting the abyss of inaction that followed from the implications of deterministic sociology.[48]

"Great Men and Their Environment" thus presented a dialectic of development in which the interaction between individual and society existed in a creative tension. In taking up the cudgels of social theory, then, James restated his general philosophical opposition to determinism. It all seemed so appropriate and apparent to James; he assumed that his readers might also wonder whether the entire debate was "nothing more than common sense" (174). But common sense was often the element most frequently lacking in those reflective individuals trapped in *tedium vitae*. They were beset by "the most ancient oriental fatalism" of metaphysical and social theories of human development (183).

Social evolutionists John Fiske and Grant Allen responded to James's spirited defense of the "great men" hypothesis in a predictable and un-enlightened way; their comments are noteworthy solely because of James's rejoinder. Fiske claimed that James's position on the interaction between the individual and the environment actually resembled the sup-positions of the arch-evolutionist Spencer. Fiske sought to claim James as one of his own by quoting Spencer's theory that heroic actions by individ-uals did affect the environment. Yet Fiske, speaking for Spencer, refused to cede to the great individual the kind of historical freedom from the environment that was the signature of Thomas Carlyle's theorizing on these matters.[49]

In his response to James's essay, Allen conceded certain minor points while continuing to maintain that James erred in neglecting how the great men represented only a statistically insignificant deviation from the mean: "genius is only a step or two above the other men of his race."[50] If the endowments of one individual be so closely aligned with those of another, then the answer to James's impassioned question about whether the early death of Robert Clive might have changed the future of England was answered in the negative. The logic of Allen's deterministic view of history—one quite similar to those forming around Marxist doctrines at about the same time—necessitated that some other individual, also a notch or two better than most other men, would have risen to the occa-sion, or been selected to respond to the demands of historical necessity. The environment selected what it needed from men, not vice versa. Or, as Allen phrased it in a letter to James, "the bubble [man] does not make the wave, but the wave the bubble."[51]

James could not allow to let stand such a sustained and confident challenge to the autonomy of the individual as a force shaping history. Although he failed to publish his response, "The Importance of Individu-als," in the *Atlantic Monthly* during the heat of the controversy, he did publish it in the philosophical journal *Open Court* in 1890. There James recounted his one of his favorite stories, about a carpenter who, when asked about the difference between one man and another, admitted that "what little there is, *is very important.*" James seconded the carpenter's sentiments. As a matter of perspective, James chose to interpret Allen's differences of a "step or two" between men as not some minor divergence from the mean, but instead as representative of a significant variation. This allowed James to maintain admiration for heroes and to claim that they significantly influenced their environment. James strongly main-tained this "zone of individual differences" was "where past and future meet. It is the theatre of all we do not take for granted, the stage of the living drama of life; and however narrow its scope, it is roomy enough to lodge the whole range of human passions."[52] James refused to allow the "philosophy of evolution" to draw the stage setting in the somber metaphysical or evolutionary hues of determinism or boredom. He wanted an action setting, where the heroic individual defined, in conjunction with the environment, the moral outlines of his or her own existence.

V

James vociferously condemned the despair bred by deterministic and mechanistic conceptions of the universe. Opposition to the bugaboo and the implications of the deterministic philosophies of Hegel and Spencer became a focal point for much of James's philosophical attention. But in his role as a public philosopher, attempting to capture the nature of the cultural crisis of his era and to present solutions to it in accessible philosophical language, James also recognized that the *tedium vitae* of his cultural formation escaped metaphysical boundaries and definitions. Indeed, it might result from a situation in which the individual jettisoned religious certitude in favor of a prolonged, introspective journey into the ultimate nature of things.

Doubt about the nature of the world and uncertainty about the autonomy of the individual became the defining characteristics of numerous young Americans in the final decades of the nineteenth century. It is the belief of later historians that the familiar Victorian odes to habit and strength of character, as well as the impassioned proofs offered for human autonomy, only served as the nervous evocations of a generation cognizant of little else other than its own doubts. The less real the autonomy of the individual became in theory and practice, the more exalted became the praise for the autonomous individual.[53] Cast adrift in a world without secure moral values, Victorians and their immediate successors were marked, in Walter Houghton's analysis, by "prolonged introspection, analysis, and indecision; or the sudden collapse of a philosophy or a religion which had been the motivation of action, with nothing to take its place; or the vision of a mechanistic universe without purpose or meaning—any or all of these possibilities latent in the intellectual situation can mean the destruction of all values whatsoever."[54]

James addressed this vexatious sense of uncertainty over belief and action in the face of the destruction of values in "Is Life Worth Living?" (1895), which was originally presented as a talk to the Harvard Young Men's Christian Association (YMCA) and later published as a slim volume. James focused on the intellectually and culturally specific context surrounding his audience and on the dangerous doubt that accompanied an "over-studious career." Young Americans appeared trapped within a "metaphysical *tedium vitae*," which brought them only "the skepticism and unreality that too much grubbing in the abstract roots of things will breed" (39–40).

Science's inroads against religious faith were partly responsible for this Hamletian situation. The logic of a narrow empiricism, especially when directed against the shibboleths of traditional theology, did devastating work. Science "frustrated religious demand" by questioning many of its more traditional and useful notions. The ideal that the natural world was the expression of the loving hand of God no longer sustained many. It was now commonly believed that the natural world was dominated by the struggle between good and evil, "nature red of tooth and claw." To accept the notion of a "God of Nature" was to place oneself in a difficult position, which might lead to despair at the dichotomy between nature and spirit, ideal and real. James sought to mediate this chasm by dropping "the worship of the God of Nature" while still proclaiming the energizing belief in God (40–41).

For those unable to overcome what James characterized as the "death-in-life paradox," borrowing the term from Carlyle, the problem of suicide loomed large. The suicidal individual, continually reflecting upon the "hard facts" of science and finding the universe to be without meaning or apparent order, was in a very difficult position; he or she stared into the "abyss of horrors," the "Maya" of illusion that had figured so centrally in James's depressive years. Empirical knowledge seemed to undermine traditional certitude and confidence, leaving little in its wake except a worship of science, a sensualism that led nowhere, or a determinism that offered only passivity—"moral holidays" was James's favored term. Armed with "our evolutionary theories and our mechanical philosophies," modern men and women understood the disorder of nature. Unfortunately, such comprehension, which Nietzsche placed at the core of Hamlet's rotten apple of perception, was sufficient cause to awaken many thinking men and women to "the nightmare or suicidal view of life" (39–40).

In speaking to the YMCA audience, James established an immediate rapport because he could identify with this "bass-note of life" view and with the plight of the suicidal individual. But the problem of suicide concomitant with excessive reflection was not confined to the hallways of the YMCA or the opium dens of *fin-de-siècle* aesthetes. Philosopher Morris Cohen recalled that when he was a young man on New York's Lower East Side, numerous young and impoverished Jewish intellectuals were afflicted with nervous disorders and melancholia. He remarked that James's "Is Life Worth Living?" also struck a resonant chord with them.[55] After all, *fin-de-siècle* suicides and potential suicides suffered from a doubting mania akin to the type that had cast its shadow over James's own life. James's grappling with the problem of the suicide was complicated by the cultural tendency to translate suicidal sensitivities into a token of modern heroism or into a paean to the ultimate proof of human autonomy in a bleak world.[56]

Intellectuals have frequently viewed suicide as the paradigmatic act of modernity. For Goethe, writing about the romantic agony that gripped his fictional Werther, suicide was a proper response to unrequited love. Romantic and sensual Werther had little choice other than to turn his passion for the ideal into the reality of suicide. Charles Baudelaire's later vision of the suicide, especially as interpreted by Walter Benjamin, stressed the logic of suicidal action as a protest against the horrors of modern knowledge. Indeed, according to Benjamin, the modern age existed most poignantly "under the sign of suicide." Suicide, therefore, was not passive resignation to the *tedium vitae* of the modern era, but an act of "heroic passion," the *passion particulerè de la vie moderne*, as Baudelaire expressed it.⁵⁷

Certainly James understood the suicidal imperative. As late as 1896 he remarked—in tones that would later be echoed by Albert Camus's *Myth of Sisyphus*—that "no man is educated who has never dallied with the thought of suicide."⁵⁸ And, as he made apparent in *The Varieties of Religious Experience* (1902), James identified more with the "twice-born" sick souls who had been tempted by despair to suicidal reflection than with the "once-born" souls who seemed congenitally, and therefore only superficially, happy and satisfied. James never lost sight of his youthful interest in Schopenhauerian pessimism; the doubts that had accompanied his suicidal urges remained a central part of his mature philosophical perspective.

James also was settling an old score with his philosophical mentor Chauncey Wright's view that physical nature was just "mere weather." The upshot of this general perception, which did much to encourage modern pessimism and possibly even the spirit of suicide, was that nothing in nature was hidden or transcendental; appearance and reality were one entity. How to confront this fact without succumbing to pessimism? "Is Life Worth Living?" turned its passion and argument toward this dilemma.⁵⁹

Unlike Baudelaire and perhaps Benjamin, James did not celebrate the "heroic passion" of the suicide, even while admitting that he fully understood the "negative state of mind" of the potential suicide in a world defined by the loneliness and horror of uncertainty or "cosmic weather." The "sign of the suicide," in James's interpretation, seemed to have been hung by modern scientists who, as he demonstrated in "The Will to Believe," cautioned a passive, almost resigned stance to the problematic choices of modern complexity. Agnostic scientists reduced life's moral chiaroscuro to little more than a waiting game. They consigned the active individual to the sidelines, a suicide within the act of living. The same type of resignation was offered by Spencerian determinism or naturalism: "For naturalism, fed on recent cosmological speculations, mankind is in a position similar to that of a set of people living on a frozen lake, surrounded by cliffs over which there is no escape, yet knowing that little by little the ice is melting, and the inevitable day drawing near when the last film of it will disappear, and to be drowned ignominiously will be the human creature's portion."[60]

James's alternative to the dilemma of passivity was to posit a vision of a universe crying out for the individual to struggle for moral ends. James presented to the student audience of "Is Life Worth Living?" a "moral multiverse" (43), in which "the instinctive springs of vitality that respond healthily when the burden of metaphysical and infinite responsibility rolls off" in the face of moral battles to be waged and won, under the ennobling sign of God (45). Here James drew the essential outlines of his philosophy of the strenuous life, his discourse of heroism, which became such a central part of his mature philosophical vision.[61]

VI

James realized that modern society appeared at first glance to be a world largely devoid of moral tension and therefore deficient in stimuli for strenuous moral activity. James thus assumed the role of social critic, someone who, under the authoritative mantle of public philosophy, sought to expose the problems inherent within his culture's willingness to build a world marked by the "iron cage" of the *tedium vitae*. James, of course, was not alone in sensing that the older heroisms of life had been written out of the modern script. His novelist friend William Dean Howells, who always tried to depict truthfully the world of the bourgeoisie, ironically commented on the new problems that challenged modern Americans. Modern heroism seemed nothing more than the search for a new apartment, the endeavor that engulfed the protagonist for six chapters of Howells's novel *A Hazard of New Fortunes* (1890). Howells found the "intellectual refinement" of Boston to resemble nothing so much as "death-in-life."[62]

James often maintained, in the language of a Puritan jeremiad, that the accumulation of material possessions threatened to corrupt the American population, thereby "increasing the sum of cowardice in the world."[63] Deterministic philosophies fed moral passivity, as James argued, but so did luxury "born of the exclusive worship of the bitch-goddess SUCCESS" also promise to raise alarmingly the level of "moral flabbiness" in America.[64] This led James to equate the frenzied drive for wealth with moral weakness; in turn, he increasingly viewed an abstract acceptance of poverty as opening the individual up to moral strength. The accumulation of wealth troubled Americans, in James's interpretation, no less than did their abject fear of losing whatever wealth they had accumulated. In this manner did corruption, cowardice, and moral lethargy seep into the individual's life. In contrast, "a man for whom poverty has no terrors becomes a freeman."[65] In summary, James charged that "the prevalent fear of poverty among the educated classes is the worst moral disease from which our civilization suffers."[66]

James associated "moral flabbiness" with a middle-class mentality that valued comfort and materialistic gain above all else; it was highlighted at the Chautauqua Assembly in Buffalo, where he spent a long week in summer 1896. He chronicled his impressions of "that sacred enclosure, [where] one feels one's self in an atmosphere of success," in the essay "What Makes a Life Significant" (1898), originally delivered as a public address to students at Bryn Mawr and Stanford. Soon after delivery, the talk was published as part of the section "Talks to Students" appended to *Talks to Teachers on Psychology*.[67]

James groaned under the weight of the probity, self-satisfaction, and luxury of the Chautauqua, that middle-class citadel of polite assumptions, culture, and education. James experienced ennui as he encountered the throngs paying homage to the values of middle-class comfort. In response to this experience, James maintained that American culture had entered a vacuous *"tedium vitae,"* a "strange pool of philistinism," which promised to rob existence "of the old heights and depths and romantic chiaroscuro." Both the material and spiritual comfort of these "once-born" Chautauqua saints threatened to spread its virus of mediocrity. America might become "in the end a mere Chautauqua Assembly on an enormous scale." Thus James worried that "even now, in our own country, correctness, fairness, and compromise for every small advantage are crowding out all other qualities. The higher heroisms and the old rare flavors are passing out of life" (154, 237).

James dreamed solely of escape during his week at the Chautauqua. His thoughts paralleled those of the doubting minister Theron Ware, Harold Frederic's fictional protagonist, who found his own "five days of the saints" at a Methodist camp-meeting to have only "bored the head off me."[68] The "ice-cream soda" atmosphere of the Chautauqua bored James equally strongly: "Even an Armenian massacre, whether to be killer or killed, would seem an agreeable change from the blamelessness of Chautauqua, as she lies soaking year after year in her lakeside sun, and showers." Even in his public pronouncements, James let his risqué humor get the better of his good sense, as when he called for something "primordial and savage" to break the horribly numbing tedium of the Chautauqua, even to the point of wanting "the flash of a pistol, a dagger . . . a crime, murder, rape, elopement, anything would do."[69]

The Jamesian critique of this utopia of middle-class existence was the same one that he had proffered against deterministic systems. Here the "lakeside" of the Chautauqua becomes the "ice pond" that defined the metaphysical world of certain determinists. The progress promoted by the Chautauqua strangled individual initiative in the same manner as the Spencerian vision of a rainbow at the end of the "yellow brick road" of evolutionary development: "The white-robed, harp-playing heaven of our sabbath-schools and the lady-like tea-table elysium represented in Mr. Spencer's *Data of Ethics*, as the final consummation of progress . . . [appeared as] lubberlands, pure and simple, one and all."[70]

James confronted a dilemma as he stridently protested against metaphysical and cultural forms of *tedium vitae*, which defined his era's *conjoncture* from 1880 until World War I. While he no doubt remained confident that his arguments against the philosophy of "elysium" would win, he worried about whether the individual—who found belief valuable and who accepted a pluralistic world—would confront a social world lacking appropriate venues for the exercise of the heroic will. This era's social realities, as James himself often depicted them, conspired to undermine the metaphysically vibrant universe that James's philosophy sought to describe. The "abyss of horrors" had translated itself, if we accept James's testimony in "What Makes a Life Significant" and *The Will to Believe,* into the weightless abyss of middle-class existence, a world all "light with no suffering and dark colors" (152–53).

To combat this presumed shift from the abyss to the "sacred enclosure" of tedium, without giving up the fight against determinism, or jettisoning moral responsibility, served as the impetus for James's discourse of heroism developed and presented during these years. Yet, at times, in his zeal to picture the individual in heroic hues, James would in the process paint himself into a philosophical corner. He would come close to not simply accepting evil as something to be fought against but to a Roycean position whereby evil was welcomed because of its pragmatic fruits, its ability to elicit heroism and strenuosity from the individual.

James occasionally argued that, without the presence of evil, heroic actions would either be tepid or not forthcoming. This perception developed from his thesis that action had to be stimulated by great resistances, leading to a ready acceptance of wars and of natural disasters, such as earthquakes, because they demanded heroic action. James stated in "The Powers of Men" (1906) that "Either some unusual stimulus fills them with emotional excitement, or some unusual idea of necessity induces them to make an extra effort of the will. *Excitements, ideas, and efforts,* in a word, are what carry us over the dam" of the tedium of our normal lives.[71] Yet James's zeal to free the individual's passions for a heroic life also threatened to evoke the imperial self, who acted without a firm sense of moral or social responsibility. The autonomous, powerful, assertive self that James labored so hard to support—as a personal, public, and philosophical enterprise—might in its worst manifestation gain a close likeness to the heroic individual that Theodore Roosevelt was then celebrating in his version of the strenuous personality. In his or her zeal, the Jamesian hero might overwhelm the realities and freedoms of other individuals.

A caveat in James's favor must first be entered before examining the excesses of James's discourse of heroism in chapter five. James did not wish to create a Frankenstein of heroism simply because he was consternated by the metaphysical and social *tedium vitae* of his era. In "The Moral Philosopher and the Moral Life" (1891), James explicitly cautioned against the notion that any desired action on the part of the individual was unencumbered by complexity and moral weight. Each act came at a cost. "There is always a *pinch* between the ideal and the actual," James warned, "which can only be got through by leaving part of the ideal behind." While he demurred from drawing up strict, abstract guidelines or categories for moral behavior—"better chaos forever than an order based upon any closet philosopher's rule, even though he were the most enlightened possible member of his tribe"—James, in his open and pluralistic manner, demanded an ethics that would satisfy as many demands as possible without unduly compromising one's own ideals or inner vision. In supporting the individual's inner vision under this sobering set of moral constraints, James established the foundations necessary for a responsible and morally valuable discourse of heroism.[72]

CHAPTER FIVE

The Discourse of Heroism

Tedium vitae was an important theme in the cultural conversation of wealthy and intellectual Americans between 1880 and World War I. Ennui, boredom, and neurasthenia became cultural commonplaces, objects for study, styles of thought, and descriptions of reality. George M. Beard initially outlined the deadening contours of the neurasthenic condition in his *American Nervousness: Its Causes and Consequences;* by the time Harold Frederic had depicted the pale colors of the religion of his fictional minister Theron Ware in 1896, the doubting figure of Hamlet and the deadening neurasthenic condition had been minted as the cultural coin of the realm. Edgar Saltus's Schoperhaurian *fin-de-siècle* aestheticism and pessimism only served to illustrate further this dissipated state of the mind.[1]

Yet the boredom that suffused American thought and culture—the doubt and inactivity that William James experienced, analyzed, and condemned—never existed as a lonely voice. A discourse of heroism was in contrapuntal arrangement with boredom. Although historians such as John Higham are no doubt correct in viewing the tempo of this heroism or revitalization movement as charging to a crescendo in the 1890s, their strong sound was readily heard in American culture in the early 1880s.[2] At the time that Beard began cataloging the neurasthenic disabilities of Americans, former Civil War general Lew Wallace published *Ben Hur* (1880). Wallace's novel of adventure and struggle wore its Christianity soaked in the blood of heroism. Ben Hur is a hero of immense proportions, clearly no Hamlet. In contrast to the doubting, inactive Dane, Ben Hur "had his plan, and, confiding in himself, he settled to the task, never more observant, never more capable."[3]

The romantic activism in *Ben Hur,* which by 1887 sold in excess of forty-five hundred copies per month, was part of a generalized discourse of heroism, not confined to any single social group. The stirring tones of the heroic and strenuous life played equally well, though not necessarily for the same reasons, in the overstuffed bric-a-brac homes of the bourgeoisie, the book-lined studies of intellectuals, and the barren apartments of workers. For those at the bottom of America's social and cultural ladder, heroism presented itself in the guise of the success myth: the belief that any young man, through strenuous and enlightened pursuit of business ideals, might gain wealth and, in the process, benefit society at large. Even Deadwood Dick—the most famous hero of the Western dime-novels developed in this period—represented, to Henry Nash Smith, "the popular ideal of the self-made man," while existing as a died-in-the-wool hero of mythic proportions. Both commerce and courage were equally written within the discourse of heroism that enthused American culture after 1880.[4]

A discourse of heroism functioned, for many in James's social and intellectual circle, as both response and alternative to the era's *tedium vitae* and Hamletism. In late-Victorian America, heroes embodied the qualities of morality and strenuosity. These attributes represented, as Walter Houghton argues, an escape from weakness that had both "psychological and nostalgic" aspects. The hero was designed to inspire other individuals to more powerful interaction with the world. Victorian heroes avoided lives beset with doubt or numbing abstractions. They lived and fought like Carlylean heroes. Even in failure, they remained unvanquished.[5]

By the 1880s the discourse of heroism in both America and Europe had transformed itself into a full-fledged revitalization movement. Ennui wrestled with strenuosity, and the latter was increasingly the victor—in both everyday life and in cultural expressiveness. Physical exercise suddenly became *de rigueur* and bicycling, rowing, and mountain climbing gained prominence. For those who preferred to experience heroic strivings in vicarious fashion, the birth of intercollegiate sports, the organization of professional sports, and even the "taming" of bare-knuckle brawling into an acceptable spectator sport all vied to supply excitement to the public. As T. J. Jackson Lears demonstrates, even those disinclined to follow the sports craze could find heroic sustenance in the world of fantasy. As an exemplar of the heroic mode of life, Deadwood Dick paraded alongside medieval and samurai warriors and biblical figures.[6]

The American discourse of heroism did not have to turn backward through the pages of history or travel to exotic locales for heroic fables or exemplars. Cultural spokesman such as painter Thomas Eakins uncovered the subject matter of heroism in everyday life. Like James, Eakins had not participated in the Civil War, but he strongly attempted to depict the heroic possibilities inherent within the postwar, middle-class experience: in the quiet strenuosity of the scullers racing down the Schuylkill

River, or in his portraits of the engraver, businessman, and physician as heroes of modern life. The strength, determinism, and confidence of Ben Hur are depicted in Eakins's famous portraits of medical heroism, such as *The Gross Clinic* (1875) and *The Agnew Clinic* (1889). Yet Eakins could just as easily do battle with the *fin-de-siècle*'s tired temperament in his own version of the Colosseum spirit in *Salutat* (1898), in which the victorious boxer or wrestler receives impassioned applause from a crowd of bourgeois gentlemen.[7]

A search for "intense experience"—be it in the paintings of Eakins, the romantic heroism of Ben Hur, or the adventurous tales of Deadwood Dick—represented not only a method for dealing with the presumed numbness of middle-class culture but also an energetic response to the bewildering change and challenge associated with modernity. The lure of primitive energy and the exercise of modern power formed the essential tension within the modern personality. Feeble Christianity and sentimental moralism fell in battle to a "moral critique of modern culture" predicated upon a cult of "romantic activism."[8] The cultural and intellectual expression of this stance took on various forms. As H. Stuart Hughes, Carl Schorske, and Eugen Weber demonstrate for the European context, the discovery of the unconscious, the emphasis upon the will, and the transfiguring power of myth were *fin-de-siècle* pronouncements of a new and active world view developed by intellectuals to enter into a dialogue with modernity.[9]

President Theodore Roosevelt came to exemplify "romantic activism," with a modern twist, in America. His conception of the "strenuous life" captured essential currents within America's cultural revitalization movement. Roosevelt celebrated the strenuous life for its intrinsic qualities: the person engaged in heroic pursuits experienced elevated feelings of power and confidence. Roosevelt's personality and ideals represented a direct assault against the religious doubt, mechanistic naturalism, and scientific skepticism that had ravaged traditional notions of individual autonomy. In Roosevelt's therapeutic of strenuosity, the neurasthenic doubter was transformed into the heroic warrior. Roosevelt personified this cult of authenticity and self-promotion—once weak, he was now strong; once afraid, he was now brave. Roosevelt tried to persuade all Americans willing to listen to his exuberant message that the cultivation of proper habits and thoughts, when accompanied by concomitant acts of the will, would re-create the individual in the heroic mode.[10] Roosevelt came to express, in Henry Adams's designation, a "singular primitive quality that belongs to ultimate matter . . . he was pure act."[11]

The ideal of personal growth through the strenuous life, as developed in Roosevelt's conception of the hero, was intended from its inception to serve as the spear of his political thrust. The Promethean hero, acting upon a malleable environment, had precise political connotations within the American context. The heroic ideal allowed Roosevelt to avoid succumbing both to the quietism of Spencerian laissez-faire social philosophy and to the pessimistic determinism of scientific naturalism. Strenuosity emerged as a rationale for Roosevelt's assault against certain aspects of corporate hegemony and, in turn, sanctioned his reform-minded revisions of the American political landscape. That Roosevelt's presumed reforms were conservative in their ultimate goals—to preserve the essentials of the political and economic system by curbing the worst abuses—should not detract from the style in which the heroic ideal, in his creative hands, helped to make social reform palatable and possible for middle-class Americans. By basking in the light of heroic imagery and a macho persona, Roosevelt was able to expand the symbolic associations of reform activity, which at the time had effeminate connotations. While this shift of reform from the realm of the weak to the arena of the heroic had little impact on the ideal of reform, at least in theory, it did make the enterprise of reform culturally and personally viable for a class of white males, primarily professionals, who had previously excluded themselves from it.[12]

The warrior ideal, Roosevelt's "belligerent nationalism," worked well with the logic of his imagery of the strenuous life. Energies directed toward domestic reforms might also expand into the theater of foreign policy. Through his guns and bluster and by dint of his policeman's mentality, the strenuous foreign policy of Roosevelt, in the evaluation of diplomatic historian Robert Dallek, "helped to renew the sense of mastery and self-confidence that the social and economic upheavals of the late nineteenth century had largely dissolved in America. His actions also spoke to the progressive preoccupation with restoring the nation's moral health."[13] In the act of war, foreign-policy objectives and personal revitalization might be united. Imperialism, then, became little more than the collective expression of the strenuous, heroic impulse that was operative within individuals. Tales of heroic individualism, dreams of empire and of economic gain, and the moral imperative "to civilize" foreigners combined in the ideology of the strenuous, the discourse of the heroic, to help subjugate Cuba and the Philippines.[14]

Many American intellectuals, especially those who had advocated a cult of heroism, joined Roosevelt on this imperial pathway.[15] In this period, James was engaged in the same conversation of heroism, yet he never responded to the imperial call, to this ode to domination and constraint. Nonetheless, James worked hard to develop a public philosophy, built out of the concerns of his professional philosophy, that would permit a discourse of heroism to be fashioned. No less than Roosevelt,

James was engaged in directing answers to a set of shared cultural questions. As Jacques Barzun has remarked, "the one thing that unifies men in a grim age is not their individual philosophies but the dominant problem that these philosophies are designed to solve."[16] Although James's philosophy sought to solve many traditional philosophical puzzles and to settle interminable philosophical disputes, it operated within a cultural context desperately in need of a discourse of heroism. Thus James sought to provide public answers to cultural questions in his writings on religious belief.

I

James's famous exclamations of the transformative, ennobling, and heroic power of religious belief appeared most forcefully in *The Will to Believe* (1897) and *The Varieties of Religious Experience* (1902). While both works existed as public documents, as originally in lectures to audiences of average educational background, their inherent philosophy was written throughout James's philosophical project. His religious and heroic view of life was both a response to a particular vision of the essential lines of the universe and an expression of James's own picture of the universe. If "philosophies are only *pictures* of the world which have grown up in the minds of different individuals," as James was fond of saying, then his picture of the world opened itself up to the Promethean activities of men and women.[17] Not intending to demean the critical import of philosophical reasoning and disputation—after all, these were the *sine qua non* of his life—James still wanted to clear a space in the cultural forest for philosophy to become a house that would "inspire our souls with courage."[18]

Philosophical positions that embraced a universe marked by *tedium vitae* starkly contrasted to James's Promethean view of human possibility. For James, the harsh colors of Nietzsche's chaos of sensations and the dull hues of Spencer's deterministic universe painted a nonheroic set of possibilities. The Nietzschean abyss offered little hope or support for heroism in the face of absolute uncertainty. The Spencerian formula, moreover, did even less to warrant heroic displays of activity. The absolutes of the abyss and of certainty pushed the individual into the Hamletian state of passivity.[19]

Although James warned, especially in his later work, which was composed under Henri Bergson's spell, against the dangers of overconceptualization—James's world remained a "chaos of experiences"—he never ceased to welcome the individual's ability to wrest order out of the swirl of experience, the "blooming, buzzing confusion" associated with the world of pure experience of "new-born babes, or men in semi-coma from sleep, drugs, illnesses, or blows."[20] A discourse of heroism required a world that was open, but not one without any possibility of order. Order emerged through active conceptualizing and respect for the complexity and concreteness of experience as a set of relations rather than as the passive given described in associationist psychologies. Assessing Spencer's theory of mind, James admitted that "I for my part, cannot escape the consideration, forced upon me at every turn, that the knower is not simply a mirror floating with no foot-hold anywhere, and passively reflecting an order that he comes upon and simply finds existing. The knower is an actor, and co-efficient of the truth on one side, whilst on the other he registers the truth which he helps to create."[21]

Man was a thinker and a doer; James never ceased to posit a teleological consciousness for man.[22] For Promethean man, a striver after ends, reality—as James conceived it in its pragmatic implications, if not in its metaphysical necessities—pulsated and grew at the edges: it "buds and bourgeons, changes and creates."[23] Deterministic or monistic conceptions of the universe inevitably failed to capture the extent to which "our spurts and sallies forward were the real firing-line of the battle . . . the thin line of flame advancing across the dry autumnal field which the farmer proceeds to burn."[24]

James once argued that the consuming problem with determinism was that it "contradict[ed] the *dramatic temperament* of nature."[25] James saw the universe as providing, through its fire and its flux of experience, a stage on which the individual participated in a "moralistic and epic kind of universe."[26] In the process, James's description of the universe was colored by his own passionate vision, and it fitted the needs of his culture, which demanded courage and heroism.

II

The personal history of James's passion for a metaphysical vision of the universe that allowed heroism to be written on its every page might have originated, as Ralph Barton Perry has suggested, in James's psychological needs. In Perry's formulation, "James's exhortation to action was addressed primarily to himself."[27] Other analysts have concurred in linking Jamesian philosophical strenuosity to the texture of his early life. Howard M. Feinstein registers the view that "action and the strenuous life were antidotes [for James] to the poison of the irrational for the student, as they would be for the psychologist he would become."[28] Similarly, George M. Fredrickson sees James's "writing in the heroic vein . . . making up in imagination for something he had missed in life."[29]

These interpretations are undoubtedly correct. After all, James's philosophical vision featured heroic, directed individuals acting in the face of uncertainty and adversity. In his initial confrontation with the call to battle, James had failed to act decisively; he had been judged by his friends "not to have lived." James's response, as his friend and philosophical interrogator Chauncey Wright remarked, was to adopt a creed, both metaphysical and practical, whereby the "heroic conditions of life" always obtained.[30] Whereas the staunchly unsentimental Wright could only deem such a view as naïve, James never ceased to declare proudly that he remained a "hero-worshipper."[31]

In its essential outlines, James's own life may be read as a testament to and expression of life's heroic possibilities. His triumph over personal and philosophical doubts certainly suggests a Herculean struggle. So, too, the explosion of important philosophical works in the last ten years of his life takes on monumental aspects, given his persistent and debilitating heart problems. Finally, James believed that the life of the mind, the heroic gymnastics of the intellect, was itself an expression of the "heroic conditions of life." In the role of public philosopher, James conceived himself as acting heroically and with great social utility. In response to his Polish philosopher friend Wincenty Lutoslawski, who had questioned the authenticity of an academic discourse of heroism, James exclaimed:

> But man as man is essentially a weakling. Heroism is always on a precipitous edge, and only keeps alive by running. Every moment is an *escape*. And whoever is sensitive as well as motor knows this, and ought not to be ashamed of it. One who should pretend to be in *possession* of a *kräftige Seele* [strong soul], would thereby prove himself a donkey ignorant of the conditions—the thing has to be conquered every minute afresh by an act, and if writing and rhetoric help us to the act, they are also part of the function and we need never be ashamed of them.[32]

The personal resonance of James's discourse of heroism and its dialogue with his earlier problems and doubts should not obscure, as he himself warned, the degree to which the need to create and to carry on despite obstructions, must "be conquered every minute afresh." Within this context, James's struggle to complete the "arch" of his philosophy partakes of the heroic. Moreover, in the context of his era's cultural and intellectual atmosphere, James's public philosophy figures as the "writing and rhetoric" designed to impel members of his audience who suffered from tedium or religious doubt to heroic acts, which were always weighted with responsibility and with awareness of the world's complexity.

As has been stated earlier, James intended that the essays collected in *The Will to Believe* and the lectures that became *Varieties* would partly function as jeremiads against the problems concomitant with scientific imperialism and religious doubt. He focused his argument toward "reflecting men and women," who were lost in a sea of "skepticism and unreality."[33] He measured his enemies carefully, finding that both determinism and scientific hubris contributed to a Hamletian state of inactivity. So, too, did James in *Varieties* analyze the weakness of modern Americans, arguing that their increasing concern with material comfort promised only the discomfort of a weightless, pallid existence. The " 'spirit' of our age," James sadly recorded in 1902, is often marked by "effeminacy and unmanliness."[34]

Analysis and condemnation of unappetizing lifestyles and philosophies did not serve as the entire focus of James's two important books on religion and religious belief. *The Will to Believe* developed a philosophical case for the right to believe and critiqued the particulars of both narrow empiricism and absolute idealism. Whether James's "will to believe" doctrine is understood as prudential or moral, he intended that his impassioned support for religious belief would transform the lives of his listeners, moving them toward a more energetic engagement with life.[35] Although James's *Varieties* stands as an important contribution to the era's increasing interest in developing a "science of religions," and as a brief favoring religious experience over theological disputation, it also represents an extended Jamesian animadversion for religion's role in supporting and extending a discourse of heroism into modern life.[36]

It is necessary to interpret James's work in religious psychology within the context of a generalized discourse of heroism, as a response to the social paralysis that he had found in his own life and culture. James offered something beyond a critique of the neurasthenic state of American and European culture in the period from 1880 to 1900; he strenuously attempted to chronicle great examples of heroism and to suggest an agenda, a therapeutic, that would encourage greater displays of heroism in the world.

III

James conveyed an important message in both *The Will to Believe* and *Varieties:* if modern men and women were to act with energy, to strive toward greater heights of thought and accomplishment, then their activities must be conjoined with those of God. The powerful push of naturalistic trends within intellectual life increasingly seemed to place the individual against a world without rhyme or reason. Whereas Nietzsche demanded a heroic response to the abyss, James more realistically warned that what might work for those blessed with "the explosive will" would only result in neurasthenic escapism for the majority of men and women. Aghast at the "abyss of horrors," all but the few *Übermenschen* would descend into a "panic fear."

Thus, James asserted, "Man is too helpless against the cosmic forces, unless there be a wider Ally."[37] At the time that Nietzsche, in his ploy to energize the individual, proclaimed God's demise, James posited God's presence for the same ends. James contended that the individual who did not believe in a God who supported energetic striving for ideal ends would continue "slumbering." In a Godless universe, "The appeal to our moral energy falls short of its maximal stimulating power."[38] God bequeathed greater sums of moral energy to the individual.

James's fullest discussion of moral philosophy, under the reassuring sign of God, appears in his essay "The Moral Philosopher and the Moral Life" (1891), reprinted in *The Will to Believe*. Here James immediately rejects dogmatically drawn ethical philosophy. Instead, he outlines a moral position that is at once utilitarian (though not in any narrow Benthamite sense of the term) and existential. James's moral ideal was all-inclusive, designed to satisfy as many demands as possible. He recognized, however, that some part of our ideal or others' ideals must be "butchered"; all good ends cannot be readily obtained.[39] For James, ethics began with recognition of the plurality of ideals and needs; he proceeded to praise those ethical ideals that least damaged the inner realities of each individual. System more than imperative, a humane plea for understanding more than a well-developed agenda, James's ethical universe intended sanctioning the heroic energies of individuals while containing them within reasonable boundaries.

In the quest for an ideal, James noted that the strenuous mood must be given priority. Struggles were required in this world, and the good could only be won by vanquishing the bad. God helped us to struggle better so long as the ends were ideal and inclusive rather than narrow and paltry. The presence of God becomes an absolute necessity for men and women: "The capacity of the strenuous mood lies so deep down among our natural human possibilities that even if there were no metaphysical or traditional grounds for believing in a God, men would postulate one simply as a pretext for living hard, and getting out of the game of existence its keenest possibilities of zest. . . . Every sort of energy and endurance, of courage and capacity for handling life's evils, is set free in those who have religious faith." The empowered individual, walking with confidence in God's presence and following the Jamesian ethical agenda, would invariably "on the battlefield of human history always outwear the easy-going type, and religion will drive irreligion to the wall."[40]

A Jamesian God promised not only a dose of moral energy but also "guarantee of an ideal order that shall be permanently preserved."[41] James found that where "God is, tragedy is only provisional and partial, and shipwreck and dissolution are not the absolutely final things."[42] God did not release men and women of their responsibility to build a better world; God helped them find the resources to act. Salvation would come through the individual's activity under the watchful and supportive eye of God.

James's God was an aesthetic conception mirroring the essential themes in Johann Schiller's aesthetics. Schiller's ruminations on Edmund Burke's inquiry into the sublime are echoed in James's religious writings. Schiller, in *On the Aesthetic Education of Man* (1792–1801), had posited two types of beauty, "melting beauty" and "energizing beauty." The former provided us with "moral holidays," whereas the latter increased one's ability to act with power.[43] James combined both stances to celebrate a God-derived universe, in which one might on occasion sit back and marvel at the Creation while equally realizing that one had to struggle with the still-uncompleted universe, to raise it to greater heights—as desired by God and as necessitated by the need to struggle against evil.

This Jamesian conception of God may not have been fully developed, but it certainly met the needs of James's audience, individuals without energy for moral action, and it also, most obviously, responded to James's own history of doubt and depression. During the late 1860s and early 1870s, that painful time in James's life when he encountered the twin horrors of a universe either fully determined or fully chaotic, James had confronted the depths of depression. At the instant when he trembled before his "panic fear," James called out to God for solace and assurance, if not for ultimate direction. The turn to God seemed a sensible alternative to a fate that otherwise might have come to resemble that of an "entirely idiotic" epileptic crouched in the corner of an insane-asylum.[44]

Although it is common to see James's recovery from the "panic fear" and its everyday manifestations of doubt and disability as a result of his acceptance of Charles Renouvier's philosophy of free will or his adoption of Alexander Bain's maxims on habit formation, salvation initially arose from an elementary and emotional appeal to God. James recalled years later that "I mean that the fear was so pervasive and powerful that if I had not clung to scripture-texts like 'The eternal God is my refuge,' etc., 'I am the resurrection and the life,' etc., I think I should have grown really insane." The God that saved James in this moment of greatest despair would later become the God that he would recommend to those without belief, to those intellectuals caught up in a Hamletian pose. While James never adhered to a traditional religious theology or cosmology, he remained, as he once remarked to his friend Thomas Davidson, "less and less able to do without" God. In his reading of his era's cultural text, James increasingly recognized that most individuals were unable to survive without belief in God.[45]

James presented a historically specific God, designed for modern men and women who had been influenced by scientific thought and method and therefore could not be expected to bow to the God of the Hebrews or the Calvinists. A God of "personal favors" or of harsh indifference did not strike James as pragmatically useful. James always returned to the conception of God as an ally in life's moral struggles. This fit in well with his own religious beliefs. While James's personal religious experience was more a "social *reality*" than a powerful emotional experience, and though he felt "foolish and artificial" when engaged in prayer, he held out for an image of God "as a more powerful ally of my own ideals."[46]

James's religious views allowed him to inhabit a ground similar to that which informed the "muscular christianity" of the period from 1880 to 1910. His religious sentiment resembled the "new theology" of Protestant liberalism then being promulgated by Theodore Munger, Walter Rauschenbusch, and other ministers; their theology promised social and religious revitalization through individual acts of heroic devotion to a cause of greater idealism than that which focused on the accumulation of wealth.[47]

IV

Although James sketched the outlines of his conception of God and detailed the salutary benefits of belief in God, he also endeavored to demonstrate how religious belief translated into a fuller, more strenuous life. In *Varieties,* James carefully described and explained, through detailed studies of the lives of the saints, how a belief in God granted the individual a sense of "absolute confidence and peace."[48] Saints of many denominations, historical eras, and geographic areas were the empirical evidence that James mustered to prove that religious belief served the ends of action rather than passivity.

Saints had undergone a religious conversion experience of particular intensity. Prior to gaining sanctification, they had wandered and suffered in a spiritual wilderness: "you must first be nailed on the cross of natural despair and agony, and then in the twinkling of an eye be miraculously released" (186). This spiritual awakening endowed saints with a fuller sense of the range of experience and opened them up to life's possibilities and problems. Mystical feeling fed into a stream flowing with the waters of "enlargement, union, and emancipation." But, in the end, such feeling was without "specific intellectual content whatever of its own" (337).

James claimed to be more interested in describing than in judging the religious experience. Nonetheless, he forcefully indicated that all religious conversions did not bring forth equally desirable results, salvation did not always inspire greater strenuosity and heroism. The "once-born" soul inhabited a world much like that described in James's critique of the Chautauqua mentality. James perceived the religion of pure healthy-mindedness, of easy and assured religiosity, as a bargain-basement product, one made of cheap fabric that would unravel at the first signs of wear (385n.). In contrast, the "twice-born" individual was blessed with the attitude of a Bunyan or Tolstoy and marked by the experience of having "drunk too deeply of the cup of bitterness ever to forget its taste." The memory of this defining experience allowed "twice-born" saints to inhabit a "universe two stories deep," where they strenuously confronted the problem of evil. Saints embraced a "wider and completer" outlook, which was an analogue to the ethical universe James drew in "The Moral Philosopher and the Moral Life." The "twice-born" saintly attitude favored by James allowed healthy-mindedness to be merged with morbidness into a "higher synthesis" that allowed "heroic" and "solemn" energy to be exuded (358n., 155).

The saint, even when only of a "once-born" mentality, demonstrated inordinate amounts of energy in confronting social, moral, and personal issues. The strenuous mode of living that James discovered in the saintly type contrasted starkly with Hamletian inaction, the weak *fin-de-siècle* attitude that he found rampant among his compatriots. Indeed, James even went so far in *Varieties* as to designate those without faith as suffering from "anhedonia" (397–98).

Unlike many middle-class Americans who wallowed in material wealth, saints practiced energetic asceticism. As James phrased it in his discourse of heroism, "Some austerity and wintry negativity, some roughness, danger, stringency, and effort, some 'no! no!' must be mixed in, to produce the sense of an existence with character and texture and power." Without such a deeply grounded sense, one too frequently absent both from the comfortable world described in certain metaphysical systems and from the realities of modern life, James comprehended that the "soul's energy expires" (219–21, 240–41).

Saints never seemed to lack for energy or to be numbed by the doubting stance of Hamlet. The religious believers described in *Varieties* achieved a "relatively heroic level" from the inducements concomitant to their faith. All sorts of ordeals, against which a nonbeliever would shriek in horror, only served as obstacles for the saint to overcome by daily ardor. "The highest flights of charity, devotion, trust, patience, bravery to which the wings of human nature have spread themselves have been flown for religious ideals" (210). While James recognized that saintly excesses could result in fits of imperial domination and moral inquisition, he maintained that such effusions were most often to be blamed on social circumstances or environmental demands. The final judgment on the specific character of any saint would have to be adduced according to the saint's ability, in largely Darwinian terms, to work for "the world's welfare." As he had emphasized in "The Moral Philosopher and the

Moral Life," James defined progress in pluralistic and expansive terms.[49]

Unlike the agnostic scientist or the absolute idealist, the "twice-born" saint enthused the world with his or her brand of passionate activity. The value of a passionate engagement with life, as James always emphasized—in *A Pluralistic Universe* (1909), he advocated philosophy as "passionate vision"—resided in the fact that religious belief called forth our natural reserves of passionate commitment in a modern world too often marked by "negativity and deadness." The saintly passion represented a wonderful "gift" to the world, one that James wished to see more widely distributed. Yet he found evidence of a saintly or heroic disposition among many nonreligious figures. For the energetic type (for example, a Garibaldi), "the obstacles omnipotent over those around them are as if non-existent." Why, James asked, could not the rest of us "so disregard them"? If this was possible, then "there might be many such heroes, for many have the wish to live for similar ideals, and only the adequate degree of inhibition-quenching fury is lacking" (230, 126–27, 215).

In stressing the value of a passionate engagement with life, James generally avoided supporting a doctrine of pure vitalism. He found that "pluck and will, dogged endurance and insensibility to danger [are not] enough, when taken all alone."[50] Yet exuberance and excitement, passion and strenuosity, often came to be seen as valuable ends in and of themselves. How could they be otherwise in a culture that James found reeking with Hamletism? Nonetheless, he had warned against the excesses of saintly moral fervor in pursuit of "paltry ideals" and remained committed to "courage weighted with responsibility." When the energy of one individual clashed with the freedom of another individual, then James clearly sided with the sanctity of the latter's "intellectual republic."[51]

A problem greater than the danger of excess continued to haunt James. How would an individual come to adopt the religious stance that would allow him or her to confront life energetically and with moral heroism? Simple, albeit fascinating, descriptions of heroic figures in *Varieties* were insufficient to impel readers to flights of heroism; exemplars might show interest and occasionally enthuse, but they did not readily convert or lift an individual from the sickbed of doubt into the hardy air of belief. James realized that his arguments might be insufficient, in and of themselves, to compel belief. After all, despite his protestations in the early 1870s in favor of Renouvier's notion of freedom, James's own recovery from depression had been uncertain and lethargic. James was enough of a believer in a doctrine of grace to realize that the process of conversion did not follow an Arminian agenda.

John Jay Chapman, a friendly but forceful critic of James, directly reproached him on this point. Chapman agreed with James that a firm religious belief would better grant American intellectuals a deeper, more strenuous attitude from which to confront life's travails. But Chapman believed that James presented religion as a commodity, something that one chose with no more difficulty than a new bow tie. If that were the case, then clearly little impeded Americans from becoming saints. James understood and admitted the validity of such criticisms, writing that "One *can't* convert a genuine disbeliever in religion any more than one can convert a protestant to Catholicism, etc. Take Santayana!"[52]

V

"Let us be saints, then, if we can," James excitedly intoned, "whether or not we succeed visibly and temporally" (299). Without either divine intervention or the strength offered by exemplars, James left the readers of *Varieties* marveling more at saints' heroism and virtue than armed with any agenda or therapy by which they might attain similar heights of expansiveness. In his most energetic jeremiads, such as "Is Life Worth Living?" James exhorted those of weak mind and body to become believers and, in the process, "Be not afraid of life. Believe that life *is* worth living, and your belief will help create the fact."[53]

Fortunately, the Jamesian discourse of heroism was built upon a foundation sturdier than the shifting sands of exhortation. In numerous popular essays, most of which were initially delivered as public lectures, James returned to the question of heroism, as he attempted to illustrate and explain its reality and possibility in the modern world. At times, he noted the presence of heroism within the lives of average men and women. Elsewhere, he discussed how habit and training might open up the individual to reserves of energy that he or she had previously thought unavailable. Finally, following upon insights that he had initially developed in *The Principles of Psychology,* whereby great resistances evoked strong feelings of effort, James analyzed how natural disasters, such as the San Francisco earthquake of 1906, elicited heroic responses. James peppered the steak of heroism with the seasoning of his philosophical vision. He intended his ideas to satisfy the appetite of a specific cultural agenda. In sum, James wanted to explore the possibilities and prospects for a heroic interaction with life.

In a remark directed toward intellectuals of his own generation, but which might apply with equal urgency and pungency to those of James's era, Philip Rieff noted that intellectuals frequently endowed the lower class with a vitality and heroism that they habitually found lacking among themselves. The upshot of such "intellectual slumming," according to Rieff, was that intellectuals, in their pathetic attempt to draw energy from the proletarian, romanticized the worker. The weakness of those residing in "penthouse apartments" contrasted strongly with the power of those inhabiting tenements.[54] Many intellectuals of James's era experienced "intellectual slumming," and he partook to a lesser degree. Indeed, George Santayana—who could never be accused of succumbing to it—wrote that James's collection of cranks and mystics in *Varieties* was reminiscent of "a 'slumming tour' in New Jerusalem."[55] Whatever the truth of this charge, James's brief appreciation of the heroic muscularity of the working class was at once a culturally commonplace event and a part of his wider concern with developing a discourse of heroism.

During the revitalization movement of the 1890s, American intellectuals became interested in the working class. Whether in quest of local color, exposés of crime and corruption, or reformist objects of sympathy, intellectuals discovered the working class. At times, the documentary veracity of Jacob Riis's photographs seemed incapable of answering the question: "What was it really like to be a worker?" Hence, writers occasionally cast off their middle-class breeding and clothing to enter into the ranks of the proletariat for a day, a week, or sometimes longer. Their accounts, such as "My Vacation in a Woolen Mill" or "Glimpses at the Mind of a Waitress," were intended to satisfy the needs of the upper class to gain new experiences and energies. In part, the interest was a pathetic but understandable attempt by elites to transcend the increasingly rigid class distinctions of the era and to achieve solidarity at a price lower than that of revolution or reform. It was also an act of voyeurism, a passive attempt by those suffering from *tedium vitae* to appropriate the energy of the proletariat.[56]

The search for life *in extremis* or *in exotica* impelled the custodians of culture upon a frenzied and invariably futile journey. Some found the energy and naturalness lacking among the New England elite in the natives of tranquil South Sea Islands or within bloody but belief-sustaining medieval history. Henry Adams was the most famous consumer of both visions. Other intellectual friends of James found energy in oriental culture or in the discovery of regionalism. Dissipated, overly studious intellectuals undertook this endeavor in order to discover a richness of life that seemed sadly absent from their own existence.[57]

James rarely donned a workman's cap in a strained attempt to lose himself among the pleasures of the working class. He did visit a gold mine near Cripple Creek, Colorado, and declared it "a decidedly new kind of experience, climbing down slippery stairs with the water dripping all over you, 400 feet below the surface."[58] When James encountered workers and industrial conditions, it was more often from a comfortable vantage point, from which he confidently assessed the credit and debit of the worker's life. In this glance, James sought to designate what was valuable about the worker's experience while carefully distancing himself from the romanticization that colored the accounts of his contemporaries.

James's fullest discussion of working-class heroism appeared in the essay "What Makes a Life Significant" (1898). Here he methodically juxtaposed the boredom and tedium of the Chautauqua, from which he had just escaped, with examples of the working-class heroism that surrounded him. James enthusiastically marveled at how workers strenuously challenged nature in attempting to wrest their daily bread. James saw poverty and material need as welcome parts of the working-class experience; they bestowed hardihood and strength upon the workers. Anticipating the critique of wealth discussed in *Varieties,* James found that poverty necessitated heroic struggle. Instead of doubting or adopting an effeminate pose, the worker strove heroically.

Speeding by train away from the Chautauqua, James experienced an epiphany as he watched "a workman doing something on the dizzying edge of a sky-scaling construction" site. Here loomed life *"in extremis,"* an intense experience rarely found in the sickbeds of the elite class in America. The Jamesian discourse of heroism attempted to place the image of the heroic worker alongside that of the saint. James exulted over the worker's sweat and strain as an illustration that "heroism and the spectacle of human nature on the rack" still prevailed within modern life.[59]

Seeing that strenuous worker awakened James to the heroic activism that surrounded him; the entire world was not confined by the problems of intellectuals. He suddenly experienced sympathy and identification with the heroism inherent in "the common life of common men." Spiritual concordance with these men revivified James.[60] Struggle brought forth heroism when any individual faced a dangerous occupation; "Italian and Hungarian laborers in the Subway" or "on every railway bridge and fire-proof building that is going up today . . . the demand for courage is incessant; and the supply never fails." Building up to a crescendo of praise for the worker not unlike that reserved elsewhere for the saint, James continued: "There, every day of the year somewhere, is human nature *in extremis* for you. And wherever a scythe, an axe, a pick, or a shovel is wielded, you have it sweating and aching and with its powers of patient endurance racked to the utmost under the length of hours of the strain." Where, James inquired further, might be found an American Kipling or Howells to chronicle these heroisms of modern life? Who might help us to recognize virtue in our midst, often unseen by us because of the workers' "horny hands and dirty skin"? In a stirring conclusion, James praised America's workers as "our soldiers . . . our sustainers, these the very parents of our life."[61]

These effusions were not simply romantic excesses for James. The excitement that these workers elicited, or his affinity for primitivism, became the core of advice that he readily offered to his own family circle. Writing in 1903 to his daughter, Mary Margaret, about the "advantages" of workers, so splendid and honest in their simplicity, James was, despite his old "degenerate soul," happy to be included as "one of the tribe." In the midst of his own physical debilities in 1899, James told his son Henry to continue his summer job as a forester. Hard physical labor was an outright good: "the wearier and longer and disconsolater this experience will seem, the more blest it will appear to you hereafter and the more it will make you understand life."[62]

James fully recognized that workers' lives had aspects that were less than heroic. But he did not examine what constituted the most obvious horrors of their lives, the grinding poverty and financial uncertainty issuing from causes quite beyond their control. Workers fell from the pantheon of true heroes, or ultimate exemplars of the heroic, because they lacked ideality. Although James would become famous for his sincere call to members of the patrician class to seek to understand and sympathize with the "inner realities" of different people, he occasionally failed miserably in this enterprise. As one critic phrased it, James demonstrated a "certain blindness" in his view of workers. In the fashion of the rationalist, his arch philosophical foe, James reduced them to one dimensionality. In the process, James projected his own insecurities and psychic needs upon the workers without fully comprehending that they might find their poverty and harsh living conditions terrible rather than heroic.

James wished that workers could only understand the joy and pleasure associated with a life of labor freed from the confines of neurasthenic doubt. His apotheosis of the workers limited them to reified objects, hands rather than hearts. Workers fell from the pedestal of heroism because they selfishly desired material comfort and security. They craved admittance into the very world that James so often dreamed of escaping. Lacking "ideal inner springs," workers failed to value the "backache, the long hours, the danger" of their lives. They "endured" these badges of honor for rewards as paltry and pathetic, in James's view, as "a quid of tobacco, a glass of beer, a cup of coffee, a meal, and a bed, and to begin again the next day and shirk as much as one can." Although workers had their appeal, they did not possess the true heroism of either military heroes or saints, both of whom combined ideality with strenuous and muscular activism.[63]

VI

James realized that his writing must contain more than exemplars in order to send those crushed by ennui on their way toward enlightened heroism. Religious experiences would no doubt help, as might recognition of the hearty struggles of workers. But, in the process of delivering his public philosophy, James also considered a variety of therapies for heroism, methodologies that might evoke the heroic propensities below the surface of mundane experience. Discipline, habit formation, and careful marshalling of resources all became part of the Jamesian agenda for the revitalization of Americans. In James's analyses, physiology and methodology combined into a therapeutic approach that would "carry us over the dam" of neurasthenic existence.[64]

James's essays "The Gospel of Relaxation" (delivered to various college audiences and first published in 1899 in Scribner's) and "The Energies of Men" (originally presented as a lecture to the American Philosophical Association and published in 1907) focused on developing a therapeutic that would enable Americans to participate in the discourse of heroism. James took the reality of tedium vitae for granted and began to present solutions, at once practical and philosophically weighted.[65]

In formulating his response to the culturally defined problem of tedium, James relied upon a combination of common-sense doctrine and psychological theory. Benjamin Franklin and Carl Lange, Annie Payson Call and Alexander Bain, all figured in James's analysis; the popular and the professional are contained within his public philosophy. Beginning with the assumption that each individual had only a limited amount of energy available, James suggested that he or she be wary of drawing too quickly from, and therefore dissipating, energy reserves. But James ultimately rejected a thesis of conservation of energy, preferring to recommend habitual exercise and cultivation as means of increasing the amount of energy available for strenuous activity.

Reflecting upon his own diminished capacity for action during his neurasthenic period, James discovered that the best policy was "to keep moving steadily and regularly" forward. Although precipitous or sudden bursts of energy might serve an immediate purpose, they would in the long term bode ill for the individual. The delicate physiological mechanism of energy dispersion should not be sacrificed through erratic action.[66]

Whatever the contradictions or gaps inherent in James's understanding and depiction of the nature of our energy reserves, he adopted a middle-ground position, finding that reasonable expenditures of energy strengthened, rather than depleted, reserves. James shifted back and forth between a dialectic of control through habitual exercises—"gratuitous" was how he phrased it in the chapter "Will" in Principles—and through "letting-go," by relaxation techniques or mystical experiences. All these methods promised qualitative benefits while also, through prudent and careful training, increasing our actual reserves of energy.[67]

Following a thumbnail sketch of his theory of emotion, James's "Gospel of Relaxation" praised the power of proper habit formation in conquering doubt and debility. Begun in the 1880s and enthusing *Principles* in 1890, his ode to habit's salutary effects on character development continued unabated in "The Gospel of Relaxation," a strong example of popular philosophy and psychology. Habit figured centrally in this essay's presentation of the James-Lange theory of emotion. James argued that right feelings followed right actions. "So to feel brave, act as if we *were* brave, use all our will to that end, and courage-fit will very likely replace the fit of fear." Through willful attention to bravery and the concomitant completion of small acts of courage, the heroic will would become habitually ingrained into the individual's character. James recommended a variant of the "positive thinking" doctrines that so impressed him at the time. He maintained that "Ideas set free beliefs, and the beliefs set free our wills." Of course, this thinking replicated James's controlling assumptions during the period when he slowly recovered from his depression. Now he reintroduced the concepts of Renouvier and Bain; James applied the new concepts of the mind-cure movement to the old ones of proper habit formation. But the cultural imperative remained the same: to help Americans break free from the prison of inactivity to lead heroic lives.[68]

Mind cure, a popular therapeutic during this period when ennui and strenuosity struggled to control American culture, promised its followers a method that would reveal reserves of energy that they had thought unavailable. The power tapped by mind cure was not unlike the subliminal energy that saints called forth through the power of belief, or that psychics obtained through their explorations of the extramarginal life. Religion, mysticism, and psychic phenomenon were joined, in part, by their promise of opening up new and exciting regions of consciousness and by their "energising of life."[69]

Mind cure's ability to energize prominently informed the discussion in *Varieties* of how a "deliberate adoption of a healthy-minded attitude" does "in countless homes" bring forth practical results. James practiced what he preached, going to mind-cure practitioners for relief from various complaints that contributed to his neurasthenia. As he understood the essentials of mind cure, its therapeutic sought to banish bad habits and thoughts from the mind. Exiled would be "the misery-habit, the martyr-habit" that evoked "fearthought" in the individual and a concomitant inability to act. The adoption and development of a correctly energetic attitude through right thinking held out hope for many Americans. This steady development of proper attitude might not be the equivalent of the complex religious experience of the saints, but it was a practical and accessible road out of the wilderness of neurasthenia.[70]

Although James never wholly embraced mind cure, he continued to believe, as he explained in 1902, that the movement might "play a part almost as great in the evolution of the popular religion of the future as did those earlier movements in their day." His optimism hinged on mind cure's ability to promote a stronger interaction, as did psychic enterprises, with regions that too often remained uncharted within daily experience. New realms of energy and new forms of experience awaited individuals willing to train themselves to discover them. Habit and mysticism, discipline and energy, placed James's writings about mind cure within his discourse of heroism.[71]

James carefully courted therapies that would unlock the secrets of the universe or increase energy reserves for the individual. He consistently searched for a method that would shift "into gear energies of imagination, of will, and of mental influence over physiological processes that usually lie dormant." This belief rested upon James's certitude that "we habitually live inside our limits of power."[72] For example, in "The Energies of Men" he attended to the possibilities that Yoga discipline held for increasing the individual's physical stamina and mental confidence to deal with life's rigors. Yoga's emphasis upon discipline and training, and its promise of intercourse with wider margins of consciousness, represented one therapeutic that would increase heroism and strenuosity.

James's enthusiasm for Yoga diminished only because he had tried it with less than satisfactory results: Yoga breathing exercises "go terribly against the grain with me . . . and even when tried this winter (somewhat perseveringly), to put myself asleep . . . failed to have any soporific effect." Nonetheless, as he admitted in print and in private communication, the narratives of Yoga disciples who had been saved from depression and weak "moral 'tone'" were too compelling to be quickly dismissed. James wrote to his friend Lutoslawski that "Your whole narrative suggests in one the wonder whether the Yoga discipline may not be, after all, in all its phases, simply a methodical way of *waking up deeper levels of will-power than are habitually used,* and thereby increasing the individual's vital tone and energy." This comment precisely captured one of the crucial intentions of James's interest in mind cure, psychic phenomena, saintly strenuosity, and Yoga: to increase "the individual's vital tone and energy" as a mode of escaping the *tedium vitae* of modern life and entering into a heroic existence.[73]

VII

A problem remained in James's discourse of heroism, unacknowledged but pressing in its dangerous implications. Therapeutics for action and heroism often appeared in James's writings as pale, almost Chautauqua-like palliatives, in comparison with the intensity demanded by the "inhibition quenching" demanded by evil or terrible events. James was forced to recognize that "Wars, of course, and shipwrecks, are the great revealers of what men and women are able to do and bear."[74] Great exertions of moral energy—the end he wished to achieve—were best evoked by worthy opponents. James first expressed this argument in "The Feeling of Effort" (1880), in which he remarked that moral initiative "is *made great by the presence of a great antagonist to overcome. . . . it is action in the line of greatest resistance.*"[75] Expanding upon the essential outlines of the heroic individual as drawn in *Principles*, James noted that in this individual the universe "finds its worthy match and mate," who through action is able to meet a world that "puts all sorts of questions to us, and tests us in all sorts of ways."[76]

Resistances such as war, earthquake, shipwreck, or moral chasms to be overcome translated into philosophical problems for James. Evil appeared as necessary and welcome precisely because it, to a far greater degree than mind cure or Yoga, demanded the presence of life-intensifying reserves of energy. Life *in extremis,* the positive flip side to the numbing negativity of *tedium vitae,* cried out for evil as a real, energizing presence in the world. James's enthusiastic applause for these rousers of the heroic spirit brought him perilously close to Josiah Royce's position on evil, which he had condemned.

In Royce's philosophical system, evil figured prominently; its necessary presence, as part of the divine plan, persistently brought forth James's wrath. Roycean evil reminded James of his deepest dislikes: monism, determinism, and absolutism. All conspired to place the individual in a passive relationship to the universe. Not surprisingly, on numerous occasions James attacked Royce's necessitarian view of evil. Although a strong case may be made for Royce's concept of evil as sounding a clarion call for individuals to struggle against it, James generally failed to see the essential affinity between Royce's view and his own.[77] In outlining his own discourse of heroism, James, by an unintended slight of hand, actually expressed what is, in essence, another version of Royce's analysis of evil. James was less a "Roycean with a bad-conscience," as Bruce Kuklick phrases it, than an unwitting "closet-Roycean."[78]

Edward H. Madden strongly argues that James came dangerously close to formulating an argument for evil in the essays of *The Will to Believe*. Madden admits that one can uncover examples of determinism that are "instrumentally good" in "The Dilemma of Determinism" (1884).[79] The appeal to evil partly resided in the medium that bore the message. To be sure, James's desire to favor the strenuous life and to support the heroic will often led him to strengthen the allure of "great resistances." In this sense, the central role of evil as instrumentally beneficial in the discourse of heroism informs much of his public philosophy and forces him down philosophical avenues that he probably preferred not to stroll. Yet James also designed his philosophy, in accord with its mission and his temperament, to bring the individual into stronger concert with life's heroic possibilities. In part, his philosophy *was* intended to fire a bullet against the target of *tedium vitae*. As James remarked on numerous occasions, a world without evil resembled only a stultifying Elysium. The paradox, which James considered central to humanity's moral nature, was expressed in the notion that "the pursuit of outward good is the breath of its [moral nature's] nostrils, the attainment of outward good would seem to be its suffocation and death. Why does the painting of any paradise or utopia, in heaven or on earth, awaken such yawnings for nirvana and escape? . . . [we are] born for the conflict, the Rembrandtesque moral chiaroscuro, the shifting struggle of the sunbeam in the gloom. . . . Not the absence of vice, but vice there, and virtue holding it by the throat, seems the ideal human state."[80]

The image of virtue holding vice by the throat wonderfully fit James's essentially romantic vision of how moral struggle made life worth living; moral strenuosity functioned as a palliative for cultural problems. A universe of moral struggle also helped James once again to define the benefits of God's presence as an ally. Freedom and choice, which always entailed responsibility, remained with individuals, who proceeded with greater confidence simply by knowing that somehow God supported their actions and that these actions would count for something when the final accounts were settled.[81]

The heroism and strenuosity of the Jamesian saint in his or her struggle against an evil foe promised to become the ideal moral agenda. The saint was released from the bonds of conformity, the allures of the material world; his or her "centres of energy" were directed toward heroic engagement with evil. James believed that part of the powerful appeal of the religious conscience rested upon the notion that "the world is all the richer for having a devil in it, *so long as we keep our foot upon his neck*."[82] James did not posit an explicit and extended metaphysical argument for the presence of evil, but he did on pragmatic principles—and in keeping with the heated nature of his cultural agenda—suggest an instinctual or moral necessity for the presence of evil in the world. Without evil impelling us to greater heights of heroism, the world descended into the boring abyss of the Chautauqua.

VIII

An argument approximating a celebration of evil for its value in evoking heroic reserves of moral energy in individuals appears in James's popular discussion of the San Francisco earthquake of 1906. Here evil is traced back to nature's terrors rather than to humanity's foibles. The essay "On Some Mental Effects of the Earthquake" (1906) combines personal experience with philosophical reflection, both filtered through a moral jeremiad against the enemies of doubt and debility. The essay's message was aimed at American youth; it first appeared in the magazine *Youth's Companion*. Designed as a didactic tale, the essay is a compelling precis of James's discourse of heroism and general philosophical concerns. It also captures the logical difficulties James encountered in evaluating the presence of evil. He was willing, almost drawn, to accept evil events for their powerful ability to force us to life *in extremis*. Compared to the fury of the earthquake, the power of mind cure was weak indeed.[83]

An intriguing circumstantial and philosophical denouement defines "On Some Mental Effects of the Earthquake." The academic suddenly finds himself thrown into the world of excitement; in effect, a Jamesian variant on the change-of-identity theme so popular in this era. James spent the academic term of spring 1906 at Stanford University, teaching an introductory philosophy course. It covered conventional Jamesian themes: the educational value of philosophical training; the need of an activist philosophy; the pluralistic nature of the universe; the necessity of mediating between empiricism and rationalism, as well as between science and religion; and, of course, the pragmatic notion of truth.[84]

James's lectures closely mirrored the content of the course's text, Friedrich Paulsen's engaging *Introduction to Philosophy* (1895). At one point in the course, James and his students discussed its section "Critique of the Teleological Argument." Here Paulsen rejected both the validity and usefulness of a teleological interpretation of human and natural history. All such arguments, he wrote, "fall infinitely short of the object of scientific argument."[85] Although James posited a teleological slant to consciousness, which was central to his conception of free will, he did not part company from Paulsen in rejecting a teleological view of human and natural history. James contended that nature tells many different stories, with a variety of endings. To hold otherwise was to reject pluralism and to adopt determinism. In the deterministic universe, everything resembled "instable molecules passively tumbling in their own preappointed way," a restatement of his earlier view, expressed during a period of philosophical doubt, that "we are Nature through and through, that not a wiggle of our will happens save as a result of physical laws."[86]

Renowned for his at times almost wanton ability to apply the most vividly provocative illustrations for philosophical positions—a valuable talent for the domain of public philosophy—James did not disappoint his Stanford students. In lecture, he spoke of the recent volcanic eruptions of Mont Pelée and the historic Lisbon earthquake in order to evaluate the problems of a teleological view of natural history. In keeping with his stern opposition to determinism and fatalism, James warned students against philosophers who perceived design in an earthquake or volcanic eruption. These thinkers were to be condemned for demonstrating humanity's passivity and for kowtowing to the fatalist position. Without Voltaire's irony, they seriously maintained that this world was the best of all possible ones.[87]

The perplexing character of these questions essentially represented a restatement of the determinism that had plagued James during his depressive years. In keeping with his melioristic, pluralistic philosophy, James maintained that one could change the world if one chose to act assertively upon that desire. Comfortable in the possibilities offered in this equation, James denounced the design argument—again using the Lisbon earthquake as an example—because it was based on the mistaken assumption that "the whole of past history had to be planned exactly as it was to bring about in the fullness of time just that particular arrangement of débris of masonry, furniture, and once living bodies." The belief in design would, in practice, only comfort those who had already surrendered their freedom and responsibility.[88]

When James discussed the teleological argument in classes at Harvard or Stanford, the topic lived philosophically but not experientially. In this sense, the earthquake illustration shared the same distance from reality as did James's analyses of religion and war; life *in extremis* remained consigned to the realm of the imagination. This dichotomy began to change when a prescient jest from philosopher Charles Bakewell augured true. Just prior to leaving Cambridge for Palo Alto, James heard Bakewell's farewell: "I hope they'll treat you to a little bit of an earthquake while you're there. It's a pity you shouldn't have that local experience."[89] James would have that special experience, as well as the chance to chronicle the heroic strenuosity that it elicited in the general populace of San Francisco.

While lying awake during the early hours of 16 April 1906 in Palo Alto, James experienced the earthquake: "it went crescendo and reached fortissimo in less than half a minute, and the room was shaken like a rat by a terrier." He recalled no sensation of fear, only excitement in experiencing the "sensible reality" of what had hitherto been only an abstract concept. Aglow in the experience, James challenged this new reality; sounding just like the saint who welcomed martyrdom as a sign of benediction, James embraced his natural opponent with the thought that the earthquake should "go it *stronger*."[90]

Later that morning, after surveying the considerable damage in Palo Alto and its environs, James accompanied a colleague, Miss. L. J. Martin, on a train trip to San Francisco to ascertain the condition of her sister, who resided there. James and Martin apparently arrived on the last train allowed into the devastated city during the earthquake's immediate aftermath. At age sixty-four, with a history of heart trouble and other maladies, James found himself energized by the disaster and became an avid observer of the destruction, activities, and emotions then regnant in the city. The day proved thrilling and exhilarating for him. James recorded, in his diary on the following day, that he had "talked earthquake all day."[91]

The earthquake experience goaded James to recognize two moral lessons, both "reassuring to human nature" and to his philosophical discourse of heroism. James marveled at the "rapidity of the improvisation of order out of chaos." Just as individuals necessarily imposed order on the chaos of sensations as a means of actively confronting a metaphysically open universe, survivors—shaken from their physical and emotional certitudes—quickly conceptualized the new reality and acted accordingly. The impetus toward survival and ordering captured the essential imperative behind James's discourse of heroism. James regaled his youthful readers with stories of "natural ordermakers" who arose from the inchoate mass of humanity to take charge in a life-threatening situation.

Such acts of heroism, initiated by individuals who had not previously displayed strenuosity, inspired James to poetic reverie. The quiescent "energies of men" had been, as James always thought they might be, called forth by a great resistance. The survivors' "universal equanimity" further impressed James. The stop-and-go motion that he had condemned in "The Gospel of Relaxation" as injurious to sustained action among Americans disappeared, replaced by a methodical form of nervous excitation channeled to useful ends.[92]

James stated that there was an explicit connection between the behavior of individuals during the San Francisco earthquake and its aftermath and the behavior of those during a state of war. In our day-to-day lives, in the iron-caged confines of our Chautauqua realities, we only pondered, always at a distance, "how people ever *do* go through battles, sieges, and shipwrecks." Survivors of these *in extremis* situations were not "superhuman," but instead individuals who had risen to the occasion. Presented with an unusual and compelling set of resistances, these individuals called forth their latent "animal insensibility and heartiness."[93]

From observing the activities of earthquake survivors, James learned that even the meekest of individuals, when challenged, exhibited a wonderful ability to expend energy with an "admirable fortitude of temper." Stressing this theme to his youthful audience, James praised these expenditures for bringing back into life "color and radiance." The discussion in "On Some Mental Effects of the Earthquake" recalled James's earlier characterization of the chiaroscuro of the fight against evil, which prominently informed the argument of *Varieties*. The earthquake was proof positive of the universe's tychistic nature. Even when violent, chance was to be welcomed for bringing forth the heroic elements in our character, which were usually hidden beneath the surface of polite, everyday reality. The earthquake reminded James, in the words of Ralph Barton Perry, that "exceptional circumstances generate exceptional inner power."[94]

There were few complaints about personal suffering during the earthquake crisis because of this inner power. Individuals "seemed to admire the vastness of the catastrophe." They worked in practical fashion to rebuild the city and to take care of immediate problems. The individual's misery merged into the communal and "all-absorbing practical problem of general recuperation." James saw this strength as the redoubtable endowment of the human race, rather than being peculiar to Californians or Americans. Pain suffered in loneliness tended to debilitate, but shared misery brought out the "temper of helpfulness."[95]

James found few examples of improper or impractical behavior during the earthquake's aftermath. "The only discreditable thing to human nature" happened when vagrants too readily devoured free foodstuffs. Cases of "petty pilfering" also occurred. James was aware of morally culpable acts, and he had witnessed the lynching of a looter in San Francisco. Moreover, he had requested a friend to keep him apprised of incidents of lawlessness and vigilante justice then prevalent in the city.[96] However, James was strangely silent on the lawlessness and crime that closely followed the earthquake. Perhaps he feared that his argument for heroism would suffer were he to detail for his youthful audience the less-than-heroic activities of some citizens. He also did not want to muddy what was in essence a perfect case study for all of the moral imperatives and hopefulness that he had earlier developed in his public philosophy. In addition, the essay was hardly meant to be exhaustive as an analysis of the earthquake's effects. Instead, it served as an illustration of how a populace that all too often remained consigned to its "drawing rooms and offices" might become inspired and heroic.[97]

Two realities impelled James to celebrate the earthquake. First, it had allowed him to experience danger, to live *in extremis*. No longer a mere onlooker, he could feel very much a part of the hubbub of life on the perilous edge. Second, he could find in the community's response to the earthquake all of the aspects of the heroism of modern life that he had detailed previously only by example, in the stories of saints or military heroes. The great resistance presented to the population of San Francisco in those initial frightening moments of violent shaking had resulted in the revelation of the best and most energetic aspects of human nature. Even if he seemed to posit a necessitarian view of evil, James did not present the response of the individual to it as a passive stance.

IX

James's discourse of heroism was developed in his analysis of religion and saints, in his search for a therapeutic to elicit energy, and in his presentation of the earthquake as one of those great resistances often needed to bring out the strength of human nature. These were all significant interventions in the struggle against the problem of *tedium vitae*. In the process of developing a response to a general set of cultural problems, James also fashioned an agenda designed to present another set of possibilities, to celebrate life under the sign of heroic struggle. Although James did not present struggle as an end in and of itself, he did at times find that strenuosity terribly welcome, if for no reason other than it allowed the individual to escape from the debility and boredom associated with religious doubt and comfortable passivity. James avoided a philosophical discourse of pure vitalism or strenuosity by contending in *Varieties* and elsewhere that he favored moral courage—that is, heroism balanced by responsibility—when it was tied to the ethical agenda as in "The Moral Philosopher and the Moral Life." Moral struggle and strenuosity along the lines of larger rather than narrower ideals formed the core of his discourse of heroism.

As an abstract formulation, James's discourse of heroism met the cultural needs of a particular sector of American society remarkably well. But he recognized that this discourse became more troublesome as political conditions within America shifted. Nothing challenged the validity and the pragmatic usefulness of this discourse more strenuously than the imperial turn that American foreign policy took in the 1890s, culminating in the Spanish-American War, which began in 1898, and the colonization of the Philippines and Cuba in the early years of the new century. This imperial tumble brought James into the public realm as a committed anti-imperialist, but one whose antiwar stance existed within the muscularity of his discourse of heroism. Thus he entered into combat against the most dangerous examples of the warlike spirit of the historical moment while fully continuing to praise the energetic activities of the soldier.

Critical problems called out for solution: How to constrain the energies unleashed by warlike fever? How could one have heroism in modern life but avoid imperialism? James's politics of anti-imperialism and his entire discourse of heroism, then, became inextricably caught up in the larger issue of foreign policy and in the entire question of imperialism and colonialism. His edifice of heroism threatened to fall like the walls of Jericho because of the noisy ranting of Roosevelt and his jingoist supporters. James battled against the excesses of these imperial warriors by developing, especially within his public philosophy, the ideal of a pluralistic universe, in which we would recognize the inner realities of individuals different from us. This concern would even make its presence felt within the text of *Pragmatism* when James used a notion of tradition as a method of counteracting the imperial excesses which some individuals might connect with a philosophy that stressed a strenuous interaction with the world.

Imperialism forms the crucial context for much of the public and professional philosophy that James composed in the years immediately following the turn of the century. He greatly feared that the ministrations of Roosevelt and other imperialists might leave Americans to face the horrible choice, described by Théophile Gautier, the sage of the decadent imagination, as "plutôt la barbarie que l'ennui" (rather the barbarism than the boredom). James would use his public and professional philosophy to contend that a more alluring and morally weightier prospect awaited Americans.

CHAPTER SIX

The Imperial Imperative

In the midst of America's years of cultural crisis from 1880 until 1910, William James built, brick by brick, the impressive walls of his philosophy. Although he never finished the building, his doctrines of radical empiricism, pluralism, and pragmatism continue to maintain strength and appeal. The crucial outlines of James's philosophical structure, by both choice and necessity, never approached the systematic. His universe, like his philosophical system, vibrantly pulsated; reality grew at the edges. Out of the dazzle of experience, the individual imposed a conceptual order based upon his or her own interests and ends. The world, however, contained many stories, all of which were narrated from different perspectives. Truth and experience were decidedly plural; truth and reality were open to possibility and revision. As James described his world shortly before his death, "All that *my* pluralism contends for is that there is nowhere extant a *complete* gathering up of the universe in *one* focus, either of knowledge, power or purpose."[1]

It is understandable that the development and expression of his philosophy dominates most accounts of James's life and thought. Brilliant philosophical formulation is, after all, the foundation for his reputation. James was a professional philosopher of great note and commitment, addressing philosophical issues in an era in which the technical and scientific language of philosophical discourse grew increasingly precise and abstract. Traditional concerns about the relationship between mind and body, the nature of consciousness, the metaphysics of the universe, the status and outlines of truth claims, the proper sphere for religion, the relational aspects of experience, the autonomy of the individual, and the implications of modern science all claimed James's energy and thought during the last thirty years of his life. While the problems he addressed may have been perennial to the philosophical enterprise, James's solutions, engagements, and discussions were modern and daring.[2]

James's philosophy and life, however, demand a fuller contextual approach than they have hitherto received. Context must be drawn in concentric circles, just as a stone tossed into a placid pond extends its presence outward. As James never tired of saying, philosophy begins with the individual philosopher. Temperament and individuality are etched deep within the texture of philosophical speculation. James never failed to emphasize that philosophical thought, in contrast to simple expressions of opinion, rested upon the not-insubstantial ground of reasoned argument. Yet he continued to maintain that behind professional speculation and argumentation was the life and passion of the philosopher: "our visions are usually not only our most interesting but our most respectable contributions to the world in which we play our part."[3] The waters of philosophical conversation were fed by the stream of personality and temperament.

Mediating between the ring of the personal and that of the philosophical is the public sphere, the realm of culture. James's identity and his philosophical corpus existed within the context of his culture and society. Much of James's work and its agenda may be viewed as responses to cultural imperatives defined by both the dangers of tedium and the development of a discourse of heroism. The discourse of heroism informed the content and language of James's philosophy. His vision of philosophy and the universe worked comfortably within the boundaries of this discourse. No doubt, too, James's temperament—his exuberant "fourteen doors" outward, as his sister, Alice, phrased it—found contentment within the universe of his professional philosophy and the discourse of his public performances.[4]

By 1895, when the nova of American imperial belligerency came into sight, James found himself increasingly drawn into the public sphere of politics, a stance that would continue significantly until the final years of his life. He proudly announced himself one of *"les intellectuels,"* dedicated to bringing the power of reasoned and impassioned intellectual discourse into the public realm. "I think that *"les intellectuals [sic]* of every country," James wrote to William Dean Howells in 1900, "ought to bond themselves into a league for the purpose of fighting the curse of savagery that is pouring over the world." In the wake of the Dreyfus affair, James took his responsibility as an intellectual more seriously. For example, he lobbied against a bill requiring the medical licensing of physicians—an act, he feared, that would eliminate alternative healing processes. Although his testimony against the bill brought down upon him the disdain of the medical establishment, James was undeterred, proudly comparing himself to Emile Zola and Colonel Marie-Georges Piquart: "I appeared at the State House yesterday against the medical profession—one of the greatest doses of virtue I have ever brought myself to swallow, not being born for such things. But I am glad I did it." Public awareness and education promised to promote social salvation and to diminish savagery. To educate the public and to oppose particular political effusions became the imperatives behind James's public philosophy from the 1890s into the early 1900s.[5]

In part, the tenor of James's period of "reform and evangelism," as Ralph Barton Perry called it, was the unexpected result of debility. Confronting a nervous condition, as well as the heart ailment that would eventually claim him as its victim, James had more leisure time to himself, time away from the demands of the classroom or the study.[6] He now perused the press more carefully than ever and was outraged at the Dreyfus affair in France, American imperialism, and the Boer War: "What times we live in! Dreyfus, Cuba, and Khartoum!"[7]

The problem with Perry's interpretation is that it is predicated upon a bogus notion of energy dissipation and also underestimates the depth of James's desire to cast off his poor health and to return from a self-imposed European exile to confront American problems. To be sure, between 1895 and 1905, the period of his greatest reform agitation, James did engage himself quite heatedly and fully in political debate—despite his physician's and family's admonitions that he curtail all types of activity. "Every excitement affects his heart unfavorably," wrote his ever-solicitous wife, Alice, to Hugo Munsterberg in 1899.[8] But this political activity hardly represents, as Perry contends, a resting point before the final explosion of energy into the development of the Jamesian philosophical legacy. This ten-year period was a prolific one for James. He presented the initial outline of pragmatism, developed and published his will-to-believe doctrine, and began work on the essays on consciousness and experience, which form the core of radical empiricism. At the height of James's political commitment to the cause of anti-imperialism, he composed *The Varieties of Religious Experience* (1902), his monumental contribution to the study of religious belief and energy. And, in two distinct periods of good health, from 1892 to 1898 and from 1905 to 1908, James delivered the majority of the addresses that form the corpus of his public philosophy.[9]

The passion behind James's political edge in the years surrounding the turn of the century, especially in his anti-imperialism, resides in the pressing and significant challenge then being issued against his philosophical and personal vision. James longed to return home from his European sojourn so that he might, as an intellectual, "influence American ideals."[10] During the 1890s James built both his public and professional philosophy. Each shared a perspective that demanded an open and expansive universe. Both required that the individual, through acts of will and attention, conceptualize this universe while not negating its plurality.

When James challenged a Cartesian model of the mind, his philosophical argument managed to serve his public ends—to reject a passive notion of the mind and to undermine dualistic systems. Concomitantly, public philosophy's discourse of heroism never wandered far from the spacious universe that James's professional philosophy consistently posited. Professional philosophy and public vision intertwined in a strong, mutually supportive bond.

The problem of imperialism dramatically highlighted certain tensions that existed in James's discourse of heroism and that would occupy a place in *Pragmatism* (1907). Imperialism led him to examine how to prevent the exuberant individual from dominating others and how to halt an energetic nation from exercising its will over an alien culture. The issue forced James to resolve, or at least to confront, the relationship between freedom and necessity, between the individual and the group, between self and society, and between the paroxysms of excitement and the rhythms of tedium. James publicly engaged all of these problems in sustained and often enlightening fashion. In the process he came to define himself politically, both within and against a Mugwmp ideology, and to follow carefully the history of America's imperial fortunes. To give full justice to the complexity of James's thought and emotion, it is necessary to move away from the common image of the absolutely self-assured opponent of American imperialism. His optimism often blunted his recognition of the centrality of America's rise to world power, and all that such hegemony implied. Moreover, the allure of the heroic—even the instinctually based loyalty of the individual to the mass and the concomitant excitement of the individual—won James's admiration and begrudging respect. However, James also feared that the imperial moment would lead to the domination of abstraction and bigness over the ultimate sublime of the individual.

Solutions to these tensions and uncertainties sometimes evaded James. Nonetheless, in two strong examples of public philosophy, the theme of imperialism and the tensions contained within his general belief about the relation between the one and the many received full discussion. A close examination of the essay "On a Certain Blindness in Human Beings" (c. 1898) indicates James's desire to retain the explosive freedom of the expansive individual while preventing that stance from resulting in blindness and domination toward others. Thus the solution, later inscribed into his philosophy of pluralism, began with a credo of openness to the variety of the world as an anodyne to the hubris of the imperial will. In addition, James's famous "The Moral Equivalent of War" (c. 1910) is studied as his attempt to retain his discourse of heroism without having its luster tarnished by the dangerous implications of imperialism and the war fever. In this chapter, the defining tensions between excitement and passivity, freedom and constraint, and individual and society are discussed within the context of the problem of imperialism as expressed through the medium of public philosophy.

Imperialism emerges, then, as one important context drawn around James's public and professional philosophy. In battling the dangerous implications of the imperial impulse, James employed pluralism and his understanding of human nature. His various discussions that analyze and condemn imperialism were of a piece, designed to blunt the consequences of a philosophy of power and domination without consigning the individual to a meaningless and passive stance. Moreover, the context of James's personal and public confrontation with the imperial will is a critical subtext of *Pragmatism*. As we shall see in chapter seven, James developed his ideal of truth and his philosophical imperative toward melioristic action under the sobering challenge of imperialism. The problem of imperialism got under the skin of James's personality, public discourse, and professional philosophy.

I

Many of James's most cherished political assumptions were influenced by New England Mugwump intellectuals. At first glance, this influence appears to be an unappealing one. Cultured to the point of excess, Mugwump intellectuals—including James's friends Charles Eliot Norton and E. L. Godkin—appear as isolated men, whose disdain for modernity and for the immigrant masses, coupled with their derision for the vulgarity of Gilded Age businessmen, takes on aspects of the marginal, if not pathological. Even in the brightest moment of the Mugwumps—that is, their opposition to American imperialism—their image looks sullied and their arguments appear unsound, specious, and racist. Christopher Lasch argues that Mugwump anti-imperialism and anticolonialism were founded upon racism, an overriding fear that America would be ruined by "amalgamating" aliens into its body politic. Such animadversions, Lasch notes, were little more than transparent analogues to the pro-imperialists' contention that human beings inhabited a Darwinian universe, which contained inferior and superior nations and races.[11] Robert L. Beisner's close study of the leading Mugwump anti-imperialists reveals similar weaknesses. Carl Schurz, for example, was haunted by the fear of America's impending demise: our tradition of freedom, he averred, would wither because of alien and inferior cultures. This frightened formulation affected his oft-repeated "law" of anti-imperialism.[12]

Overt racism, coupled with disdain for ignorant individuals, led to the formation of powerful and irrational mobs. They fell prey to the manipulative and self-serving pronouncements of yellow journalists, venal politicians, and vulgar capitalists, who constituted the bogeymen in the anti-imperialist jeremiads of Godkin and Norton. Godkin's recitation of the principles of the Declaration of Independence and George Washington's Farewell Address and his bemoaning of America's rejection of cherished ideals appear as hollow and tiresome sentiments of an isolated intellectual. Godkin claimed that America stood "in danger of the endorsement of a gross fraud for the first time by a Christian nation."[13]

Racism, fear of the mass, and regret for vanished ideals situates the Mugwump intellectual within what literary historian Patrick Brantlinger labels "negative classicism." The mythology of "negative classicism" connects the rise of mass culture—and imperialism was certainly an aspect of that advent—with perceived conditions for the decadence and decline of the Roman Empire. America's implosion into imperialism, then, was only one aspect of a troubling set of circumstances that, to the status-conscious Mugwumps, boded poorly for America's survival, at least as they conceived it.[14]

Certain lines connect James to the Mugwump anti-imperialists. Henry Steele Commager's thumbnail sketch of the typical Mugwump could easily apply to James: "They had gone to the best schools—one sometimes feels that a college degree was a prerequisite to admission to their club—associated with the best people, belonged to the Century or Harvard Club, read *The Nation* and *The Independent,* and knew politics, for the most part, at second hand."[15]

James was a close friend of Norton and other leading Mugwumps, as well as a frequent participant in the functions of their flagship organization, the New England Anti-Imperialist League. Furthermore, James's important debt to Godkin issues from his own admission that "in the earlier years I must say that my whole political education was due to the *Nation.* . . . You have the most curious way of always being *right,* so I never dare to trust myself now when you're agin me."[16] James's identification with the Mugwump ideal often intruded into his public philosophy. For instance, in "Great Men and Their Environment" (1880), he went so far as to predict the eventual triumph of the reform cause.[17] More significantly, he spiced his speech in honor of the Civil War hero Robert Gould Shaw with an encomium to the "civic courage" of the modern reformer.[18] This insertion of "mugwumpery" at the end of the address, William admitted to his brother Henry, "was very difficult to manage."[19]

Mugwumps found their cultural, political, and social ideals in the British nation. For the Mugwumps, the mother country represented the repository of wisdom, the ideal of empire with restraint, and, above all, a national culture to be emulated. William James's Anglophilia, especially when compared with that of his expatriate brother, Henry, was moderate. Nonetheless, William frequently praised the British for their "strength of character," which he believed was trained by sober judgment, healthy traditions, and strenuous physical exercise.[20]

James also appears to have Mugwump sympathies in his private correspondence when he reveals the class prejudices that were common to the elite, who swelled the Mugwump ranks. James referred to the Haymarket Riot as little more than the "work of a lot of pathological Germans and Poles." Elsewhere in his correspondence, his language reveals racial and ethnic stereotypes.[21] Such eruptions were infrequent and were usually later tempered by reflection and recantation. He chided Godkin and the *Nation* for failing to see the sobriety of the program of the Knights of Labor, and he wrote to his friend Thomas Davidson to protest the anti-Semitism of a hotel, adding: "I propose to return the boycott."[22] Interestingly, his tendency to lapse into patrician prejudice was strongest when he wrote to his brother Henry. Perhaps unconsciously William sought in those letters to communicate with Henry on the latter's terms of intense uneasiness about immigrants and America's paucity of culture.[23]

Most importantly, James departs from Mugwump assumptions in significant and unusual fashion. His openness to others, including the odd and the unusual, brought him into the company of individuals from diverse backgrounds—and he exulted in their multiplicity. James did not cultivate prejudices of class or taste or religion. Godkin, as well as many other Mugwumps, never tired of denouncing the intelligence of the American populace; indeed, Godkin was almost apoplectic about the manners and culture of those inhabiting the West.[24] In contrast, James maintained an unwavering faith in "the essential soundness" of the American people.[25] Whereas the Mugwumps shared Theodore Roosevelt's voracious hatred for the Populists and their standard bearer, William Jennings Bryan, James could—in his moments of severe frustration with the Republican party's support for imperialism—commit himself in letters to gushing words of respect for Bryan or even to vow to vote for him if the occasion should present itself, an incredible act of apostasy for a Mugwump.[26] Although his ideas were clearly nurtured within the Mugwump milieu, James could not tolerate imperial certitude, be it political, scientific, or philosophical. James was always a party of one.

We should not dwell too long or too confidently on the debits of the Mugwump ideology; it balanced a backward perspective, a sense of loss, with a forward-looking program. According to this evaluation, Mugwump intellectuals sought to bring structure and order to America's economic and social development. In regard to the issue of anti-imperialism, alongside of their "negative classicism" existed a sober assessment of the meaning of America's colonial adventures and an understanding that the future of the American experiment might well hang in the balance.[27] James was enough of a Mugwump to recognize that the imperial controversies of the 1890s and early 1900s marked a turning point in American history. American imperialism emotionally assaulted James, who recalled that he had "cried *hard,* when the hostilities broke out & General Otis refused Aguinaldo's demand for a conference,—the only time I've cried in many a long year." But tears would not silence James's commitment to action and public education; he would, as one of *"les intellectuels,"* strenuously bring his philosophical insights to the cause of anti-imperialism.[28]

I I

The backdrop for James's famous public intervention against the imperialist actualities of the Spanish-American War occurred first during the tempest-in-a-teapot Venezuelan crisis of 1895–1896. The details of this minor boundary dispute between Venezuela and British Guiana, as well as the resultant imperial posturing between Great Britain and America, need not concern us here.[29] However, it is important to note that the shadow of imperialism first presented itself to James during this dispute. The jingoism that arose during this crisis brought a number of insights— to be developed more fully at the turn of the century—to James: a recognition of America's inevitable entrance into the class of world powers; a realization that society, through jingoist hysteria, could unite individuals into an excited mass; proof positive of the continuing power of instinctual demands for glory and excitement; and the acrimony of James's initial confrontation with his former student Roosevelt over the citizen's responsibility to the state during war and crisis.

The war hysteria in 1895–1896 claimed James as one of its victims. In a heated letter—"I haven't slept right for a week"—to Godkin, written on Christmas Eve, James praised the editor's "glorious fight against the powers of darkness," displayed by the prowar jingoists. The outbreak of war fury reminded James of the initial days of the Civil War: "I swear it brings back the days of '61 again, when the worst enemies of our Country were in our own borders."[30] Although James had not participated in the earlier conflict, he now fought alongside the forces of light.

The conflict brought James into sharp public controversy because he opposed the jingoism of Roosevelt. Writing to the Harvard student newspaper in January 1896, James railed against this jingoism. Roosevelt's claim that those who failed to rally to President Grover Cleveland's war message were betrayers of America struck James—who steadfastly refused to answer the call—as a silly and dangerous assertion. The essence of patriotism, lectured James, was to speak out against the "fighting-drunk" war hysteria. Thus James reversed the tables on Roosevelt and thereby brought himself out of the stance of passivity, to which Roosevelt

sought to consign him. James refused to play Hamlet to Roosevelt's Fortinbras. Instead, James characterized Roosevelt and prowar students as
those "easily swayed by phrases," somnambulists who were "hypnotized" into their political positions. James, in contrast, would "be patriotic enough *not* to remain passive." The discourse of heroism required that
he speak out and that he publicly oppose the war sentiments. Rational
thought and concerted action represented the only proper and valuable
course. James forthrightly announced that he and all other patriotic citizens must "consult our reason as to what is best, and then exert ourselves
. . . with all our might."[31]

Despite his rejection of Roosevelt's patriotic frenzy, James wavered
between the problems and promise inherent within jingoism, just as he
would later be uncertain about the benefits of the Spanish-American War.
The activity and loyalty of the individual in the crowd contrasted against
the sobering reality that such an individual was hypnotized and blinded
by fury. But James preferred the positive side of war jingoism: the sense of
unity that it instilled in the population, as well as the powerful instincts
for excitement suddenly crashing through the *tedium vitae* of the modern
world. The Venezuelan crisis led in the direction of the perception that
would eventually be the center of "The Moral Equivalent of War"—that
the fighting instincts of Roosevelt and the crowd proved how "We are all
ready to be savage in *some* cause."[32] The constructive, quite as much as
the destructive, potential of unleashed instincts fascinated James. This
interest separated James from his fellow Mugwumps, each of whom was
repelled by the instinctual cravings of the individual and the crowd.
James, however, celebrated the hints of heroism in the jingoist temperament. Even if his analysis of the politics of imperial expansion remained
weak, as early as 1895 he was well aware of what historian Lewis Wurgaft
notes in another context: that imperialism's mythology and mystique
"presented a dimension of human experience felt to be missing at home—
the daily encounter with death that forces self-mastery and personal
insight."[33]

In the mid–1890s, James offered no solution for the dangerous implications of the imperial and emotional outburst engendered by the
Venezuelan controversy. All he could do was to reiterate the familiar
Mugwump nostrum of public education as the cure for most ills associated with the behavior of the masses, bedeviled political leaders, and
sensationalist newspaper editors. Education represented "the only permanent safeguard against irrational explosions." The power of education
to nurture enlightened leaders and to control instinctual urges never
faded from James's anti-imperialist arsenal. But he was not naïve in arguing for the expectation of elite leadership to always pursue the right
course. As he admitted in the address "The True Harvard" (1903), educa-

tion often stood condemned for simply training the intelligent individual to "invent reasons for what he wants to do . . . Harvard men defend our treatment of our Filipino allies as a masterpiece of policy and morals." Education in conventions and prejudices only promised "cleverness in the service of popular idols and vulgar ends."[34]

James righteously identified education with "the party of civilization," the party of light. Although his formulation of this party, especially in the essay "The Social Value of the College Bred" (1907), revealed Mugwump elitism—"Our better men *shall* show the way and we *shall* follow them"—he held to democratic ideals and, most importantly, obliterated the line traditionally drawn between elite and mass. To James, the masses were differentiated from the leadership only by the degree of education and discipline available to them for the control of the instincts. Everyone, leader no less than the individual in the mass, was prone to fall victim to instinctual urges. And, as he further developed his understanding of the fighting instincts, James came to identify with the liberating call sounded by these instinctual urges. Thus he parted company from Mugwump critics of war by finding them prone to neurasthenic hollowness, which distanced them from the excitement of conflict and instinct. He could not fail to acknowledge that newspaper accounts of the war were "more entertaining than all the various Kritiks of Em. Kant."[35]

III

The end of winter 1897/98 brought the bluster of war to James's door. Yellow journalism, months of diplomatic threats, and the explosion of the *Maine* in the Santiago harbor rendered war with Spain a foregone conclusion. In the weeks before the formal declaration of war by Congress on 25 April, James accepted the coming hostilities with complacency, if not confidence. Perhaps his was the reaction of a trapped mountain climber awaiting another avalanche. More likely, James was simply attempting to look at the positive side of a sordid affair, a case of his willingness to grant the best motives to his philosophical or political opponents and to find a philosophical or political pot of gold behind storm clouds. His analysis of war fever had few hints of Mugwump "negative classicism." Nor did his initial response to the early days of the war correspond well with the popular image of James as a redoubtable, consistent opponent of the imperial temper.

"The war is undoubtedly the very best thing that could have befallen us," exulted James only two weeks before the formal declaration of war. War presented itself as an initiation ritual, which would introduce America into the brotherhood of powerful nations. Rather than viewing involvement as tinged with imperial aims or rapacious appetites, James stressed, in the familiar tones of a "benevolent imperialist," that "new and diversified responsibilities" would force the American nation to "*have* to put our very best qualities foremost." The war even promised good cheer, in James's initial logic, for the cherished Mugwump causes of enlightened leadership and nonaggression. Out of the ashes of war would arise "a magnificent chance" for the Mugwumps to make "the virtues of country *live* once again."[36] After all, when James examined the motivation behind the public's clamor for a military crusade against the Spanish, he chose to see only honorable intentions, just as he would later report mainly favorable impressions on the aftermath of the San Francisco earthquake. Americans fought simply to rid Cuba of Spanish ruffians. In May, James confided to his brother Henry that "Not a soul thinks of conquest or wishes it."[37] The only negative aspect of this analysis was the possibility that a lengthy, dragged-out conflict might result in annexation of Cuba.[38]

Even before the reality of America's colonial aims became clear, unadulterated praise for American intentions was colored by James's distrust of the press. James echoed the familiar Mugwump cry of villainy against yellow journalism. Diplomacy would have worked to force concessions from the Spanish in Cuba if only the sensationalist press had not stirred up the passions of the populace. James maintained that war fever had infected almost every American, largely because of "deliberate newspaper criminality." The grand ideal of *"vox populi"* had been stilled, if not killed, by the editors of the "New York *Journal* (a Harvard Graduate millionaire named Hearst) and *World,* ought to be hung higher than any criminals."[39] These editors, with the help of conniving politicians, had managed to create "a genuine hysteric stampede" for war, a perfect "case of *psychologie des foules.*" Newspapers were but one leg of the monster that threatened to continue this *psychologie des foules* in the modern world. The day of " 'big'ness—by national destinies, political parties, trade-combines, newspapers, is sweeping every good principle and quality out of the world."[40]

James's passing reference to the war stampede as a *"psychologie des foules"* was undoubtedly the result of his reading of Gustave LeBon in late 1896 or early 1897. However, the use of LeBon's terminology does not indicate appreciation for the work. Reviewing the English translation of LeBon's book for the *Psychological Review,* James found the essential argument of *The Crowd* marred, if not crippled, by a biological reductionism bordering on the "misanthropic and pessimistic in the extreme."[41] While James certainly consented to LeBon's contention that even in individualistic nations, such as America, the crowd phenomenon was of greater moment than ever before—in light of the Venezuelan and Cuban excitements, this reality could not escape James's consciousness—

he could not accept LeBon's absolute denigration of the crowd. Rather than bemoaning the loss of individual will and autonomy, which many commentators saw as an essential evil of the individual in the mass, James highlighted the value of directed group action toward beneficent ends.[42] The individual within the crowd cast off Hamletian inaction in order to move with confidence. James's criticisms were not against the crowd itself, but those who sought to manipulate its good will. Leadership demanded restraint and ethical standards, not wanton excitement and demagoguery.

The phenomenon of the individual in the mass thus escaped James's barbs during the initial months of the Spanish-American War. Although essentially narcotized, the individual in the crowd often acted with good intentions and in accord with instinctual needs. This perception fit in well with James's earlier theoretical musings on the crowd. Elaborating on some of the insights in the section "Play" in the chapter "Instinct" in *The Principles of Psychology* (1890), as well as insights gained from the spectacle of the Venezuelan controversy, James stressed the socially valuable components of crowd behavior. Festivals and organized rituals appealed to our instinctual urges. In 1890, James found that the formation of armies and various ceremonies offered the individual "the excitement of concerted action as one of an organized crowd." Within the abstract and safe confines of his psychology text, James remained unconcerned with the loss of individual autonomy or sense of self in a collective situation.[43]

Disdain for tedium, for a generalized inability to act without absolute certitude, had been the *bête noire* that James challenged in his discourse of heroism in *The Will to Believe* (1897) and that he would continue to' attack in *Varieties*. At the least, the crowd allowed the individual to cast off doubt and hesitation and to act in concert with other individuals. In a sense, the crowd's hunger for excitement was the other side of the coin of the doubt-ridden intellectual that figured so prominently in James's own life and public philosophy. This recognition tended to lessen his distaste for the theoretical excesses of the crowd. Contemplation bred only more contemplation, soon plunging the reflective individual into a state of abulia and inaction: "too much philosophy acts as a kind of narcotizer of the active faculties," wrote James in 1903.[44]

A new danger presented itself in the arousal of the crowd; each act of excitement necessitated a need for more stimulation. Having learned from his observations of the crowd during the Spanish-American War, James noted that the gravest danger occurred when the "psychologic factor" came into play after a crowd had become energized.[45] This "psychologic factor" indicated the tendency of the crowd, once inflamed with violence or heightened ideals, to have increased cravings for excitement.

The spiral of action that broke the inertia now threatened to degenerate into dangerous hedonism and savagery.

James's brief discourse on the crowd mentality forced him to reconsider the role of human nature in the political realm and within the culture of imperialism. In the late 1890s, the notion of human nature as a causative factor in activity did not figure as deadeningly in James's analysis as it did in LeBon's. To be sure, James wrote to François Pillon in 1898 that "human nature is everywhere the same; and at the least temptation all the old military passions rise and sweep everything before them."[46] Writing to his psychologist friend Carl Stumpf in 1901, after the Spanish-American War had ended, James gave succinct expression of this reality: "Man is essentially an adventurous and warlike animal, and one might as well preach against the intercourse of the sexes as against national aggrandizement by piracy."[47]

James was not extremely frightened about eruptions of human passions. Given his long struggle to implant passion into a prominent place in his own life, the life of his culture, and the life of philosophy, this reaction should hardly seem shocking. Indeed, James's fascination with the infusion of passion into the public arena is one of the benchmarks of his modernity. For James, no less than for Sigmund Freud or Georges Sorel, the undercurrents of consciousness both repelled and attracted. James also gave vent, in his writings on instinctual passions and the crowd, to what one analyst later labeled "the ordeal of civility"; that is, the belief that the bourgeoisie made a religion out of repression, comfort, and confidence about its status. Like Freud, James chose to resist the allure of instinctual passion while respecting its power. Unrestrained passion fascinated, but it needed to be directed into viable actions. This insight would, of course, later receive full analysis in "The Moral Equivalent of War."[48]

The Spanish-American War revealed to James that "passion is the key . . . the great passion undeniably now is the passion for adventure." He reflected that excitement, passion for war, and even savagery "are the deepest things in the race!"[49] The worship of contemplation and ease— the staples of the Chautauqua—had suddenly been overthrown by the worship of excitement. This rendered Roosevelt's strenuous life, full of warlike heroics, logically appealing to a populace long stunted by tameness. James recognized as much: "Civilization, properly so-called, might well be termed the organization of all those functions that resist the mere excitement of sport." Thus, continued James, "what is life for, except for opportunities of excitement?! It makes all humdrum moralizing seem terribly dead and tame!"[50]

Roosevelt's discourse of heroism fully recognized and played upon this generalized perception. Victorian culture was one of tedium and resistance to passions. The need for heroism was recognized by the apostles of war, and Americans responded accordingly. James, too, found it difficult to resist calls to be heroic, to break out of the confining boundaries of the *tedium vitae*. Decry though he would the results of imperialism, James nevertheless listened to its proponents. Yet he remained acutely aware of the responsibility of the philosopher, intellectual, and citizen to evaluate the implications of the heroic will in its various expressions. In carrying out this imperative, he found himself with no choice other than to battle American imperialism and its defenders.

James's calm understanding of the tensions between energy and tedium, freedom and constraint, broke down once the imperial aspects of the war became apparent to him in summer and fall 1898. His worst fears about America's imperial aims suddenly came to the fore when the annexation of Hawaii was followed by discussions of similar claims upon the Philippines. In 1899, following the war news from his European retreat, James sadly learned that America had thrown off any pretense to working for the freedom of the Philippines; instead America had taken up the cause of colonialism. American forces were suddenly engaged in destroying the Filipino national resistance, which was led by Emilio Aguinaldo. This "infamy" forced James into his active, consistent, and impassioned anti-imperialist stance.[51] He developed his program within the assumptions of his philosophy and without severe damage to his discourse of heroism. James intended to stall the progress of imperialism by awakening Americans to the validity of others' experiences and by dispelling the blindness that gave moral pretense to calls for beneficent imperialism. And James would eventually come to respect the instinctual allure of the warlike spirit while fashioning a method or therapeutic to blunt its sharpest dangers.[52]

IV

The perspective that would inform James's most important works in public philosophy arose from diverse sources. The Jamesian temperament of openness to difference and of tolerance for diversity cannot be attributed to the books that he read or the philosophical theories he developed. As a young man, he experienced profound depression and uncertainty, which greatly influenced his understanding of life's variety and problems. James's temperament is evident in the development of his doctrines of pluralism and radical empiricism in the 1890s. At the same time, temperament and philosophy joined together to battle imperialism. James's ideas of pluralism and openness, which he would employ to undermine imperialist ideology, gained critical support from the readings he undertook in the mid-1890s.

The sanctity of experience and the ideal of pluralism constituted a significant part of James's rapidly developing professional philosophy. Although his famous philosophical formulations existed in embryonic form as early as the 1870s, his involvement in anti-imperialism helped to bring into stronger relief those ideas that would later predominate his philosophy. Pluralism enthused James's philosophical vision; it also worked its way into his political and cultural writing. Respect for the individual fact or experience, as well as rejection of the blinding aspects of overconceptualization, strengthened the spheres of public and philosophical discourse: "Individuality outruns all classification," James stated in *A Pluralistic Universe* (1909).[53]

James's genetic or experiential inclination to a spirit of openness and acceptance was, nevertheless, seconded by the reading that enthused him in the mid-1890s. He was a voracious reader, as indicated by the immense number of citations gracing the pages of *The Principles of Psychology* and *Varieties*. Especially during periods of debility, when he was weary from heart disease and depression, James sought sustenance in novels and in works of cultural analysis, as well as in his regular fare of autobiographies. Leo Tolstoy's novels and H. Fielding's examination of Burmese culture particularly influenced and supported James's already existing fund of concepts. These nonphilosophical books helped to bring James's pluralism and respect for others' experiential reality more into the open, and in turn helped to develop the core of his philosophy of openness and his critique of the imperial temper. In addition, they gave James a language of protest and analysis, which he would employ in his public philosophy and which he would replicate in his professional philosophy after 1900.

Soon after the war howls of the Venezuelan controversy had abated, James read Tolstoy's *War and Peace,* "undoubtedly the greatest novel ever written," an "infallible "representation of human life" in all of its complexity and vastness. Through his art and religious conversion, Tolstoy had transcended his aristocratic background and captured the "immense" diversity of the Russian people in his novels.[54] Tolstoy's veracity in recording the rhythms and realities of the Russian peasantry helped to lighten James's haughty judgments of America's "peasant" class. Tolstoy's work deepened James's inclinations toward openness. Traveling across the nation in summer 1896 to present public lectures on pedagogy to "hulking rustics" and "creaking and groaning teachers," James had occasionally condemned these individuals with a Brahmin glare that would have made his brother Henry or friend Charles Eliot Norton proud. Thanks in part to Tolstoy's promptings, James came to realize that even if these rustic and urban teachers were intellectual dead weight, at least their weight was real. This observation encouraged James's increasing tendency later in his life to celebrate the plurality of cultures. In contrast, the imperialist rejection of openness and pluralism led to domination, just as surely as rejection of religious faith led to anhedonia.[55]

Fielding's now-forgotten *The Soul of a People* (1898) proved more important than Tolstoy's novels in seconding James's best intentions and in furnishing him with the language, if not the perception of openness, that informed his public philosophical perspective. James read Fielding's book during the period that America's imperial flag unfurled. James's approach in his Gifford Lectures on religious experience was shared by Fielding, who also emphasized that religious belief was best understood as religious experience rather than as theology or ecclesiastical structure. Even more significant, Fielding lectured prospective scholars interested in diverse cultures that they needed to cease viewing those of alien cultures as "strange creatures from some far-away planet." Only by casting off cultural hubris or traditional blindness might an observer hope to gain access to "the very soul of a people," the inner realities of a different culture. In an ode to the concepts of pluralism and openness—which would be central to James's mature philosophy—Fielding concluded his volume with this message: "Let each man but open his eyes and see, and his own soul shall teach him marvelous things."[56] These sentiments supported and inspired James's tendency to remain open to cultural diversity. Thus, at the moment when he shuddered at the McKinley administration's blindness and moral turpitude toward the Filipinos, James uncovered in Fielding's volume a complex of ideas "destined to dispell [sic] the blindness."[57]

By 1900 James was engaged in a public, polemical assault against the blindness, hubris, and danger of American foreign policy, especially as directed against the Filipino. In a series of letters to editors of New England newspapers, James chided politicians who cloaked their discussions of the Filipino question in the cloth of ignorance ("dim, foggy, abstract good will"). He believed that such benign disdain to the inner realities of the Filipinos was worse than a policy predicated upon "Cynical indifference, or even frank hostility." James argued:

> Surely any reflecting man must see that, far away as we are, doomed to invincible ignorance of the secrets of the Philippine soul [Fielding's language] (why, we cannot even understand one another's souls here at home), desirous moreover of results of a sort with which we are domestically familiar, and expressing our aspirations through an Executive which is only too true to our own type, our good will can only work disaster, and work the more disaster to the Filipinos the more conscious it gets of itself and the more *exalté* it grows over its "responsibilities."[58]

James uncovered significant Hegelian undertones in the imperialists' assumptions. Hegelianism in politics as much as in philosophy drew forth James's strongest ire. He explicitly connected the Hegelian, abstract mode of thought with the imperialists' view of the world and their destiny. Of course, James's antipathy to the Hegelian language and assumptions was already a staple of his philosophical career. Interestingly, James's polemics against the imperialists coheres neatly with his cherished, developing philosophical conceptions. In his famous essay "On Some Hegelisms," published in 1882 but reprinted in *The Will to Believe*, James mockingly took Hegel to task for his totalistic, abstract mode of philosophizing, whereby the individual item was lost in the unity of all other facts. This imperial, abstract method did violence to the sanctity of the individual fact upon which empirical philosophy must rest.[59] James, in contrast, maintained that "[a] true philosophy must clear itself from . . . smugness. It must keep in touch with the *character* of reality." Close contact with reality was one of the essentials of radical empiricism; failure to keep in close touch with reality only resulted in dangerous, blinding conceptualizations.[60]

The juggernaut of the imperial attitude did similar violence to the individual, both American and Filipino. Imperialists commonly reduced Filipinos to "painted pictures." With "imperialism under full headway," "the impotence of the private individual" in America to stop it or to act in a democratic fashion was rendered obvious. James believed that the Hegelian aspects of the totalized, imperial state resulted in the loss of individualism in the name of philosophical abstractionism. No one was more guilty of such Hegelian politics than Roosevelt. He was a Hegelian in James's political lexicon because he preached "abstract war worship," a devotion based on a principle of "aesthetic abstractness," which had the same unerring appeal that Hegelian aesthetics had for many individuals and nation-states. Rooseveltian, imperialist abstractions— such as "America's destiny," "the white man's burden," or "modern civilization"—all had the effect of expressing, and helping to create the conditions for, our "big, hollow, resounding, corrupting, sophisticating torrent of mere brutal momentum and irrationality."[61]

James's most important attempt to dispel the blindness that made imperialism possible appeared in the essay "On a Certain Blindness in Human Beings," written probably in late summer 1898 and presented that October to students at an Episcopal school. The talk's theme of openness to cultural and personal diversity, as well as its emphasis upon the expansive cultivation of inner feelings, represented James's intervention, through the vehicle of public philosophy, into America's controversial war policy. The essay remained one of James's favorites. He announced more than once that it "was better loved by me than any of my other productions." It expressed "the perception upon which my whole individualistic philosophy is based."[62]

"On a Certain Blindness" is a formidable example of James's public philosophy. He perceived in the wake of the Dreyfus affair that American philosophers must become versions of *"les intellectuels"* of France, educating and leading the public in a judicious, enlightened manner. James's activities as a philosopher-citizen did not preclude polemical interventions of a partisan nature—as he revealed forthrightly in a variety of impassioned letters to editors against imperialism in the Philippines. Polemics were useful when one wanted to rally the troops or glorify in the destruction of an enemy. Such words, however, rarely converted unbelievers or edified the general public. Public philosophy proceeded in a different fashion. The public philosopher conceived his audience as students; effectiveness grew out of reasoned and calm analysis.

Public philosophy transformed heated issues of the moment into enduring problems of life and philosophy. The public philosopher did not intend to avoid issues; he sought to diffuse the blinding passions connected with them as a prelude for reasoned solutions. If the audience—composed of students in the case of "On a Certain Blindness"—would listen, then they might grasp the allegorical point without being put off by explosive polemics. Once understood, the value of the public philosopher's solution might be applied to the controversial issues of the day; the public philosopher would not allow vituperation to substitute for education. "On a Certain Blindness" never mentions American foreign policy toward the Philippines, but that subject is at the heart of the essay's allegorical structure. In the discourse of public philosophy, James intended to confront a problem that deeply concerned him: blindness as it related to imperialism.

In its general contours, "On a Certain Blindness" also addressed a baffling, perennial theme for American social theorists—the relation between self and society—which would later have reverberations in James's philosophical dilemma of reconciling the one and the many. Ralph Waldo Emerson, who exemplified the station of public philosopher in America, "solved" the relation of self to society only by carefully balancing the demands of the individual with those of society; this, at least, was the doctrine formulated by the mature Emerson as he traveled across America giving popular addresses.[63] The tension between self and society—central to the American intellectual tradition—would be made concrete and especially pressing by James's confrontation with the reality of imperialism.

Writing thirty years after Emerson, James faced a society at once more pervasive and demanding in its influence. James believed that its tentacles, which fastened to bureaucratic structures of immense size and power, also were capable of strangling the individual with regulations, manipulation, and power. James's antagonism to bureaucratic structures should not be seen as confined to social or political creations. In his philosophy, especially in *The Will to Believe*, he strongly opposed the institutions of science and the concomitant hubris and blindness of scientists such as John Tyndall, W. K. Clifford, and Thomas Huxley. In this formulation, the coterie of scientists who sought to define what constituted truth had set themselves up as bureaucratic arbiters limiting experience and, in the process, dominating thought. James also found that the general bureaucratic tendency in modern life that he had stripped bare in science was also increasingly prevalent in the "bigness" and power of modern social structures. He perceived "bigness" in society as one of the essential problems behind the imperial attitude; it threatened the reality and potentiality of human autonomy. He phrased it most famously and succinctly in a letter written soon after the composition of "On a Certain Blindness":

> I am against bigness and greatness in all their forms, and with the invisible molecular forces that work from individual to individual. . . . The bigger the unit you deal with, the hollower, the more brutal, the more mendacious is the life displayed. So I am against all big organizations as such, national ones first and foremost; against all big successes and big results; and in favor of the eternal forces of truth which always work in the individual and immediately unsuccessful way, under-dogs always, till history comes, after they are long dead, and puts them on the top.[64]

Society (artificial and blinding) represented for James what tradition had symbolized for the young Emerson—the Emerson of "The American Scholar" and *Nature*—a roadblock in the way of the individual's communion with nature and transcendence of the self. James seconded Emerson's "matchless eloquence" in proclaiming the "sovereignty of the individual" despite the demands of the modern state. Yet James also wondered how to control the imperial impulse within humanity and the state, which surely helped to explain America's imperial attitude toward the Philippines. James chided Howells in a letter for his surprising silence over America's role in the Philippines. Here James also announced the essentials of his pluralistic, empiricist philosophy: "I am becoming more and more an individualist and anarchist and believer in *small* systems of things exclusively. Small things can be veracious & innocent." Once things grow large, as with nations, then "falsity and crime" suddenly appear, along with "the curse of savagery that is pouring over the world."[65]

The harsh polemical air that dominated James's letters to the editors against Roosevelt faded from the tone and text of the public style of philosophy as exemplified in "On a Certain Blindness." Intention and purpose, however, remained the same. James quickly set the tone for his audience by stressing the centrality and vibrancy of the excitement experienced by the individual. What each individual most deeply feels and regards as most significant represents a "vital secret." The specificity of these experiences and their particular character remained a central theme throughout James's thought. Certainly the essentials of his discourse of heroism were based upon the "vital secrets," the energy-inducing feelings that arose from strenuous labor, mystical experiences, or battles against evil. The reality of such feelings must never be doubted, James further emphasized in "On a Certain Blindness," repeating the point he had made earlier in *Principles: "whatever excites and stimulates our interest is real."*[66]

James understood that unconstrained interests were dangerous because they blinded the individual to the validity and reality of others' feelings. James was not unconcerned or unaware of the difficulty of adjudicating conflicting inner realities; this had, after all, been a theme in "The Moral Philosopher and the Moral Life" and in his discussions of saintly excess in *Varieties*. But he was convinced that the essential first step toward better relations among individuals resided in the learned ability of each person to empathize or sympathize with the inner realities, the "vital secrets," of individuals different from them (132). In intent and expression, this notion nicely paralleled the doctrines outlined in James's essays on radical empiricism. There, speaking about the experience of activity in purely pragmatic terms, James made this summation: "Everything real must be experienceable somewhere, and every kind of thing experienced must somewhere be real."[67]

In his public philosophy, James used allegory to communicate the depths of experiential reality, variously perceived, and to condemn the "hegelian" blindness of imperialists. Allegory slowly and carefully outlined the story of a North Carolina homesteader clearing a small patch of land in the midst of a breathtakingly beautiful mountain setting. In creating his farm, the homesteader had built a ramshackle house, irregularly planted Indian corn, and constructed a "zigzag rail fence." James's first impression was that this homesteader was guilty of desecrating virgin land; the farm was an outrage against James's well-developed sense of beauty and an affront to the sublimity of nature. But James noted how he soon came to realize that his vision of beauty did not correspond with that of the homesteader, who was certain that he had achieved a personal victory over the environment, and in the process, brought the beauty of civilization to the wild mountains. "In short," James now understood, "the clearing which to me was a mere ugly picture on the retina, was to them [homesteaders] a symbol redolent with moral memories and sang a very paean of duty, struggle, and success" (133–34). James did not, in the manner of a political philosopher, seek to consider the possibility that each individual's vision of beauty and pursuit of it might undermine others' enjoyment. This question, of course, was at the heart of the imperialist temper. However, James granted it secondary importance; of primary importance was the need for a laissez-faire approach to other individuals and cultures, one predicated on some degree of understanding of the inner realities of those individuals. James sought to convey, in the form of a simple parable, two essentials of his professional philosophy: the perspectivism central to pluralism and the sanctity of the individual fact, which was so important in radical empiricism.

The sentiments of "On a Certain Blindness" reappear with more depth elsewhere in James's professional philosophical essays. In *A Pluralistic Universe,* he warned his audience not to conceive of themselves as passive readers of a cosmic novel. Instead, each individual played a starring role in the "world-drama. In your own eyes each of you here is its hero, and the villains are your respective friends or enemies. The tale which the absolute [Hegelian] reader finds so perfect, we spoil for one another through our several vital identifications with the destinies of the particular personages involved."[68] Overconceptualization and vicious intellectualism represented the philosophical counterpart to the blindness of imperialism in the political sphere. Thus, the political and the philosophical were never far removed from each other in James's life or cultural perceptions.

The necessity to grasp others' inner realities was related to James's emphasis upon the heroic, upon opening up the individual to new experiences as a method of escaping the *tedium vitae* of modernity. Indeed, the excited language and the reductionist logic that might be read into his discourse of heroism sometimes seemed to implicate James as accepting almost anything that helped to bring forth heroic endeavor. "On A Certain Blindness," however, pointed toward a "higher vision of inner significance" that was peaceful and mystical in its expansive possibilities. The essay concluded in an Emersonian epiphany describing those transcendent moments of religious conversion or poetic insight when certain experiences are suffused with a reality above all others. Passion or love served as James's paradigm for such intense, mystical feelings. The veracity of mystical feelings of expansiveness should not issue forth in a desire to force others into one's own mold. An answer to the paradoxical problem of the imperial self reemerged in James's essay. Predicated upon blindness, America's imperial attitude toward the Filipinos grew out of prejudice and ignorance; it was abstract and unreal.

James argued that truly enlightening experiences—that is, strong mystical communions—opened up the individual to others' experiences. Anticipating the language of a religious conscience "two stories deep," which would appear in *Varieties,* James found in "On a Certain Blindness" that the individual with a valid "higher vision" was transformed into someone with an impassioned respect for the experiences of others. Or at least James hoped so. If not, there appeared to be no way out of the conundrum of needing to respect the plurality of experiences and the attendant danger of conflicting visions seeking hegemony over each other. Again, James anticipated the later language of his pluralist, perspectivist philosophy in this public and popular essay; how different, after all, are the sentiments of "On a Certain Blindness" from the imperatives behind *A Pluralistic Universe:* "We have so many different businesses with nature that no one of them yields us an all-embracing clasp. The philosophic attempt to define nature so that no one lies outside the door saying 'Where do *I* come in?' is sure in advance to fail. The most a philosophy can hope for is not to lock out any interest forever."[69] The point of "On a Certain Blindness" and of James's anti-imperialistic ideal of openness was to keep all doors unlocked.

James never desired to weaken intense, liberating experiences, because they made possible the escape from boredom and passivity. As "practical creatures," Americans had frequently paid the price of deadened feelings (138). They had distanced themselves from nature and became encumbered with the trappings of the artificial and conceptually abstract. James invoked a romantic vision, reminiscent of Emerson's, to support his call for openness and expansion. Directly addressing his audience, James announced that "we of the highly educated classes (so called) have most of us got far, far away from Nature. We are trained to seek the choice, the rare, the exquisite, exclusively, and to overlook the common. We are stuffed with abstract conceptions, and glib with verbalities and verbosities" (146). Continuing with the tone prevalent in his discourse of heroism, but without seeking to allow its expression to become a will to domination, James told his listeners to return to primitive joys of struggle and hardihood, even going so far as to suggest the value of shipwreck or imprisonment or military service to "show the good of life to many an over-educated pessimist" (146).

James illustrated one aspect of his call for a return to nature with a lengthy quote from W. H. Hudson's *Idle Days in Patagonia* (1893). The excerpt is an ode of escape from society to the remote and solitary wilderness. In Patagonia, where silence dominates and where one's reveries are never interrupted by the unwelcome din of confining modern civilization, an individual can experience an elation of the senses and "perfect harmony with nature" (148–49). James's use of Hudson's passages recalls the famous transparent-eyeball image of Emerson's *Nature,* in which the individual is suffused with the rhythms of nature. James's eyeball does not dominate the surrounding landscape; it actually becomes part of the natural environment. The individual who achieves transcendence of the sort James recommended is under a "magically irresponsible spell," one of the "holidays of life" (149).

James concluded his address by warning that these "special revelations" significantly differ for each individual, though each retains its own truth. Respect for the "special revelations" of others, including those in "prisons and sick-rooms" (and, James might have added, in the Philippines), remained an absolute credo. Here James only repeated what he had written in his *Introduction to the Literary Remains of the Late Henry James* (1884): "The sanest and best of us are of one clay with lunatics and prison-inmates."[70]

Each of us, therefore, had a duty to "tolerate, respect, and indulge those whom we see harmlessly interested and happy in their own ways, however unintelligible these may be to us." James believed that such strictures were in stark contrast to the imperial and Hegelian attitude of a Roosevelt. The imperial stance in politics and society well paralleled James's philosophical opposition to a monistic universe. He condemned both for threatening to overwhelm the validity of a fact or experience. The final sentence of "On a Certain Blindness" is a veiled criticism of the Rooseveltian discourse of heroism's mechanisms for conquest and domination: "It is enough to ask of each of us that he should be faithful to his own opportunities and make the most of his own blessings, without presuming to regulate the rest of the vast field" (149). Thus James expressed, in an acceptable way, his famous "individualistic philosophy," with emphasis upon the plurality of experience—the perspectivism that respected the individual unit, while it posited an openness necessary not only for scientific and philosophical work but also for political imperatives. As James phrased it, in the aftermath of the Venezuelan controversy, to his activist friend Wincenty Lutoslawski, "I am growing myself, more and more pluralistic and individualistic in my general view of things. . . . Probably the rest of my life will be devoted to defending it more and more."[71]

V

In his works of public philosophy and in expressly political interventions, James advocated openness as a method of diminishing the imperial domination central to the discourse of heroism and blindness preached by Roosevelt and his followers. James recognized, however, that a doctrine of openness alone was insufficient as the cultural response to the mythology and excitement of imperialism. Nor could he submit that rational argument would, in and of itself, be sufficient to counteract war fever. However, James did not intend to celebrate the irrational. But he sadly recognized that, compared to the war fever, "Reason is one of the very feeblest of Nature's forces."[72] From his earliest analyses of the mob psychology in *Principles* and in letters on the Venezuelan controversy, James indicated that the will to dominate and the desire for military conquest had deeper, instinctual roots.

Whatever the attractions pacifist socialism might have held for James, he backed away from the its utopianism because he believed that it could not eliminate humanity's need for private gain: "Man's instincts are rapacious," wrote James to socialist Ernest Howard Crosby, "and under any social arrangement, the *rapatores* will find a way to prey."[73] Indeed, the essence of James's discourse of heroism worked to free these instinctual urges from the repression associated with the ease and boredom of modern life. Heroism and strenuosity were important within James's life and cultural lexicon. Unfortunately, especially as embedded in Roosevelt's political ramblings, the implications of these stances seemed to point dangerously in the direction of an imperial self. To retain the emphases of his discourse of heroism and to undermine the instinctual foundations of the imperial attitude constituted James's agenda in his famous essay "The Moral Equivalent of War" (1910).

James's recourse to the instinctual was largely a reaction against what he regarded as the "hollow" and pathetic qualities of his anti-imperialist allies. By 1903, James and the public generally viewed anti-imperialists in low esteem; they perceived them as "pure idealists." He found an 1899 meeting of the anti-imperialist league to be a "'pathetic' affair," while a later encounter reinforced James's idea that many anti-imperialists were unworthy of popular support and respect. He realized that pure talk, pure ideals, and even the invocation of the sacred Declaration of Independence would not dissipate the appeals of war, conquest, and domination. The psychology of jingoism was too well entrenched in the popular spirit— and in the human psyche—for it to be wished away.[74]

The strength of James's emphasis upon the heroic passions was both a function of his own inner need to face the abyss resolutely and his self-imposed duty to help his culture overcome the *tedium vitae* of modernity. The imperialists' expressions of strenuosity struck a resonant chord for James. Nonetheless, he always realized that stirring militarism endangered the very structure of his entire discourse of heroism, threatening to make it appear little more than a philosophically sophisticated version of Rooseveltian jingoism.

Soon after completion of *Varieties,* James focused on attempting to understand the military mentality and the appeal of war. He contemplated a work to be entitled either "Psychology of Jingoism" or "Varieties of Military Experience." In all probability, such a volume would parallel the approach that had been central to the *Varieties*—to examine, through military biographies, the essential outlines of war fever, though less for condemnation than for a full and sympathetic hearing. The volume would probably have focused upon an attempt to retain the zeal of the soldier without narrowness and fanaticism and to cherish the strenuosity and heroism of the military spirit without its destructive energies and imperial aftereffects.[75]

James had first broached this imperative within *Varieties*. There he compared military and religious sensibilities, finding that the two had much in common. After all, both emphasized "self-severity" and flourished under harsh and demanding conditions. James found the "beauty of war . . . is that it is so congruous with ordinary human nature." It allowed the individual to marshal the "soul's heroic resources" and to confront evil directly. In his discourse of heroism he could not entirely discount militarism as a response to "the worship of material luxury and wealth."[76] The point, however, as James made clear, was not to transform the militarist into a saint. The haunting experience of the Spanish-American War reminded James—and here he seconded the archmilitarist Helmuth von Moltke—that the end of soldierly heroics was "destruction, and nothing but destruction."[77] The pressing need was for a "moral equivalent of war," an ideal that would retain the qualities of the discourse of heroism while channeling certain of its dangerous implications into an arena where "the need of crushing weaker peoples" would no longer be necessary.[78]

In language strange, if not inappropriate, for a self-professed pacifist and anti-imperialist, James continued in his writings after 1901 to dwell upon the pressing reality and allure of the "bellicose constitution of human nature."[79] Wars helped to release an "explosion of imaginative energy." They were capable of producing in an individual feelings quite similar to those of "vague religious exaltation." The "sacrament" of war was bred, by the evolutionary process, into the very "bone and marrow" of human beings. Although entrapped in *tedium vitae*, modern men and women were not immune—when the situation presented itself—to return to their instincts. Indeed, "periodical excitement" is primarily what made life worth living, James wrote in "Remarks at the Peace Banquet" (1904); it represented "relief from Habit's tediousness." Most tellingly, James only somewhat ruefully admitted: "The plain truth is that people *want* war."[80]

The Darwinian flavor of James's philosophy was strongest in his discussion of the enticement and evolutionary necessity of war in furthering the development of the human race. War had selected out for preservation the traits of "heroism, martyrdom, endurance," as well as organization, loyalty, patriotism, and obedience to authority. Because many of these traits were central to James's discourse of heroism and to his personal battle against the "abyss of horrors," he could not in good conscience

reject them out of hand; they represented the "blood tax" of our development as a species. However, he respected peaceful civilization enough to
know that the time had long passed for their expression in militaristic
endeavors. James preferred to search for "preventative medicine" rather
than for a "radical cure."[81]

The essential structure of "The Moral Equivalent of War" (an essay
that appeared in *McClure's, Popular Science Monthly,* and *Atlantic Readings*) perfectly fits into the general contours of Jamesian professional and
public philosophy: to heighten awareness of the validity of experiences
different from those usually centered within our individual conceptual
universe. Blindness either to the experiential reality of others or to the
instinctual realities within ourselves resulted in only shortsighted policy
and narrowed experience.[82] But James made clear that mere exclamations
of good feelings or odes to peacefulness would not satisfy the blood lust of
the imperialists. Nor did James want to fool anti-imperialists into false
confidence about humanity's pacifistic nature. Instead, James felt a compelling need to justify his discourse of heroism to those who remained
beholden to Victorian notions of life as all "sweetness and light." James
certainly had no antagonism to "sweetness and light" as such, but he did
recognize that they were confining in large doses. James found the discourse of many anti-imperialists "mawkish and dishwatery." The world
the anti-imperialists championed was that of *tedium vitae.* As James
phrased it most strenuously in "The Moral Equivalent of War," to the
"reflective apologists for war," war's " 'horrors' are a cheap price to pay
for rescue from the only alternative supposed, of a world of clerks and
teachers, of co-education and zoophily, of 'consumers' leagues' and 'associated charities,' of industrialism unlimited, and feminism unabashed.
No scorn, no hardness, no valor any more! Fie upon such a cattleyard of a
planet!" (166). James followed this exclamation with the common-sense
observation that "no-healthy-minded person, it seems to me, can help
partaking of it [war] to some degree." Anti-imperialists were blind and
were incapable of recognizing the warrior's "esthetical and ethical point
of view" and of respecting the important contribution that war had made
to the development of society (166–68).

James found himself caught between two worlds. He appreciated the
strenuosity of Rooseveltian imperialists as much as he identified with the
peaceful aims of the anti-imperialists. To mediate this dilemma, James
engaged in a bit of prestidigitation in "The Moral Equivalent of War."
Military conquest and domination were no longer to be viewed as instinctual necessities. He believed that they could easily be separated from
the instincts of heroism, endurance, and discipline. These instinctual
desires would be retained by becoming part of the heroism that James
associated with "civic passion" (162, 165).

A new spirit of "civic passion"—exemplified by strenuous and satisfying work in "iron mines, freight trains, . . . fishing fleets in December . . . dishwashing"—became the logical replacement for the destruction of war in the argument of "The Moral Equivalent of War." Excitement and the opportunity for heroism remained paramount, but attention would now be focused upon socially useful enterprises (171–72). James intended his conscripted citizen-soldiers to be engaged in a battle against nature, which he now presented as an "immemorial" enemy.[83] The Emersonian vision of the beatitudes of nature, emphasized in "On a Certain Blindness," was gone. The quest for the control of nature was to replace the domination of individual over individual, of nation over nation, which was so deeply and unfortunately imbricated in the imperial spirit.[84]

James barely indicated how the line between control of nature and domination over other individuals would be maintained. His prescription of substitute activities hardly inspired with the zeal that Roosevelt's bellicose posturing seems to have raised in American youth. As Gerald E. Myers notes, James's suggestions at first appear "perhaps naive," especially when compared with the heroic hardihood and excitement that he often connected with wars and natural disasters.[85] Moreover, James called for young men, and only young men, to be conscripted into this army of citizen-soldiers. He did not suggest any therapy for older, already confirmed jingoist or Hamletian individuals. Perhaps habit had been too ingrained in these individuals for their "civic passions" to be aroused. And, in addressing these problems, James usually spoke in the future tense and in ideal terms. After all, much of his earlier public philosophy had been concerned with the tedium of modernity and had suggested a variety of nostrums.

James's solution of psychological sublimation or transference apparently was primarily directed to those individuals from the elite class who suffered from doubt, a sense of unreality, and Hamletism. In his thesis of a conscripted work force, James returned to the line of argument that he had first used in "What Makes a Life Significant." There he had distinguished between the weakness of the Chautauquans and the strenuosity of the working class. However, James found the idealism of the former lacking in the latter. In "The Moral Equivalent of War," he appeared to offer to the "luxurious classes" a chance to supplement their ideality with directed strenuosity. This would knock the childishness out of them and, in the process, transform elite young Americans into more serious and widely sympathetic adults. The hardihood of directed labor would have the same effect on American "gilded" youth as religious experiences had on the saints; it would make their nature more expansive and humane. Yet James did not examine how industrial or agricultural workers would gain idealism from working side by side with the "luxurious classes." All he promised the working class was that its hardy labors might be lessened by an expanded work force; this was hardly a compelling prospect in a time when labor suffered from many problems, not the least of which was a surplus of able workers (171–72).

Although the solution offered little for the working class, it promised much for the elite who had been roused out of their slumbers to answer Roosevelt's clarion call. In his version of strenuous sublimation, James was careful to maintain that its ardor need not undermine any other individual or nation. In this imperative, he demonstrated the consistency of his moral philosophy. "The Moral Equivalent of War," no less than *Varieties,* resuscitated the ethical program first outlined in the 1891 essay "The Moral Philosopher and the Moral Life." There James presented his strenuous moralism as a goal, always with the view that energy must be directed in an expansive and socially useful manner. By positing a fight against nature, and in the process bringing strength and expansive sympathies to the elite youth of America, James anticipated that the results would give full play to the all-inclusive heroism that he found so appealing in the ethical values of the "twice-born" saints. "The Moral Equivalent of War" seemingly offered a generation of "twice-born" young Americans not only the avoidance of the "blood tax" of war but also the benefits to be derived from strenuosity, discipline, and ideality.[86]

Although "The Moral Equivalent of War" is James's fullest entry into the realm of social theory, it is a weak, albeit a psychologically innovative and instructive, response to the problems posed by war. Even on James's own terms, its comparisons between civic passion and military excitement are not equivalent. The necessity of great resistances to elicit tremendous reserves of heroic energy might be offered by war, but it is unclear if the chores recommended in this essay would elicit the same degree of excitement. Nevertheless, it is important to remember the context in which James's essay was composed. Faced with the painful recognition of the fatal attraction of the warlike instincts and their salutary role in helping modern men and women to overcome *tedium vitae* and fears of the abyss, James was compelled to search for a formula that would enable them to be warlike and strenuous without deleterious effects—a noble but difficult task. He was more enthused by the vision of heroism, despite its obvious excesses, as well as by the strenuosity that military ideals offered, than by conscious sublimation. James would have been forced to agree with Freud's apt and sobering formulation: "It is easy . . . for a barbarian to be healthy; for a civilized man the task is hard."[87]

The essays "The Moral Equivalent of War" and "On a Certain Blindness" are enduring examples of James's attempts in his public philosophy to come to terms with the imperial attitude. The problem of imperialism, and its reverse, Hamletism, continuously nagged James. No sooner had he published *Pragmatism* in 1907 than critics began to suggest that its definition of truth represented a dangerous apology for the imperial will, a philosophy in which "iron clads and Maxim guns" functioned as the "ultimate arbiters of metaphysical truth."[88] Of course, James did not harbor such intentions. *Pragmatism* must be understood as yet another exclamation of James's discourse of heroism (with all of its attendant problems), whose subtext contained a powerful argument against imperialism. Although *Pragmatism* had purely professional intent, it could not avoid the context of James's desire for activism and his fear of imperialism.

CHAPTER SEVEN

The Politics of Pragmatism

Much of William James's life as a philosopher, at least when viewed in retrospect, may be seen as leading toward publication of *Pragmatism* in 1907. As early as 1884, in "The Function of Cognition," James had begun to develop a realist epistemology that stressed the critical role of belief and the significance of a concrete notion of truth in bringing the individual into closer contact with reality. Although this essay, as James later admitted, was marred by numerous "defects," it remains an important initial examination of pragmatism.[1] In 1898, hard on the heels of publishing *The Will to Believe,* in which pragmatism was expressed in all but name, James delivered a fuller explication of it. In "Philosophical Conceptions and Practical Results," after tracing pragmatism's lineage to Charles Peirce and the British empirical tradition, James posited the central pragmatic maxim that concepts are to be evaluated according to what difference they might or might not make in the realm of practical experience and conduct. Considering the relative merits of theism or materialism, James found the former pragmatically more advantageous because it promised an ultimate moral order and sanctioned a life of active struggle for moral ends. From its point of origin, Jamesian pragmatism walked hand in hand with moralism.[2]

Soon after the intensity of his involvement in the fight against American imperialism had abated, and following publication of *The Varieties of Religious Experience* (1902), James continued to consider the meaning of truth and the function and consequences of ideas. In essays such as "Humanism and Truth" (1904) and in "A World of Pure Experience" (1904), James further advocated the pragmatic vision. In 1905 he delivered public lectures at Wellesley College, the Lowell Institute, the University of Chicago, Glenmore Summer School, and Columbia University; these lectures composed most of what would later be published as *Pragmatism* (185–86).

James was confident that this extended exploration of philosophical issues would result in an event as "epoch making" as the Protestant Reformation. Although he recognized that the unconventional and popular nature of his presentation of ideas would rankle his fellow philosophers, he nonetheless harbored few doubts that the publication of *Pragmatism* would force them to retreat from their stultifying rationalist and abstractionist heights and confront the full implications of the pragmatic theory of meaning and truth. He confidently pictured himself as the leader of a revolutionary movement in developing a philosophy "with *no* humbug in it."[3]

The response from the world of professional philosophy was immediate and widespread. Unfortunately, except for John Dewey, Giovanni Papini, F.C.S. Schiller—that is, the initial coterie of James's followers—many influential philosophers either ignored pragmatism or formed the opposition. Criticism of *Pragmatism* centers around the imprecise nature and implications of James's philosophical position: Did he intend to conflate meaning and truth? Did he believe that the truth of a concept should be considered according to its "cash-value"? Was truth to be viewed solely a function of the individual's subjective needs? Are true ideas true only for a finite length of time? Finally, are only true ideas marked by utility?[4]

The strenuous debate over the meaning and import of *Pragmatism* continues unabated and will no doubt remain a source for philosophical discussion in the future;[5] what is instructive in analyzing James as a public philosopher is to recognize how considerably the immediate reception of his pragmatic ideas was filtered through social analysis and contextualization. Evaluations of *Pragmatism* never focused solely upon the doctrine's philosophical import; they consistently turned to the social or political implications of the Jamesian view of truth and meaning. Most of James's contemporaries uncovered a social message embedded within *Pragmatism*. Yet all that James claimed was the intention to write a volume that would settle old and specifically philosophical scores against the abstractionists while promoting a method that promised to resolve otherwise unending philosophical disputes. Of course, the opposite happened.

All philosophical texts may be, and often are, evaluated according to multiple criteria. The conventional method requires the analyst to consider the philosopher's ideas according to their contribution to the solution or illumination of traditional philosophical puzzles. In this narrative, philosophical discourse is contained within a universe of one great philosopher conversing with previous philosophers about presumably shared questions and concerns. Occasionally, however, the sanctity of philosophy as an internal quest, one largely separate from the world of passion and politics, is undermined by the proposition that there is an important relationship between epistemology and politics, metaphysics and social attitudes. In the view of intellectual historian James T. Kloppenberg, "strong elective affinities connect conceptions of knowledge and responsibility with conceptions of politics, and the historical bond between these categories of thought is indisputable." Indisputable, even if inexact. Certainly one might profitably analyze the nexus between John Locke's empiricism and the development of British liberalism, or the relationship of Martin Heidegger's metaphysics to Nazi political ideology.[6] A closely related approach to the history of philosophy seeks to understand philosophy within its social context. The value of this endeavor is aptly captured by one of its advocates, Albert William Levi: "The social anchorage of philosophy in any given epoch gives the clue to the intentions of its major practitioners."[7]

In our postmodernist age, the correspondence between epistemology and politics is, of course, highly controversial. Yet the act of reconstruction—the historical examination of the acknowledged context or code of debate for a philosophical doctrine at its time of reception—does demand consideration. This task is made easier when the contemporaries of the philosopher under study quite readily construct and accept the social and political context, the connection between epistemology and politics, as a given within the work. Few contemporary reviewers of *Pragmatism* doubted that its epistemological foundations had important political and social implications. Moreover, many were assured that pragmatism represented a philosophy expressive of a particular historical epoch. Thus, Bertrand Russell found that pragmatism embodied "the prevailing temper of the age better than any of its older rivals," and Alfred E. Taylor described it as "*très chic . . . très fin-de-siècle.*"[8]

I

James's philosophical expressions of pragmatic doctrine were anchored in a social and political context. As his attention increasingly turned toward the political realm, beginning with the Venezuelan controversy of 1895, he became an outspoken advocate for anti-imperialism. His delivery of the lecture "Philosophical Conceptions and Practical Results" to the Berkeley Philosophical Union on 26 August 1898 occurred at the time when his deepest concerns were centered on the Spanish-American War. This may, of course, have been simply happenstance, coincidence. Yet in the emerging text of pragmatism, philosophy and politics might also have been explicitly and implicitly connected.[9]

In the months prior to the composition and presentation of "Philosophical Conceptions," James constantly faced the "idiotic blundering business" of imperialism. At dinner parties he could not avoid impassioned and acrimonious discussions of America's imperial turn; with great suspense and anticipation, he awaited each day's news of battles and policy changes. His correspondence during spring and summer 1898 is generously spiced with news of the Spanish-American War and concerns for America's future foreign policy. James's analysis of these early months of the war was both optimistic and pessimistic. Optimism arose from faith that the experience of an imperial interlude would bring Americans into the fraternity of nations, thereby bequeathing to them a new set of responsibilities. However, he realized that America had entered into the age of abstractionism and the mass, as well as that the crowd's desire for excitement (admirable in an abstract sense) might eventuate in a dangerous and increased lust for domination and power.[10]

The reality of the Spanish-American War explicitly appears in "Philosophical Conceptions." The controversial term "jingoism" occurs in the context of James's attack upon the "ponderous artificialities" of the German rationalist and abstract cast of mind, as exemplified by Kant's influence. Here James ironically deployed the language of imperialism to undermine a philosophical tradition that he would, a few years hence, come to view as providing aid and comfort, a philosophical rationale, to the imperialist cause. James believed that abstractionism and rationalism—that is, "vicious intellectualism"—in philosophical debate tended to blind one to concrete realities; the rationalist mania to fit everything into a "block universe" of interpretation resulted in violence against the individual entity. In his strong critique of the "hegelian" aspects of Theodore Roosevelt's imperialist raving, James made the same connection, condemning Roosevelt as an abstractionist. In "Philosophical Conceptions," which was composed and delivered while the Spanish-American War raged and America's future as an imperial power tipped precariously in the balance, James recommended his variant of "practicalism" as a philosophical and political palliative for Kant's presumed abstract, antique thinking.

James further announced his "imperial" desire to form an Anglo-American alliance in order to wrest control of the philosophical world from a Kantian theoretical imperialism deadened by "ponderous artificialities." James warned that pragmatic doctrine arises "not out of national jingoism, for jingoism has no place in philosophy," but out of a conviction that "the English spirit in philosophy is intellectually, as well as practically and morally, on the saner, sounder, and truer path" (269). He concluded his address by recognizing that "our race," presently taking "possession" of "this wonderful Pacific Coast," must work upon "the principle of practicalism" if Americans are to be successful in their "struggle towards the light" (270).

James ironically blended the language of imperialism with a critique of its very presumptions and mode of perception. The success of pragmatism would evolve not from national jingoism, but from its methodology's purely philosophical power and practical benefits. The strength of pragmatism—its tremendous ability to reveal the practical consequences of different concepts—guaranteed that it would be victorious and beneficial in the marketplace of ideas. In "Philosophical Conceptions," pragmatism paraded as a mediator and peacemaker: its promise "in philosophical disputations tends wonderfully to smooth out misunderstandings and to bring in peace" (259). In this regard, James might have pointed to his discussion of the One and the Many within the lecture as proof positive that the pragmatist properly and fairly evaluated the debits and profits of all philosophical position.

Despite James's best intentions, the force of his language and the favoritism he clearly showed for theism over materialism, as well as for pluralism over monism, unfortunately undermined the presumptive force of pragmatism and its claims to mediator status. Indeed, James's language of pragmatic peace sometimes descended into a philosophical hitting of one's opponent beneath the belt. His description of Kant is an appropriate illustration: "Kant's mind is the rarest and most intricate of all possible antique bric-a-brac museums . . . I believe that Kant bequeathes to us not one single conception which is both indispensable to philosophy and which philosophy either did not possess before him, or was not destined inevitably to acquire after him" (269). Not surprisingly, George Holmes Howison, James's host for the "Philosophical Conceptions" talk at the University of California at Berkeley, found this attack gratuitous and unfair—"Will James has come and gone, and pleased everybody, of course. But most thought his assault on Kant futile and foolish."[11]

Politics again appears explicitly within the context of the development and expression of pragmatic theory in James's important 1904 essay "Humanism and Truth," reprinted in his sustained defense of pragmatism, *The Meaning of Truth* (1909). James condemned "all noble, clean-cut, fixed, eternal, rational, templelike systems of philosophy." These systems stood accused of undermining "the *dramatic temperament* of nature" and of rejecting a humanist perspective. Most importantly, in a footnote accompanying this critique, James quoted in French from Mme. Em. D. Laval's *La Vie de Emile Duclaux*. Duclaux was a French biochemist and passionate Dreyfusard. James's affinity for the Dreyfusard cause had been intense; its tone and timing exactly paralleled his political engagement against imperialism. In both cases, he saw the political enemy waving the flag of abstractionism. As he proclaimed in this footnote, the "contrast between humanist and rationalist tempers of mind" had political implications. At the time of the Dreyfus affair, two camps had devel-

oped in France. The traditionalist cadre held to abstractionist or rationalist principles: "*poseurs de principes, chercheurs d'unité, constructeurs de
systèmes* a priori*.*" Abstractionist views in the political realm led to the
sacrifice of the individual upon the altar of the state. In contrast, Drey-
fusards adhered to open and individualistic political perceptions that
stressed the same essential features of James's pragmatism.[12]

Finally, the crucial issue of imperialism even insinuated itself within
Pragmatism in the familiar context of a battle between the rationalist and
the pragmatist. James admitted that his pluralistic metaphysics represented a frighteningly "loose universe," a "tramp and vagrant world," to
the rationalist. The pragmatic pluralist universe affects the rationalist "as
the swarm of protestant sects affects a papist onlooker"; that is, with
abject terror. The rationalistic type of philosophy professor viewed the
individual working within an experiential world, with salvation coming
"only from its own intrinsic promises and practices," as a proposition
quite as absurd as the opinion that "the Filipinos are fit for self-
government." Just as the rationalist in philosophy could accept only a
universe of order, which was classic and unchanging in its metaphysical
outlines, the rationalist in politics could not accept freedom and democracy in the Philippines. One might surmise that pragmatism in politics
would undermine America's imperialist domination over the Philippines.
In contrast, the rationalist emphasis upon a world of a "doctrinaire and
authoritative complexion" translated into a politics of domination. The
rationalist believed that a "respectable" world would be one where Filipinos were ruled by their superiors and protectors, a world of the white
man's burden. In the pragmatically open and freedom-filled universe that
James recommended, freedom for the Philippines would appear to the
rationalist as "a trunk without a tag, a dog without a collar" (124–25).

II

When published in 1907, *Pragmatism* immediately struck its readers as a
controversial work whose implications expanded far beyond the confines
of philosophical discussion. To traditionalists everywhere, and to James's
supporters as well, the ideas of pragmatism directly assaulted the certitude and beauty of rationalist systems of philosophy. Opponents viewed
James's notion of truth as vague and nonsystematic. Indeed, Jamesian
pragmatism seemed to destruct the foundations which philosophy had
worked so painstakingly to build. Not surprisingly, such radical questioning and methodological openness brought forth an avalanche of criticism, much of it claiming that pragmatist philosophy was epistemologi-
cally unsound and politically dangerous.

Some critics believed that pragmatism's questioning of traditional metaphysics and of certain ideals of truth as absolute had transformed James into a philosopher of power and imperialism. Bertrand Russell strongly contended that pragmatism, "although it begins with liberty and toleration, develops by inherent necessity into the appeal to force and the arbitrament of the big battalions." He believed that basing the evaluation of truth upon success or expediency, and having these truths engage in a struggle for existence, was little more than a call for "iron clads and Maxim guns" to function as the "ultimate arbiters of metaphysical truth." Jamesian pragmatism became a philosophy adapted "to imperialism abroad." Russell hesitated in placing James firmly in the camp of Nietzschean celebrants of the will to power. Nevertheless, Russell found that "the excessive individualism of the pragmatic theory of truth is inherently connected with the appeal to force." In essence, he uncovered a "Bismarckian belief in force" within pragmatic epistemology. In the arena of international politics, pragmatism would have a devastating effect on the peace movement, because power rather than peaceful negotiation now figured as the essential arbiter of disputes. Pragmatism's triumphantly proclaimed power to resolve philosophical disputes itself came into dispute as Russell invoked it as a destroyer of peace and as a weapon against mediation.[13]

Russell's criticisms placed pragmatism within the social and political realms. James recognized the prevalence of this interpretation of pragmatism while regretting that so many had chosen to see it "as a philosophy got up for the use of engineers, electricians and doctors." He protested that the imperative behind pragmatism was to analyze "the function of knowing" more fully and subtly "than previous philosophers" and to make readers take seriously the purely theoretic aspects and consequences of thought.[14] James's protestations notwithstanding, the history of pragmatism always was tinged with social meaning. But the precise social meaning of pragmatism need not be consigned to an unproblematic assertion of imperialism, and its epistemology should not be seen as unavoidably leading to forceful domination. Instead, the social expression of pragmatism evolved from James's discourse of heroism and worked comfortably, if controversially, with his politics of anti-imperialism. As many critics have contended, professional philosophy and public discourse did coexist within *Pragmatism*, but that intertwining is quite different in its origins and implications than has generally been recognized. James's central discourse of heroism and his emphasis upon voluntarism, strenuosity, and action are present in *Pragmatism*'s narrative line and cultural imperative. The exuberance of James's language, as well as the uncertainty surrounding his doctrine of the meaning of truth, attuned readers to hear the dangerous cannons of imperialism pounding within his text. Read in this manner, James's definition of truth as *"only the expedient in the way of our thinking, just as 'the right' is only the expedient in the way of our behaving"* (106), as well as his repeated assertion that truth must be judged according to its "cash-value," were, not surprisingly, seen by many readers as justifications for solipsism or, at the very least, indications of a tendency toward pure subjectivism.[15]

The critics' condemnation of pragmatism as an imperialist agenda in philosophical garb grew out of the metaphysical universe that James described in *Pragmatism* and *Essays in Radical Empiricism*. This connection is important. In the words of Gerald E. Myers, an analyst of James's technical philosophy, he "made pragmatism coincide with and support his metaphysical vision of the universe as loosely knit, open to chance and novelty, a cosmos ever in the making."[16] To James's critics, pragmatism's metaphysics and epistemology portrayed a philosophical method and a world that appeared better suited to the imperialist's battlefield than to the philosophical mediator's drawing room.

The rationalist metaphysics of a unified, perfectly ordered universe drew mainly condemnation from James. "The alternative between pragmatism and rationalism," he wrote, *"concerns the structure of the universe itself."* For the rationalist, reality *"is ready-made and complete from all eternity"* (123–24). Moreover, rationalistic descriptions of the universe invariably led to passivity, treating as they do "abstract principles as finalities, before which our intellects may come to rest in a state of admiring contemplation" (49). The universe they present is a completed one; as a political or religious philosophy, rationalism and monism tended toward "quietism." Although James occasionally offered praise for rationalism and monism—for, after all, they had been vindicated by history and did "sanctify the human flux"—the brunt of his exposition pointed in the direction of pragmatic pluralism as a philosophy more wide-ranging and strenuous in capturing the details of our future experience (133).

In contrast to the rationalist belief that "the belly-band of its universe must be tight," Jamesian metaphysics dwelled on the open and unrestrained nature of the universe (124). The Jamesian universe was described as "wide open," full "of novelties and change," and "imperfectly unified still . . . of *additive constitution*" (20, 60, 79–82). In his jauntier moments, James described the pluralistic universe as one with a "happy-go-lucky anarchist" bent (124). While James had no desire to position himself firmly in a harsh positivistic camp, which conceived metaphysical reality as simply "cosmic weather" or an abyss, he remained committed to celebrating precisely what horrified the rationalist about the pragmatist's vision of a "tramp and vagrant world, adrift in space, with neither elephant nor tortoise to plant the sole of its foot upon. It is a set of stars hurled into heaven without even a centre of gravity to pull against" (125).

James's metaphysics of pragmatism developed fully and logically from the writings later collected in *Essays in Radical Empiricism*. For example, in "A World of Pure Experience," he favored a pluralistic universe without any single type of connection between its parts; it is "to a large extent chaotic." This did not mean, James emphasized, that the world of the radical empiricist was without any connections, only that his doctrine of relations gave fair consideration to both the unity and disunity of the universe, in a manner alien to most rationalists. James believed the unification of the flux of experience would have to be a future event, one in the process of possible realization. However, he conceded in his more confident moments "that the unity of the world is on the whole undergoing increase," but this increase came about solely as a result of experiences being grafted onto the mass. For James, the world as we experience and know it remained both pluralistic and without firm foundations that transcended our experiences.[17]

James's essentially pluralistic metaphysics offered little confidence to those who read *Pragmatism* for an enduring vantage point from which to decide questions of truth. In a favorable evaluation of Jamesian metaphysics and epistemology, philosopher Richard Rorty goes so far as to proclaim that James's project actually ripped asunder the foundational aspects of philosophy, especially its claim to ultimate, transcendental truths.[18] What might appeal to Rorty did not enthuse James's contemporaries. Most philosophers thought that a world of experiential flux and chaos suggested a jungle atmosphere in which only brute power imposed order. James's epistemology, with its vocabulary of the market place and its emphasis upon the instability of truth claims, only heightened the sense that pragmatism might ultimately be a philosophy of imperialism or dangerous subjectivism. John E. Russell found radical empiricism to be nothing more than a invitation to solipsism: thus, radical empiricism "contains no principles by means of which it is logically admissible to reach other reality than the individual's own experience."[19]

Pragmatism questioned traditional notions of truth. In Lecture Six of *Pragmatism,* "Pragmatism's Conception of Truth," James rejected the popular idea that truth must copy reality or what is contained in "the Absolute's way of thinking." In contrast, intellectualists incorrectly posited truth as "an inert static relation," which led to the epistemological position of "stable equilibrium" (96). Such a view, of course, undermined the open metaphysical and moral vision that James sought to develop. For him, truth became something that "*happens* to an idea," a process of verification and validation. The key questions that the pragmatist asked of a proposition or belief were: "[W]hat concrete difference will its being true make in anyone's actual life? How will the truth be realized? What experiences will be different from those which would obtain if the belief were false? What, in short, is the truth's cash-value in experiential terms?" (97).

James at times argued that truth content resided in the degree of satisfaction that a concept, belief, or desire contributed to the individual's relationship with reality. He complicated this idea by his tendency to speak of truth in terms of the satisfaction or "cash-value" that it offered. His critics thought that James left truth without adequate foundations. G. E. Moore complained that James's description of truth was so muddled as to either be found guilty of the most obvious truisms or to be condemned as a variant of absurd subjectivism.[20] James's examples, no less than his language, seemed to intransigently banish truth from the realm of the theoretical and thus consign it to that world of the practical and temporal:

> Our account of truth is an account of truths in the plural, of processes of leading, realized *in rebus,* and having only this quality in common, that they *pay.* They pay by guiding us into or towards some part of a system that dips at numerous points into sense-percepts, which we may copy mentally or not, but with which at any rate we are now in the kind of commerce vaguely designated as verification. Truth for us is simply a collective name for verification-processes, just as health, wealth, strength, etc., are names for other processes connected with life, and also pursued because it pays to pursue them. Truth is *made,* just as health, wealth and strength are made, in the course of experience. (104)

The metaphysics of pragmatism, which evoked for rationalists "a sort of wolf-world absolutely unpent and wild" (128), as well as the antiessentialist epistemology of pragmatism, suggested to Bertrand Russell a definition of truth as the expedient, dependent upon who has the power to impose one version of reality and truth upon another. Not surprisingly, this perspective moved certain interpreters to characterize pragmatist politics as an intellectual rationale for imperialism. This interpretation was heightened by what appeared, especially in *Pragmatism*'s final two chapters, as a voluble call to action, a jeremiad in favor of strenuosity and action. In addition, the enthusiasm of James's philosophical exposition tended to blur the logic and hide the conditions that he attached to the verification process for truth.[21]

III

Pragmatism exists in that uncertain, complex space between public and professional philosophy. One agenda in pragmatism points toward the technical development of a new conception of truth; another, toward a public imperative. This is hardly surprising. James's philosophical project often resonated with his personal and cultural concerns. In an era of cultural malaise and tedium, he fittingly determined to develop a philosophical universe where individual initiative and action accounted for something. Philosopher Julius Bixler correctly read pragmatic doctrine as seeking to transform "the search for truth from a sedentary to an aggressive, experimental occupation which enlisted the more active energies." A more recent observer, historian David A. Hollinger, goes so far as to find that James's message in the final chapter of *Pragmatism* "is devoted to an impassioned, even evangelical formulation" for activism. Whereas Bertrand Russell and other critics interpreted the Jamesian emphasis upon action in *Pragmatism* and his other public work as giving vent to an imperialistic or vitalistic philosophy, James consistently presented a concept of action that was colored by responsibility, complexity, and morality.[22]

Early in *Pragmatism,* James announced that his philosophy "stands for no particular results." Pragmatism claims "no dogmas, and no doctrines save its method" (32). Armed with pragmatic methodology, individuals realize that in "our cognitive as well as in our active life we are creative. We *add*, both to the subject and to the predicate part of reality. . . . Man *engenders* truths" upon the world (123). The chapters of "Pragmatism and Humanism" and "Pragmatism and Religion" are, at the very least, sustained odes to a life of energetic activity in a world marked by victories and losses.

What are the practical benefits of the pragmatic method in the world of experience? How would this method express itself politically, for example? Some of James's answers offered little confidence to those who craved an epistemology that presented an absolute, well-defined political program. Borrowing the formulation of the Italian pragmatist Papini, James described pragmatism as "a corridor in a hotel. Innumerable chambers open out of it. In one you may find a man writing an atheistic volume; in the next someone on his knees praying for faith and strength; in a third a chemist investigating a body's properties. In a fourth a system of idealist metaphysics is being excogitated; in a fifth the impossibility of metaphysics is being shown. But they all own the corridor, and all must pass through it if they want a practicable way of getting into or out of their respective rooms" (32). Bertrand Russell, who saw an imperialistic "worship of force" written into the pragmatic methodology, might well have extended Papini's analogy to include a sixth room in which someone composed a pacifist tract while in a fateful seventh room an imperialist conspired to dominate all the other inhabitants of the hotel, though still claiming to operate under the aegis of pragmatic method.

"Philosophy, like life," James wrote in *Some Problems of Philosophy,* "must keep the doors and windows open."[23] A critical question confronted the pragmatist: How wide must the door and window be left open; could they be closed enough to prevent the imperialist storm from blowing into the temple of philosophy and politics with the winds of pragmatism? Despite its weaknesses, James's argument in *Pragmatism* did erect a foundation that would allow the philosophical window to be reasonably open, while attempting to prevent imperialism from ripping apart its edifice. Within the context of professional philosophy, James developed an argument that complemented his opposition to imperialism. In this sense, pragmatist epistemology and anti-imperialist politics were closely connected.

IV

James made quite clear that pragmatism began by associating itself with the proven experimental method of modern science. The essence of this method, under whose banner pragmatism proudly marched, demanded close attention to facts, as well as an openness to the revision of hypotheses in the light of experimental negation. Pragmatism was forthrightly opposed to the narrow, scientific positivism of scientists such as W. K. Clifford and Thomas Huxley; in their blindness to nonempirical realities, religious belief was too often considered as superstition or primitivism. James believed that the neo-positivists of his era were unduly proud of their unwillingness to jettison doubt. But James did not intend his pragmatism to be a sop to opponents of science and empiricism; his goal was quite the opposite. As he later noted in his rejection of the charge that pragmatism was antirealistic: "The pragmatizing epistemologist posits there is a reality and a mind with ideas. . . . He [the pragmatist] finds first that the ideas must point to or lead towards *that* reality and no other, and then that the pointings and leadings must yield satisfaction as their result" in a concrete and particular manner.[24]

Contrary to Richard Rorty's suggestion, James did not reject epistemology; he noted in "The Pragmatist Account of Truth and Its Misunderstanders" (1908) that "One of pragmatism's merits is that it is so purely epistemological." Its verification process for truth remained intent, in theoretical matters no less than in practical ones, upon being concrete and particular. This was the centerpiece of James's conception of science and of his philosophical description of himself as "a natural realist."[25] He maintained that science—hard, experimental, and open to the world's reality—would replace abstractionism and rationalism.[26]

In contrast to the false apostles of science, such as Huxley and Clifford, James believed that in the scientific, pragmatic point of view truth was attainable but not absolute, a process rather than a conceptual strait jacket. As James phrased it in one of his unpublished philosophical notes, the pragmatist's stated intention always remained to "keep in touch with

the *character* of reality."[27] The scientific style of testing involved in pragmatism's evaluation of competing conceptions of truth also contrasted
with the rationalist belief that truth existed as a timeless, abstracted
entity. The rationalist habit of mind, in common with the imperialism of
Roosevelt, looked "backward to a past eternity. True to her inveterate
habit, rationalism reverts to 'principles,' and thinks that when an abstraction once is named, we own an oracular solution" (108). This was the
stance of the closed mind, which could not recognize the sanctity of the
individual fact in the face of the overwhelming power of rationalist conceptualization.

Of course, James regularly attempted to deflect criticisms of the pragmatic idea that truth was fleeting and solipsistic. After all, he did not see
the world as simply an extension of the individual's will. As James put it in
an engaging metaphor, though the individual organized the stars into a
constellation known by a particular name, this characterizing was never
meant to suggest that the stars did not exist apart from the individual's
conceptualization of them (121). James also rejected the charge that the
pragmatic notion of truth was relative, solipsistic, or simply expedient to
the individual's subjective needs. Truth was not simply what one chose
to believe. James warned that the dangers and consequences were grave to
the person who ignored the world's concrete and long-term realities. True
ideas would bring the individual closer to reality, in a "progressive, har-
monious, satisfactory manner" (97). James emphatically declared "Woe
to him whose beliefs play fast and loose with the order which realities
follow in his experience; they will lead him nowhere or else make false
connexions" (99). In the essay "Humanism and Truth," James reiterated
that reality has an ultimately convincing effect upon "licentious thinking."[28] Again and again in *Pragmatism* James proclaimed that one cardi-
nal tenet of pragmatism was "to agree with reality is seen to be grounded
in a perfect jungle of concrete expediencies" (111).

Despite his adherence to a realistic epistemology, faith in the scientific
method, and emphasis upon carefully testing the efficacy and complexity
of ideas against reality, James could not win the argument. Philosophers
of a more technical or exacting bent contended that James's definition of
truth as that which worked in the long run, led to a satisfactory passage
into the flux of reality, or paid out in "cash-value" remained too vague
and individualistic. How long, G. E. Moore asked, must an idea "work"
in the Jamesian sense of the term before it might be designated "true"?
Whatever the force of Moore's criticism, which was hardly atypical,
James was attempting to develop a pragmatic conception of truth that did
not have its ultimate test simply within the subjective realm of the individual; the imperial will was always to be tested and constrained by the
powers of reality.[29]

Most significantly, James carefully anchored the credibility of different truth claims not only in the proud methodology of science and the pressing demands of reality but also in the realm of common sense, tradition, and accepted truths. He never sanctioned a wholesale overthrow of "intellectual forms or categories of thought" (84). Without this baggage, the individual would hardly function; forced to test each and every concept against experience, he or she might constantly reinvent the wheel. This perception fitted well with James's Darwinian conception of the survival value of ideas. Many, if not most, of our inherited ideas had survived because they had been selected and tested in the environment. James thus framed his Darwinian thesis in *Pragmatism: "Our fundamental ways of thinking about things are discoveries of exceedingly remote ancestors, which have been able to preserve themselves throughout the experience of all subsequent time.* They form one great stage of equilibrium in the human mind's development, the stage of *common sense"* (83).

This Darwinian-influenced analysis was linked to a psychological interpretation of how the individual receives new truths. James recognized, in an anticipation of cognitive dissonance theory, that change and continuity define the individual's method of conceptualization. New truths are added on to older ones; they do not necessarily overthrow and banish older truths. "The most violent revolutions in an individual's beliefs leave most of his old order standing. . . . New truth is always a go-between, a smoother-over of transitions" (35). James believed that the process of mental growth was ultimately one of slow change. "We patch and tinker more than we renew" (83).

James noted that critics of pragmatism too often overlooked the role of older, tested truths in the pragmatic conception of reality. He argued that the individual reasonably accepted as valid most facts and concepts on the basis of a presumption of truth. The influence of older truths in the process of deciding meaning and truth figured as "absolutely controlling" (35). Thus James could note that "Truth lives, in fact, for the most part on a credit system" (100). Only when older truths failed to work or did not pay off in "cash-value" did the individual need to develop a new conceptualization that would better lead him or her into the realm of experience, in which the pragmatic verification and validation of the truth process would come into full play.

Whether it was described in psychological, common-sense, or Darwinian terms, tradition constrained the individual who wished to engage in a will to deceive. In the "manner of belief," James submitted, "we are all extreme conservatives" (35–36). He continued to connect truth with the individual's subjective needs, yet he never confused the two. And throughout *Pragmatism* he stressed that an individual who abandoned inherited truths would be cast adrift in the "cosmic weather" and "wolf-world" that rationalists so rightly feared.

V

In *Pragmatism* James recognized and respected tradition's essential role in constraining the individual and the nation. For both of them, truth was slowly grafted onto an existing tree of tested truths and assumptions. This melding of old with new helped the individual and the nation to deal with the cacophony of possible truths demanding attention every day. In his political analysis, which paralleled closely his philosophical understanding, James emphasized that America possessed a common and useful core of ideals—a tradition of democracy. American ideals of respect for others, acceptance of diversity, and refusal to sanction domination of the individual in the name of *"bigness"* struck James as the national stock of opinions. Odes to openness and sublimation may have been at the center of his politics of anti-imperialism, but his political views were strongly joined by a firm belief in tradition as a force mitigating the will to dominate in politics, in philosophy, and in science.

James found that America's exuberant tumble into imperialism in the 1890s had severely damaged its democratic tradition. Writing at the time when *Pragmatism* was being published, James indicated how haunted he was by the alacrity by which imperial fever had undermined this tradition's assumptions and practices and how quickly "the country pucked up its ancient soul at the first touch of temptation."[30] James perceived the problem in typical Mugwump fashion: American traditions of humanity and civilization had fallen victim to bloodthirstiness and to the public's instinctual need "to be savage."[31] In an age dominated by tedium more often than strenuosity, yellow journalists, as well as short-sighted politicians such as Roosevelt, manipulated the mob instinct. This desire for excitement apparently overwhelmed James's political emphasis upon the sobering reality of tradition. Yet, in pragmatic fashion, James believed that the "truth" of the imperialist would be undermined by the power of past tradition and that imperialism would be unable to maintain itself over a long period of time. James anticipated that the traditions of freedom, democracy, and fair play in America, when combined with the responsibility of intellectuals to educate and lead, would return it to its proper place; the forces of light would eventually vanquish those of darkness. "[W]e intellectuals in America," James wrote during the heat of the Spanish-American War, "must all work to keep our precious birthright of individualism, and freedom" away from the corrupt institutions and rampaging jingoists.[32]

James was convinced that each nation had its own ideals and traditions. These formed, in part, the foundation of ethical and moral values. Even if his epistemology was antifoundationalist, it recognized fully the importance of local and national traditions as the basis of perception and activity. The durable reality of tradition was true in both an organic and a political sense. "Every nation has its ideals which are a dead secret to other nations." America was proving itself blind to the ideals of the Filipinos, while ignoring its own traditions. Although the war threatened American innocence and democracy, James contended that Americans— at least in comparison with the French, who had demonstrated corruption in the Dreyfus affair—were capable of returning to their tradition of nonentanglement in the affairs of other nations.[33]

Perhaps James's support for a concept of national tradition first appears to oppose the firm individualism that enthuses his life and philosophy. Indeed, an anarchistic perspective was behind much of his philosophical and political reasoning. But his idea of tradition was tied to a notion of community. His was essentially a romantic vision, a belief in the organic nature of the American experiment. James saw openness to diversity and acceptance of individualism as the birthmarks of this natural ideal of community and tradition. However, he trembled at its modern opposite—the institutionalization of political opinion, scientific belief, and philosophical doctrine. Marked by blindness, *"bigness,"* and domination, these trends were the tricks of the trade of imperialists, philosophical absolutists, and scientific positivists.

Not all readers found James's emphasis upon tradition and community to be realistic. It had an anachronistic air to some. In perhaps the strongest rejoinder to such a fanciful notion of an idyllic American tradition of innocence, George Santayana ridiculed James's "false moralistic view of history." Santayana submitted with his typically Olympian air that not only individuals but also nations were swept along by the tide of historical necessity. He believed that James's plea to respect and honor a tradition of liberty and tolerance, as outlined in documents such as the Declaration of Independence, pathetically missed the reality that such vaunted traditions constituted only "a salad of illusion."[34]

James was not as naïve as Santayana contended. Unlike many of his Mugwump associates, James did not seek to transform a tradition of liberty, real or imagined, into a new form of abstractionism or absolutism. In keeping with his pragmatic ideals, James posited that viable traditions combined a respect for past assumptions with an openness to new influences and possibilities. He realized the anomaly of America's praise of ideals of liberty when contrasted with its historic support for the institution of slavery. But James perceived in the ideal of a tradition of liberty an important antidote to the reality of slavery. Even when ideality and reality did not perfectly conjoin in American history, he continued to uphold the tradition of liberty and equality as the very type of idealism that a pragmatist must sanction; in the long run, American idealism would work its efficacious effects. Pragmatism, with its readily available methodology for testing of truth, was designed to lead toward, rather than away from, democracy.

Democracy always stood on trial. In pragmatic fashion, James accepted its positive elements while realizing that it must grow in an inclusive rather than an exclusive sense. He tended to believe that "civic courage" might save America from those whose narrow interests threatened its social stability. Although tradition was a contested terrain, James emphasized two crucial elements in the American tradition that boded well for the future success of both the nation and the individual: a doctrine of good will toward others and a "fierce and merciless resentment towards every man or set of men who break the public peace."[35] James associated public peace and well-being with doctrines of openness and liberty. Jamesian anti-imperialism viewed tradition, just as Jamesian pragmatism regarded common sense, as the bank account upon which to draw funds against dangerous enemies of the public peace. This constituted the "cash-value" of tradition in both philosophy and politics.

The energy and emphasis of pragmatic, pluralist philosophy was directed against the enemy of abstractionism or rationalism, both of which James condemned for presenting a world of fixed qualities and concomitant blindness. As James made clear in *A Pluralistic Universe* (1909), in philosophical debate the rationalist or abstractionist uses concepts in a blinding rather than a revealing manner. "The misuse of concepts begins with the habit of employing them privatively [sic] as well as positively, using them not merely to assign properties to things, but to deny the very properties with which the things sensibly present themselves." This type of "vicious intellectualism" resulted in tyranny; it confined the individual concrete entity to a "block universe" of explanation. In contrast, Jamesian pragmatism and pluralism promised to respect the individual entity while "unstiffening" theories and assumptions. The pragmatic method brought its employer into closer and more satisfactory contact with reality. Even if such "unstiffening" did not bring forth exact answers or certitude, it would remain useful for undermining the hubris that James associated with absolutist and rationalist philosophies.[36] The pragmatic method, with its emphasis on concrete and particular results, promised to undermine the hazy thinking of the abstractionists in both philosophy and politics. Likewise, pluralism portended a greater willingness to accept variant visions of the universe and to recognize the rights and realities of others (for example, the Filipinos).

In plotting his pragmatic maxims, James did more than simply attempt to effect a Protestant Reformation in philosophy and to halt American imperialism. *Pragmatism* explodes with the strenuosity of his discourse of heroism. Its possibilities begin with his unmasking of the *tedium vitae* inscribed into the rationalist conception of the universe. In contrast to this constrained view, his pluralistic metaphysics offered an arena necessitating heroic struggle and moral action. The discourse of heroism thus constitutes yet another public message within *Pragmatism*'s enduring philosophical content.

VI

Strenuous morality remained a centerpiece of *Pragmatism* by combining "scientific loyalty to facts and willingness to take account of them" with "the old confidence in human values and the resultant spontaneity, whether of the religious or of the romantic type" (17). Pragmatism was a form of scientific romanticism confronting a world of flux and novelty, a world open for humanity to engender its truths upon it. The ultimate "cash-value" of pragmatism was its ability to realize that "True ideas lead us into . . . useful sensible termini. They lead to consistency, stability and flowing human intercourse. They lead away from excentricity [sic] and isolation, from foiled and barren thinking" (103). In this sense, truth became the essential attribute of energetic men and women. After all, in *Pragmatism* James continued to proclaim the teleological aspects of human consciousness as a selector and seeker after ends. The "foiled and barren thinking" of Hamlet facing the metaphysical abyss vanished in the face of the self-confident individual working with the pragmatic method and under the sign of a moral God.[37]

James argued that his pluralistic metaphysics and pragmatic epistemology were best suited for a strenuous life. He based this contention on the assumption that absolutist philosophies too readily sanctioned "moral holidays" for individuals. In a universe already formed, or in a process of perfect formation, the individual's active energies appeared superfluous. In "The Absolute and the Strenuous Life" (1904), James admitted that monism permitted action as readily as it promoted quietism. This admission by definition was weak and largely negative. In evaluating the absolute's ability to instill a strenuous stance, James concluded that it "suits sick souls and strenuous ones equally well." But monistic or absolutist systems of thought allowed for strenuous activity only when the individual was already prone to action. For the individual of a Hamletian temperament, monism translated into a passive stance. Monism achieved this dual support system because "it will *sanction* anything and everything after the fact, for whatever is once there will have to be regarded as an integral member of the universe's perfection."[38]

Pragmatism and pluralism were James's preferred vehicles for initiating a strenuous attitude. They did this by presenting a universe in the making, one in which morality was added, rather than inert within the realm of experience. Indeed, the point our ideals "ought to aim at [is] the *transformation of reality*—no less!"[39] Pluralism demanded emotional strength, rather than "fatty degeneration," from the individual. James claimed that the pluralist world "demands" a strenuous stance, "since it makes the world's salvation depend upon the energizing of its several parts, among which we are."[40] The pragmatic individual, living in a universe of chance and change, plastic to his or her will, became, by definition, a reformer. The world stood "malleable, waiting to receive its final touches at our hands" (123). This partly constituted what Gerald E. Myers has called James's "ethics of optimism," his strenuous refusal to accept passivity in psychology and the world, thus translating into "a philosophy of action."[41]

In the chapter "Pragmatism and Religion," James fully developed this idea of the Promethean, reformist individual in his doctrine of meliorism.[42] Meliorism represented an essential "attitude," balanced between the Schopenhauerian pessimism of his youth and the absolutist optimism of his cultural and intellectual milieu. In some ways, his doctrine of meliorism was an analogue to his "twice-born" saints, who were strenuous in their activities, blessed with a sober perspective on the world's diversity, and deeply aware of their ultimate responsibilities to reform the world under the friendly gaze of God. As presented in *Pragmatism*, meliorism began with the pluralistic perception of an "unfinished world" (52). This world was a stage for heroism and strenuosity, because it was "still pursuing its adventures." Individual activities designed to reform the world became the crucial components of conscious existence. Such acts constituted "our turning places, where we seem to ourselves to make ourselves and grow" (138).

The Jamesian pragmatic, activist world banished Hamlet. In his place were men and women actively engaged in a process of wresting salvation, both personal and collective, from the universe. James purposefully defined salvation in vague terms, not wanting theological or political disputes to interfere with his emphasis upon a strenuous morality. He only suggested that the process of salvation—that is, the reformation of the individual and the world—demanded that the individual add his or her "*fiat* to the *fiat* of the creator." Here James essentially repeated the argument of *The Will to Believe*. Anchored in compassion, energy, and cognizance of each individual's truths, melioristic reform was buoyed by an alliance with God. As James reiterated throughout his discourse of heroism, God's presence meant that "tragedy is only provisional and partial, and shipwreck or dissolution not the absolutely final things" (140, 55).

In opting for a world where moral struggle was omnipresent and conducted under the sign of a supportive God, James built a reformist, activist theology upon the foundations of pluralism and pragmatism. In so doing, however, he recognized that his vision was ultimately a personal belief, which he favored for pragmatic reasons. In the concluding pages of *Pragmatism,* James praised the assumption that the individual working for salvation must pay a price. This world was marked by conflict and suffering, which initiated the individual's moral strenuosity. James's world demanded action, whereas the monists' "saccharine" world tended toward passivity. James conceded that his was a personal belief: "In the end it is our faith and not our logic" that decides whether pluralism is "a serious hypothesis." If serious, then the addition of strenuosity would determine that "there should be real losses and real losers" in the world (141–42). James developed his philosophy with this hearty vision of the world always in view. In presenting his melioristic attitude and his conception of the universe's immense possibility, he avoided some important political questions: What form should strenuous activism take? What does it mean to say that "Man engenders truth upon" the world? These concerns return us to the question contained in Papini's formulation of pragmatism as a hotel corridor. Are the truths engendered upon the world by the believer and the atheist, the pacifist and the imperialist, equally valid, equally welcomed? In sum, does a specific political agenda exist within the social expression of *Pragmatism*?

Pragmatism's conception of truth wedded to a pluralistic philosophy did little to sanction an imperialist politics. While James celebrates action and strenuosity in his text, his pragmatic assumptions and requirements demand that action be constrained by tradition, common sense, and long-term gains. All of these desiderata are further supported by James's oft-held belief that an individual lessens the possibility of domination by viewing the object in a concrete manner and by deciding truth in a particularistic one. In this sense, pragmatism fit into James's anti-imperialist politics without jettisoning his discourse of heroism.

Although intended to be anti-imperialist, the politics of pragmatism remains vague and unimpressive in various ways. Many analysts have noted that James's political theorizing was occasional at best and that its exposition was never sustained. In the strongly worded opinion of Bruce Kuklick, "James did not even develop a reasoned account of moral argument, and his social and political philosophy was negligible." Kuklick explains this lacunae in the thought of James by stressing that philosophy was institutionalized and professionalized during James's life. In America, the study of logic and of the natural and physical sciences increasingly dominated both the form and content of philosophical practice.[43]

Weakness in political theory need not, of course, adversely affect political activism or undermine political influence. James was clearly active, within the proprieties demanded for a Harvard professor, in his opposition to the American imperialism. It is also apparent that the ideas within his public philosophy attracted a wide audience and proved to be of more than passing moment. James T. Kloppenberg has made a compelling and extended case for James as an influential spokesman for a philosophy and politics of the *via media*. James's radical theory of knowledge and his questioning of epistemology proved suggestive and supportive to a generation of political theorists and reformers who fought for progressive change in America. Jamesian meliorism, with its emphasis upon voluntary action and freedom as crucial elements in the realm of experience, contributed to a willingness to reform, an acceptance of change in the social and political realm. Kloppenberg summarizes James's political influence: "Through his radical empiricism and his pragmatism he helped to nurture the seeds of a new political sensibility, which reached fruition in the writings of John Dewey and other like-minded American radicals between 1890 and 1920, by insisting that knowledge begins in the uncertainty of immediate experience and that all ideas must remain subject to continuous testing in social practice."[44]

James's ideals did influence numerous philosophers and reformers. For example, W.E.B. DuBois was guided out of the "sterilities of scholastic philosophy to realistic pragmatism." Chicago School sociologist and reformer Robert Park, a student of James, remembered his emphasis on tolerance and openness as crucial methodological foundations for the study of sociology and the reform of the urban environment. During his early flirtation with socialism and reformism, Walter Lippmann found James a heroic figure, "so very much of a democrat."[45] This influence was as much a result of James's position as a public philosopher as it was his famous openness as a human being.

Santayana was undoubtedly correct in finding that James's personal politics "shared the passions of liberalism. . . . He was one of those elder Americans who were still disquieted by the ghost of tyranny, social and ecclesiastical."[46] The mission that James urged upon Harvard graduates, and took as his own credo, called upon educated individuals in a democracy to take responsibility for leadership. There was no implicit denigration of democracy embedded in this message. James perceived that the problem of democracy was to assure that the right men be placed in positions of leadership. By right, he meant those who might take an enlightened view of political affairs and who would not be beholden to the passions of the moment or to the enthusiasms of the jingoist crowd. But James was never one of those "pessimistic prophets" bewailing the fate of American democracy in the age of the masses. The masses, led and educated by "les intellectuels," would progress. Errors would be made and corrected in the march of triumphant democracy until America's institutions would "glow with justice."[47]

James's ideal of leadership and responsibility may be seen, on one level, as corresponding well with the Progressive movement's belief in elite leadership. Yet he always differentiated between leadership and certitude. His pragmatic doctrine was not simply to become a political tool for progressive engineers to rule more efficiently. The pragmatic frame of mind was ultimately democratic in its imperatives, and it was confident that future progress would arise because of the workers' proud endeavors rather than from the bureaucrats' assured calculations.[48]

Born as they were in Mugwump and liberal traditions, James's politics might be seen as developing in the direction of socialism. He concluded his analysis of the labor problem in "What Makes a Life Significant" (1898) with the admission that society will "pass towards some newer and better equilibrium, and the distribution of wealth has doubtless got to change."[49] As a public philosopher, James confidently predicted the advent of socialism in "The Moral Equivalent of War": "I will now confess my own utopia. I devoutly believe in the ultimate reign of peace and in the gradual advent of some sort of a socialist equilibrium."[50]

James did not rest content with such musings, however. In his practical and individualistic fashion, he then criticized those "socialistic peace-advocates" whose only concern was for a world graced by a greater distribution of comforts. This utopian desire for an "ease economy" upset James's discourse of heroism and weakened the energies of the individual to fight against various evils. In sum, "present-day utopian literature tastes mawkish and dishwatery to people who still keep a sense for life's more bitter flavors. It suggests, in truth, ubiquitous inferiority."[51]

Utopias were valuable to James only if they remained ideals to be fought for, goads to strenuosity. Excitement was more in the striving than in the realization. Utopian visions such as those embraced by the socialists had pragmatic value. "Utopias are the noblest work of man," wrote James to William Dean Howells, "out of them all some effect comes, for if we *want* enough, we get it."[52] In the same manner, James could praise Jane Addams's progressive undertakings for their pragmatic aspects. She was no fuzzy-minded reformer; James wrote to her: "You *inhabit* reality." He did not agree with all of the details outlined in her book *Newer Ideals of Peace* (1907); nonetheless, it remained valuable for its "New perspectives of hope!" and its strenuosity.[53] Beyond such excited support for reformers and utopians alike, James had almost nothing to do with the progressive and socialist movements that became major forces in American life after 1900. His public philosophy could not be contained by the politics of the moment, even when those politics so logically approximated his own perceptions.

James's interest in socialist utopias was connected, perhaps paradoxically, to his support for anarchism. Freedom required cooperation and community, but the ever-increasing concentration of power in modern life translated all too readily into new modes of domination. Anarchist communalism best captured James's sympathies. He declared himself at one with philosophers as dissimilar as Herbert Spencer and Thomas Davidson in their shared antagonism to centralized, bureaucratic systems of government. James was convinced that the best way to maintain freedom, as well as to protect the rights of the individual unit, remained "for lovers of the ideal [of freedom] to found smaller communities . . . through small systems, kept pure, lies one most promising line of betterment and salvation. Why won't anarchists get together and try it. I am too ill (and too old!) or I might chip in myself."[54]

Existential anarchism better suited James's personality, philosophy, and politics. "I am becoming more an individualist and anarchist," he wrote in 1900 to his friend Howells.[55] James admitted to following a mild form of anarchism, in part because its practitioners, in contrast to monists and absolutists, were well aware of the world's evil and hesitant of solutions granting absolute power to the state or to philosophical dogma. In *Pragmatism,* he prefaced a quote by the anarchist and anti-imperialist Morrison I. Swift by noting that "Mr. Swift's anarchism goes a little farther than mine does" (21). James's sympathetic understanding of Tolstoy's Christian anarchism responded most appropriately to the perceptions and lessons he had learned from the Spanish-American War.

"Bigness"—whether in military might, philosophical systems, scientific certitude, or government bureaucracies—led to blindness and domination. But James also condemned socialists for not dealing adequately with the unyielding realities of human nature. "Man's instincts are rapacious, and under any social arrangement, the *rapatores* will find a way to prey."[56] In one of his more somber moments during the aftermath of the Spanish-American War, James wrote that in any social situation the "'Ubermenschen'" would find a way to claw to the top. The modern technocratic hope and vision of vast, efficient bureaucracies, which captured the imagination of great thinkers such as Thorstein Veblen, left James cold: human nature could not be changed by technology. Technology only promised to chain the individual in the iron of abstraction. James was attracted to small, concrete, and particular realities, rather than to larger organizations in life, politics, and philosophy.

I am against bigness and greatness in all their forms, and with the invisible molecular moral forces that work from individual to individual, stealing in through the crannies of the world like so many soft rootlets, or like the capillary oozing of water, and yet rending the hardest monuments of man's pride, if you give them time. The bigger the unit you deal with, the hollower, the more brutal, the more mendacious is the life displayed. So I am against all big organizations as such, national ones first and foremost; against all big successes and big results; and in favor of the eternal forces of truth which always work in the individual and immediately unsuccessful way, under-dogs always, till history comes, after they are long dead, and puts them on the top.[57]

James preferred to base his personal, public, and professional philosophy upon essentially anarchistic grounds—they better suited his temperament and his imperative for a world of pluralism and possibility, a world of individual moral responsibility under the sign of a personal God. Writing in 1896 to political activist and fellow philosopher Wincenty Lutoslawski, James noted that "I am growing, myself, more and more pluralistic and individualistic in my general views of things; and I think that against the monism which dominates everywhere the philosophic mind, men are needed to stand stoutly up for that opposite view. Probably the rest of my life will be devoted to defending it more and more."[58] In both his philosophy and politics, James proved true to his word.

VII

As a public philosopher, James demanded that his readers and listeners understand almost intuitively the essentials of his political and social position. To have been more obvious and sustained in developing a politics of anti-imperialism or even the polite anarchism suggested in his philosophy would have transformed public discourse into partisanship; it would have turned James into one of those "closet-philosophers" of morality that he had condemned in "The Moral Philosopher and the Moral Life" (1891). The adoption of such a stance might have compromised his ability to fashion a wide-ranging cultural agenda designed to lead public opinion away from jingoism and absolutism. James devoted himself to freeing the public from these dangerous perceptions in both political and philosophical discourse and to replacing them with a pragmatic philosophical position that allowed room for strenuous action, with due recognition of the complexity and consequences involved in any act that paraded under the banner of truth. In the opening pages of *Pragmatism*, James emphatically captured this imperative. Although he admitted that the common view that philosophy " 'bakes no bread' " was largely true, he stated that philosophical discourse should strive to "inspire our souls with courage" (10). This courage would entail making decisions based upon belief, rejecting all-embracing propositions in favor of uncertainty and change, being moral and responsible, resisting imperialism's excitement and clamor, and philosophizing in the face of the abyss.[59]

Confronted throughout his entire life, and the life of his culture of tedium, by the dread of a universe either fully indeterminate or determined—the Nietzschean abyss or the evolutionary Elysium—James sought to avoid the numbing calm of passivity. He refused, and wanted his fellow citizens from the elite class to refuse, to fall into the role of Hamlet. He therefore constructed his philosophy to emphasize an active, sustained, and sober engagement with life: "How I exult in this forward movement along the whole empiricist line, towards something which must be recognized in the end as more concrete and vital than any possible Absolutism!"[60]

James sometimes indicated that it was better for the individual to follow any of the open doors that pragmatism's "corridor in a hotel" offered than to succumb to a culturally commonplace willingness "to rest in a state of admiring contemplation" (49). The strength of James's discourse of heroism, rooted as it was in his own life and in the problems of his culture, sometimes overwhelmed his good judgment, though the essential outlines of his philosophy and moralism did tend to mitigate against such effusions. James had not participated in the Civil War and he had experienced long years of depression and debility. Hamletian existence had little to recommend it; the individual imprisoned within such a nightmare reality could only answer the Jamesian question "Is Life Worth Living?" with a resounding negative. Excitement and heroism made life worthwhile. James preferred to confront a strong opponent, someone or something whose resistances would call forth his greatest powers of endurance and energy in a fight for salvation. This was the message of *The Will to Believe,* and it continued to resonate in *Pragmatism.* Indeed, the message's tocsin rings heroically and perhaps instructively throughout the entire corpus of James's public philosophy.

Notes

CHAPTER ONE
Introduction: The Varieties of Context

1. Quoted in George Steiner, *In Bluebeard's Castle: Some Notes towards a Redefinition of Culture* (New Haven: Yale Univ. Press, 1971), 11.

2. On the placement of James within a modernist or postmodernist perspective, see Sanford Schwartz, *The Matrix of Modernism: Pound, Eliot, and Early Twentieth-Century Thought* (Princeton: Princeton Univ. Press, 1985); and Frank Lentricchia, "The Return of William James," *Cultural Critique*, no. 4 (Fall 1986): 5–31. See also Harold Bloom, *Agon: Towards a Theory of Revisionism* (New York: Oxford Univ. Press, 1982), 30–31; Ihab Hassan, "On George Steiner," *Salmagundi*, nos. 70–71 (Spring–Summer 1986): 318; and Hassan, *The Postmodern Turn: Essays in Postmodern Theory and Culture* (Columbus: Ohio State Univ. Press, 1987), 204–9.

3. Jacques Barzun, *A Stroll with William James* (New York: Harper and Row, 1983). On the politics and poetics of James's project, see Frank Lentricchia, "On the Ideologies of Poetic Modernism," in *Reconstructing American Literary History,* ed. Sacvan Bercovitch (Cambridge: Harvard Univ. Press, 1986), 200–249.

4. An internal approach predominates the otherwise commendable and impressive work on James's physiological psychology by Gerald E. Myers, *William James: His Life and Thought* (New Haven: Yale Univ. Press, 1986).

5. Alasdair MacIntyre, *After Virtue* (South Bend, Ind.: Univ. of Notre Dame Press, 1984), 11. Although MacIntyre is to be commended for attempting to return to a contextualist rendering of the history of philosophy, his depiction of context is often blurred and insufficiently established in the historical concrete of cultural circumstances.

6. The strongest expression of a deconstructionist reading of texts is Dominick LaCapra, "Rethinking Intellectual History and the Reading of Texts," in *Rethinking Intellectual History: Texts, Contexts, Language* (Ithaca: Cornell Univ. Press, 1983), 23–71. It appears that some scholars working in a postmodernist vein are attempting to reintroduce context, albeit by the back door. See Stephen W. Melville, *Philosophy beside Itself: On Deconstruction and Modernism* (Minneapolis: Univ. of Minnesota Press, 1986).

7. This is the argument of John P. Diggins, "The Oyster and the Pearl: The Problem of Contextualism in Intellectual History," *History and Theory* 23 (1984): 151–69;

and *The Lost Soul of American Politics: Virtue, Self-Interest, and the Foundations of Liberalism* (Chicago: Univ. of Chicago Press, 1986), 359–62.

8. Quentin Skinner, "Meaning and Understanding in the History of Ideas," *History and Theory* 8 (1969): 3–53; and John Dunn, "The Identity of the History of Ideas," *Philosophy* 43 (April 1968): 85–116. A sustained case for a contextualist approach, drawing upon speech-act theory, is in Bruce Kuklick, "Studying the History of Philosophy," *Transactions of the Charles S. Peirce Society* 18 (Winter 1982): 18–33.

9. LaCapra, "Rethinking Intellectual History," 35. In fairness to LaCapra, he does not apotheosize the text; instead, he posits that one must follow Mikhail Bakhtin's lead and seek a dialogic relationship between text and society mediated through language. See LaCapra, "Bakhtin, Marxism, and the Carnivalesque," in *Rethinking Intellectual History*, 291–324.

10. Diggins, "The Oyster and the Pearl," 153.

11. William James, *Pragmatism* (Cambridge: Harvard Univ. Press, 1975), 34. Typical of the recent revival of interest in Jamesian pragmatism as a pluralistic approach to the study of literature and society is Lentricchia's "The Return of William James," 3–31.

12. The strongest and most strident case for the public intellectual is in Russell Jacoby, *The Last Intellectuals: American Culture in the Age of Academe* (New York: Basic Books, 1987). Some intellectuals applaud the decline of the public philosopher, associating such a presence with a desire to encompass, and thus dominate, through a monistic vision, the plurality and chaos of existence. James's pluralistic and individualistic philosophical position clearly allowed him to battle monism while maintaining cultural credibility and importance. For an argument against the tradition of the public intellectual, see Jean-François Lyotard, *Tombeau de l'intellectuel* (Paris: Galilée, 1984).

13. The thesis of the philosopher as artist is presented fully by Daniel W. Bjork, *William James: The Center of His Vision* (New York: Columbia Univ. Press, 1988).

14. Howard M. Feinstein, *Becoming William James* (Ithaca: Cornell Univ. Press, 1984); Cushing Strout, "William James and the Twice-Born Sick Soul," *Daedalus* 97 (Summer 1968): 1062–82; Strout, "The Pluralistic Identity of William James: A Psychohistorical Reading of *The Varieties of Religious Experience*," *American Quarterly* 23 (May 1971): 135–52; R.W.B. Lewis, "The Courtship of William James," *Yale Review* 73 (Winter 1984): 177–98. Also noteworthy as evaluations of James's early life are James William Anderson, "In Search of Mary James," *Psychohistory Review* 8 (1978): 63–79; Anderson, "'The Worst Kind of Melancholy': William James in 1869," *Harvard Library Bulletin* 30 (1982): 369–86; and John Owen King, *The Iron of Melancholy: Structures of Spiritual Conversion in America from the Puritan Conscience to Victorian Neurosis* (Middletown: Wesleyan Univ. Press, 1983).

15. This thesis is strongly presented in Feinstein, *Becoming William James*.

16. In his dated but still important account, Ralph Barton Perry stressed the importance of philosophical questions in James's depressive years. While not neglecting tensions over vocation, Perry did not emphasize the father-and-son conflict. See Perry, *The Thought and Character of William James*, 2 vols. (Boston: Little, Brown and Co., 1935), 1:237–377. Similar accounts are in Gay Wilson Allen, *William James: A Biography* (New York: Viking Press, 1967); and F. O. Matthiessen, *The James Family: A Group Biography* (New York: Alfred A. Knopf, 1947).

17. Feinstein alludes to, but does not sufficiently consider, the generational aspects of neurasthenia and vocational problems. See Feinstein, *Becoming William James*, 118–22.

18. Oliver Wendell Holmes, Jr., "Memorial Day," in *The Mind and Faith of Justice*

Holmes: Speeches, Essays, Letters and Judicial Opinions, ed. Max Lerner (Boston: Little, Brown and Co., 1951), 10. On the importance of the Civil War to this generation, see the excellent analysis in George M. Fredrickson, *The Inner Civil War: Northern Intellectuals and the Crisis of Union* (New York: Harper and Row, 1968).

19. On the cultural contradictions and problems of this era, see T. J. Jackson Lears, *No Place of Grace: Antimodernism and the Transformation of American Culture, 1880–1920* (New York: Pantheon Books, 1981), 32–46; and Alan Trachtenberg, *The Incorporation of America: Culture and Society in the Gilded Age* (New York: Hill and Wang, 1982), esp. 140–81.

20. The term *social expression* indicates that philosophical ideas are statements, often veiled, that evolve from and respond to society. The fullest statement of this position is in Albert William Levi, *Philosophy as Social Expression* (Chicago: Univ. of Chicago Press, 1974), 1–37. A similar thesis on the homologous relationship between ideas and society is Lucien Goldmann, "Genetic-Structuralist Method in History of Literature," in *Marxism and Art: Writings in Aesthetics and Criticism,* ed. Berel Lang and Forrest Williams (New York: David McKay, 1972), 234–55. An excellent discussion of Goldmann's methodology is Martin Jay, *Marxism and Totality: The Adventures of a Concept from Lukács to Habermas* (Berkeley and Los Angeles: Univ. of California Press, 1984), 300–330.

21. A forceful statement of this thesis is offered by James Turner, *Without God, without Creed: The Origins of Unbelief in America* (Baltimore: Johns Hopkins Univ. Press, 1985).

22. On the centrality of doubt to Victorians, see Walter E. Houghton, *The Victorian Frame of Mind* (New Haven: Yale Univ. Press, 1957), 54–89. On the resolution of Darwinism and religion, see James R. Moore, *The Post-Darwinian Controversies: A Study of the Protestant Struggle to Come to Terms with Darwin in Great Britain and America, 1870–1900* (Cambridge: Cambridge Univ. Press, 1979); and Daniel Walker Howe, "American Victorianism as a Culture," *American Quarterly* 27 (December 1975): 507–32.

23. See the excellent discussion of the crisis of autonomy in Lears, *No Place of Grace,* esp. 17–20, 26–32. On how this crisis was revealed in the anxiety over the question of insanity, see Charles Rosenberg, *The Trial of the Assassin Guiteau: Psychiatry and Law in the Gilded Age* (Chicago: Univ. of Chicago Press, 1968).

24. William James to Tom Ward, March [?] 1869, *The Letters of William James,* 2 vols., ed. Henry James (Boston: Atlantic Monthly Press, 1920), 1:152–53.

25. William James, "The Dilemma of Determinism," in *The Will to Believe* (Cambridge: Harvard Univ. Press, 1979), 114–40. James specifically addressed his ideas to the crisis of belief and individual will. See James's "Preface," 5–10.

26. Freidrich Nietzsche raises this possibility in the context of a discussion of Hamlet in *Ecce Homo,* trans. and ed. Walter Kaufmann (New York: Vintage Books, 1969), 246.

27. William James, "Diary," 4 April 1873, James Family Papers, Houghton Library, Harvard University. Hereafter cited as JFP.

28. James, *Pragmatism,* 123–25. Pluralism and freedom as the center of James's philosophy is stressed by John E. Smith, *The Spirit of American Philosophy* (New York: Oxford Univ. Press, 1963), 38–43; and John J. McDermott, "The Promethean Self and Community in the Philosophy of William James," in *Streams of Experience: Reflections on the History and Philosophy of American Culture* (Amherst: Univ. of Massachusetts Press, 1986), 44–58.

29. Lears, *No Place of Grace,* 159–67, 210–15, 302–9. See also John Higham, "The Reorientation of American Culture in the 1890s," in *Writing American History: Essays in Modern Scholarship* (Bloomington: Indiana Univ. Press, 1970), 73–102.

30. Henry Adams, *The Education of Henry Adams: An Autobiography* (Boston and New York: Houghton, Mifflin Co., 1918), 379–90.

31. Sean Wilentz, *Chants Democratic: New York City and the Rise of the American Working Class, 1788–1850* (New York: Oxford Univ. Press, 1984); Lawrence Goodwyn, *The Populist Revolt: A Short History of the Agrarian Revolt in America* (New York: Oxford Univ. Press, 1978); and John L. Thomas, *Alternative America: Henry George, Edward Bellamy, and Henry Demarest Lloyd and the Adversary Tradition* (Cambridge: Harvard Univ. Press, 1983), 5 passim.

32. George Cotkin, "William James and the 'Weightless' Nature of Modern Existence," *San Jose Studies* 12 (Spring 1986): 7–19.

33. The best account of the bureaucratic imperative on the part of those who fought is Fredrickson, *Inner Civil War*, 199–216.

34. On this shift from philosophy to literature, see the suggestive comments in Richard Rorty, "Professional Philosophy and Transcendentalist Culture," in *The Consequences of Pragmatism* (Minneapolis: Univ. of Minnesota Press, 1980), 66.

35. David A. Hollinger, "William James and the Culture of Inquiry," *Michigan Quarterly Review* 20 (Summer 1981): 264–66. Hollinger reiterates the important connection between philosopher and audience in his essay "American Intellectual History: Issues for the 1980s." Both essays are in his *In the American Province: Studies in the History and Historiography of Ideas* (Bloomington: Indiana Univ. Press, 1985), 3–22, 176–88.

36. Bruce Kuklick, *The Rise of American Philosophy: Cambridge, Massachusetts, 1860–1930* (New Haven: Yale Univ. Press, 1977), 172.

37. William James to his brother Henry, 12 July 1905, and to his wife, Alice, 6 July 1905, both in JFP.

38. See the discussion of the publishing history of these lectures in the editorial apparatus to William James, *Talks to Teachers on Psychology* (Cambridge: Harvard Univ. Press, 1983), 256, 271.

39. Charles H. Compton, *Who Reads What?: Essays on the Readers of Mark Twain, Hardy, Sandburg, Shaw, William James, the Greek Classics* (1934, Freeport, N.Y.: Books for Libraries Press, 1969), 91–98.

40. Josiah Royce, "William James and the Philosophy of Life," in *William James and Other Essays on the Philosophy of Life* (New York: Macmillan, 1911), 3–6. A similar analysis of James is offered by Walter Lippmann, then a socialist, in "An Open Mind: William James," *Everybody's Magazine* 23 (December 1910): 800–801. George Santayana, "The Genteel Tradition in American Philosophy" (1911), in *Documents in the History of American Philosophy: From Jonathan Edwards to John Dewey*, ed. Morton White (New York: Oxford Univ. Press, 1972), 419.

41. A full discussion of the tradition of public philosophy, especially as practiced by Emerson and James, is in my "Ralph Waldo Emerson and William James as Public Philosophers," *Historian* 49 (November 1986): 49–63.

42. Quoted in Kuklick, *Rise of American Philosophy*, 306.

43. James's complaints about the problems of public philosophy are in his various letters. See William James to Théodore Flournoy, 3 January 1908, JFP; William James to his brother Henry, 10 September 1906, *Letters of William James*, 2:259; William James to F.C.S. Schiller, January [1908], Perry, *Thought and Character*, 2:583. I discuss the problems and advantages of James's style in my "William James and the Cash-Value Metaphor," *ETC: A Review of General Semantics* 42 (September 1985): 37.

44. William James to his brother Henry, 6 August 1895, JFP.

45. Richard Rorty, *Philosophy and the Mirror of Nature* (Princeton: Princeton Univ. Press, 1979), 365–94.

46. William James, "The Ph.D. Octopus" (1903), in *Essays, Comments, and Reviews* (Cambridge: Harvard Univ. Press, 1987), 67–74; William James to G. C. Ferrari, typescript, 22 February 1905, Special Collections, Stanford University Library; William James to Edwin D. Starbuck, 12 February 1905, and to Dickinson S. Miller, 6 December 1905, both in *Letters of William James*, 2:217, 235–37.

47. William James used the expression "passionate vision" in his *A Pluralistic Universe* (Cambridge: Harvard Univ. Press, 1977), 81.

48. This was the established practice for public lecturing in America. "The unwritten law on the Lyceum circuit," Gay Wilson Allen notes, "was that highly controversial subjects must be avoided." See Allen, "Emerson's Audiences: American and British," *Ariel: A Review of International English Literature* 7 (July 1976): 96. See also Wilson Smith, *Professors and Public Ethics: Studies of Northern Moral Philosophers before the Civil War* (Ithaca: Cornell Univ. Press, 1956), 88. On the importance of the lecture within nineteenth-century American culture, see Donald M. Scott, "The Popular Lecture and the Creation of a Public in Mid-Nineteenth Century America," *Journal of American History* 66 (March 1980): 781–809.

49. I discuss this in my essay "Ralph Waldo Emerson and William James," 57–63.

50. The strongest statement of this position is Max C. Otto, "On a Certain Blindness in William James," *Ethics* 53 (April 1943): 184–91.

51. In this regard, my analysis of a philosophical classic parallels certain scholars' examination of canonical works of literature. See Jane Tompkins, *Sensational Designs: The Cultural Work of American Fiction, 1790–1860* (New York: Oxford Univ. Press, 1985).

52. The connection between James's epistemology and the politics of reform at the turn of the century is the focus of the impressive analysis of James T. Kloppenberg, *Uncertain Victory: Social Democracy and Progressivism in European and American Thought, 1870–1920* (New York: Oxford Univ. Press, 1986).

53. Quoted in Perry, *Thought and Character*, 2:510. William James, *Essays in Radical Empiricism* (Cambridge: Harvard Univ. Press, 1976), 85–86n.8.

CHAPTER TWO
"Judged Not to Have Lived"

1. Quoted in M. O'C. Drury, "Conversations with Wittgenstein," in *Ludwig Wittgenstein: Personal Recollections*, ed. Rush Rees (Totowa, N.J.: Rowman and Littlefield, 1981), 121.

2. William James, *Pragmatism* (Cambridge: Harvard Univ. Press, 1975), 11–15.

3. Quoted in F. O. Matthiessen, *The James Family: A Group Biography* (New York: Alfred A. Knopf, 1947), 69.

4. The hectic educational experiences of the family are recounted in Gay Wilson Allen, *William James: A Biography* (New York: Viking Press, 1967), 12–63.

5. Howard M. Feinstein, *Becoming William James* (Ithaca: Cornell Univ. Press, 1984). Feinstein engagingly presents this dispute as a recapitulation of vocational struggles played out between Henry James, Sr., and his father. Gerald E. Myers rejects this interpretation, finding evidence—and perhaps in the process making too much of a single letter—conceiving William James's initial vocational tendency as directed toward science rather than art. See Myers, *William James: Life and Thought* (New Haven: Yale Univ. Press, 1986), 3–4, 19–20. For more on the James family connection, see Paul Jerome Croce, "Money and Morality: The Life and Legacy of the First William James, 1771–1832," *New York History* 68 (April 1987): 174–90.

6. Ralph Barton Perry, *The Thought and Character of William James*, 2 vols.

(Boston: Little, Brown and Co., 1935), 1:125–45; and Matthiessen, *James Family*, 101–12.

7. This argument is excellently developed in Richard Hocks, *Henry James and Pragmatic Thought: A Study in the Relationship between the Philosophy of William James and the Literary Art of Henry James* (Chapel Hill: Univ. of North Carolina Press, 1974).

8. William James, *The Principles of Psychology*, 2 vols. (Cambridge: Harvard Univ. Press, 1981), 1:282 passim.

9. Josiah Royce, "William James and the Philosophy of Life," in *William James and Other Essays on the Philosophy of Life* (New York: Macmillan, 1911), 31.

10. Oliver Wendell Holmes, Jr., "The Soldier's Faith" and "Memorial Day Address," both in *The Mind and Faith of Justice Holmes: His Speeches, Essays, Letters and Judicial Opinions,* ed. Max Lerner (Boston: Little, Brown and Co., 1951), 18, 10.

11. Ralph Waldo Emerson, "Voluntaries," in *Poems,* in *The Complete Works of Ralph Waldo Emerson,* 12 vols. (Boston and New York: Houghton, Mifflin Co., 1904), 9:207.

12. The concept of adolescent crisis and vocational doubt is taken from Erik Erikson, *Identity: Youth and Crisis* (New York: W. W. Norton and Co., 1969), 129, 132. Erikson specifically considers James's adolescent crisis on 151–53.

13. Quoted in Barton J. Bledstein, *The Culture of Professionalism: The Middle Class and the Development of Higher Education in America* (New York: W. W. Norton, 1976), 159.

14. George M. Fredrickson interprets the vocational uncertainty of this Brahmin youth cohort as a function of its having been cast adrift in an "aimless literary and scholarly existence." See Fredrickson, *The Inner Civil War: Northern Intellectuals and the Crisis of Union* (New York: Harper Torchbooks, 1968), 146. On the prevalence of vocational uncertainty among James's generational cohort, see the passing remarks in Feinstein, *Becoming William James,* 118–22.

15. On the Puritan concept of a calling, see Daniel T. Rodgers, *The Work Ethic in Industrial America, 1850–1920* (Chicago: Univ. of Chicago Press, 1978), 7–11.

16. Emerson's early years and crisis of vocation are intelligently discussed in David Robinson, *Apostle of Culture: Emerson as Preacher and Lecturer* (Philadelphia: Univ. of Pennsylvania Press, 1982).

17. On this shift of the economy in Massachusetts, see Jack Tager, "Massachusetts and the Age of Economic Revolution," in *Massachusetts in the Gilded Age,* ed. Jack Tager and John W. Ifkovic (Amherst: Univ. of Massachusetts Press, 1985), esp. 5–9.

18. Robert Wiebe, *The Opening of American Society: From the Adoption of the Constitution to the Eve of Disunion* (New York: Alfred A. Knopf, 1984), 143–67, 323, 347. See also Daniel H. Calhoun, *Professional Lives in America: Structure and Aspiration, 1750–1850* (Cambridge: Harvard Univ. Press, 1965), 185–97. I differ with John Higham's argument that the "boundlessness" of the Jacksonian years was played out by the 1840s. The term seems appropriate for the vocational possibilities open to young men of the elite classes right up until the Civil War. See Higham, *From Boundlessness to Consolidation: The Transformation of American Culture, 1840–1860* (Ann Arbor: William L. Clements Library, 1969).

19. Adams, *The Education of Henry Adams* (Boston and New York: Houghton, Mifflin Co., 1918), 210, 240–41. Adams indicated that career choices were few but the vocational narrative in his autobiography and in his friends' lives reveals a different story.

20. Edward W. Emerson, *The Life and Letters of Charles Russell Lowell* (Boston and New York: Houghton, Mifflin Co., 1907), 8–13, 119.

21. Adams, *Education,* 240–41; and Emerson, *Lowell,* 119. On American roman-

tic writers and the marketplace, see Michael T. Gilmore, *American Romanticism and the Marketplace* (Chicago: Univ. of Chicago Press, 1985).

22. Bliss Perry, *Life and Letters of Henry Lee Higginson* (Boston: Atlantic Monthly Press, 1921), 64–71.

23. Royal Cortissoz, *John LaFarge: A Memoir and a Study* (New York: Da Capo Press, 1971), 89, 120.

24. Charles Francis Adams, *Autobiography* (Boston: Massachusetts Historical Society, 1916), 12–15, 19–21.

25. Percy Mackaye, *Epoch: The Life of Steele Mackaye, Genius of the Theatre, in Relation to His Times and Contemporaries,* 2 vols. (New York: Boni and Liveright, 1968), 1:79–80. The list of young men suffering vocational uncertainty and neurasthenic symptoms could be enlarged to include George Herbert Palmer, James's colleague in the Harvard philosophy department. See Palmer, *The Autobiography of a Philosopher* (New York: Greenwood Press, 1968), 10–11, 25, 32.

26. Adams, *Autobiography,* 19, 28.

27. Quoted in Catherine Drinker Bowen, *Yankee from Olympus: Justice Holmes and His Family* (Boston: Little, Brown and Co., 1944), 199. The concept of "vague benevolence" is used to excellent effect by Howard M. Feinstein to explain Henry James, Sr.'s relationship with William. Feinstein, *Becoming William James,* 115.

28. Jay Fliegelman, *Prodigals and Pilgrims: The American Revolution against Patriarchal Authority, 1750–1800* (London: Cambridge Univ. Press, 1984), 9–10. See also Joseph F. Kett, *Rites of Passage: Adolescence in America, 1790 to the Present* (New York: Basic Books, 1977), esp. 111–43.

29. Perry, *Higginson,* 66–71.

30. In *Becoming William James,* Feinstein makes the same point about the varied maladies that afflicted James's friends, but he does not pursue the insight. The shared nature of these problems indicates that the internal dynamics of the James family, though real and enduring, are not the entire story. See 117–22.

31. George M. Beard, *A Practical Treatise on Nervous Exhaustion (Neurasthenia): Its Symptoms, Nature, Sequences, Treatment* (1888; reprint, New York: Kraus Reprint Co., 1971), 25–31. Beard first outlined these theories in his classic *American Nervousness: Its Causes and Consequences* (1881; reprint, New York: Arno Press, 1972), esp. 96–192, an exhaustive and, in retrospect, humorous look at the causes of American nervousness.

32. An excellent account of the relationship between neurasthenia and work is James B. Gilbert, *Work without Salvation: America's Intellectuals and Industrial Alienation, 1880–1910* (Baltimore: Johns Hopkins Univ. Press, 1977), 31–43. See also Rodgers, *The Work Ethic,* esp. 103–6 passim.

33. Perry, *Higginson,* 7, 25, 43, 52–53, 120–21, 141. Higginson's eye ailment was never taken seriously, at least according to the Agassiz family, into which he married. See Louise Hall Tharp, *Adventurous Alliance: The Story of the Agassiz Family of Boston* (Boston: Little, Brown and Co., 1959), 157–58.

34. Emerson, *Lowell,* 130–31, 156–57.

35. Mackaye, *Epoch,* 63.

36. Adams, *Education,* 249.

37. Emerson, *Lowell,* 204.

38. Perry, *Higginson,* 141–42, 154.

39. Mackaye, *Epoch,* 97.

40. Adams, *Autobiography,* 114–29.

41. Perry, *Higginson,* 179, 232–33.

42. Adams, *Autobiography,* 129; and Fredrickson, *Inner Civil War,* 175–76.

184   Notes to Pages 29–35

43. *Touched with Fire: Civil War Letters and Diary of Oliver Wendell Holmes, Jr., 1861–1864*, ed. Mark DeWolfe Howe (Cambridge: Harvard Univ. Press, 1947); and Holmes, "The Soldier's Faith," in *Mind and Faith*, 21.

44. Feinstein, *Becoming William James*, 103–45.

45. Fredrickson, *Inner Civil War*, 229, 232; and Marian C. Madden and Edward H. Madden, "The Psychosomatic Illnesses of William James," *Thought* 54 (December 1979): 385.

46. Leon Edel, *Henry James: The Untried Years, 1843–1870* (New York: Avon Books, 1978), 170.

47. Henry James, *Autobiography* (Princeton: Princeton Univ. Press, 1983), 282.

48. Allen, *William James*, 72; Perry, *Thought and Character*, 1:203; and Myers, *William James*, 31.

49. On the chronology for James's onset of illness and its connection to his vocational struggles, see Feinstein, *Becoming William James*, 104, 140–41.

50. Madden and Madden, "Psychosomatic Illnesses," 85.

51. Quoted in Allen, *William James*, 71–72.

52. A biography of Robertson and Wilky argues that they enlisted because they simply wanted to serve and because by 1863 the war had been transformed from a narrow sectional conflict into an impassioned crusade to end slavery, a goal that Henry James, Sr., found appealing. See Jane Maher, *Biography of Broken Fortunes: Wilkie and Bob, Brothers of William, Henry, and Alice James* (Hamden, Conn.: Archon, 1986), 15–27.

53. Allen, *William James*, 72.

54. Perry, *Higginson*, 192.

55. William James to Mrs. Katherine James, 12 September 1863, *The Letters of William James*, 2 vols., ed. Henry James (Boston: Atlantic Monthly Press, 1920), 1:44.

56. Henry James, *The Bostonians* (Middlesex, Eng.: Penguin Books, 1983), 13.

57. William James, "Is Life Worth Living?" in *The Will to Believe* (Cambridge: Harvard Univ. Press, 1979), 56. James's emphasis upon a discourse of heroism and his fascination with the military life also support this contention. See chapters five and six of this work.

58. Quoted in Tharp, *Adventurous Alliance*, 158–59. See the excellent discussion of the stay-at-homes in Fredrickson, *Inner Civil War*, 151–65.

59. Oliver Wendell Holmes, Jr., to his mother, 7 June 1864, *Touched with Fire*, 142.

60. Emerson, "Voluntaries," 207.

61. Edel, *Henry James*, 172.

62. "Notebook R" (1863), James Family Papers, Houghton Library, Harvard University. Hereafter cited as JFP.

63. Feinstein, *Becoming William James*, 114–16 passim.

64. Henry James, Sr., "The Social Significance of Our Institutions: Oration Delivered by the Request of the Citizens of Newport, R.I., July 4, 1861," in *American Philosophical Addresses, 1700–1900*, ed. Joseph L. Blau (New York: Columbia Univ. Press, 1946), 234–56. Fredrickson discusses Henry James Sr.'s position on the war in *Inner Civil War*, 68–69.

65. Ibid., 252.

66. James Bradley Thayer, *Letters of Chauncey Wright: With Some Account of His Life* (Cambridge: Press of John Wilson and Sons, 1878), 5–6, 49. See also Edward H. Madden, *Chauncey Wright and the Foundations of Pragmatism* (Seattle: Univ. of Washington Press, 1963), 3–21. Wright's philosophical ideas are confidently surveyed in Philip P. Weiner, *Evolution and the Founders of Pragmatism* (Cambridge: Harvard Univ. Press, 1949), 31–69.

67. Thayer, *Chauncey Wright*, 50–52.

68. William James to his mother, c. September 1863, *Letters of William James*, 1:45–47.

69. Discussions of the expedition and James's role in it are in Feinstein, *Becoming William James*, 169–81, and in Allen, *William James*, 101–16. James would later come to view Agassiz as "a man on the heroic scale, not to serve whom is avarice and sin" (48). The connection between this necessity to serve Agassiz and his own unspoken failure to serve in the Union army is too obvious for comment. See William James, "Louis Agassiz" (1896), in *Essays, Comments and Reviews* (Cambridge: Harvard Univ. Press, 1987), 48. A full account of the trip, much of it culled from James's diaries, is in Charles Sprague Smith, "William James in Brazil," in *Four Papers Presented in the Institute for Brazilian Studies, Vanderbilt University*, ed. Charles Wagley et al. (Nashville: Vanderbilt Univ. Press, 1961), 97–137.

70. On Agassiz's concerns for this expedition, see *The Intelligence of Louis Agassiz*, ed. Guy Davenport (Boston: Beacon Press, 1963), 119; Feinstein, *Becoming William James*, 169; and Edward Lurie, *Louis Agassiz: A Life in Science* (Chicago: Univ. of Chicago Press, 1960), 345–50.

71. Allen, *William James*, 102.

72. John Owen King, *The Iron of Melancholy: Structures of Spiritual Conversion in America from the Puritan Conscience to Victorian Neurosis* (Middletown, Conn.: Wesleyan Univ. Press, 1983), 149–53.

73. Feinstein, *Becoming William James*, 170.

74. William James to his mother [30 March?] 1865, *Letters of William James*, 1:56–59.

75. Holmes, *Touched with Fire*, 27. William James to his parents, 21–25 April 1865, *Letters of William James*, 1:60.

76. William James to his father, 3 June 1865, *Letters of William James*, 1:62–63. James would, no doubt, have been pleased to learn that his travels and hard work were later used to illustrate a point against the argument from design in correspondence between Chauncey Wright and Charles Darwin. Wright compared James's fishing in the Amazon region as "not far removed from the conditions of primeval man." In Thayer, *Chauncey Wright*, 332–33.

77. William James to his father, 12–15 September 1865, *Letters of William James*, 66.

78. William James to his parents, 21–22 October 1865, and to his mother, 9 December 1865, quoted in Perry, *Thought and Character*, 1:224–26.

79. Feinstein, *Becoming William James*, 182–83.

80. William James to Bliss Perry, 3 October 1905, JFP.

81. Charles Baudelaire, *The Painter of Modern Life and Other Essays*, trans. and ed. Jonathan Mayne (New York: Phaidon, 1970), 28–30.

82. Adams, *Education*, 314.

83. Perry, *Thought and Character*, 1:324.

CHAPTER THREE
From Hamlet to Habit

1. William James to Hugo Munsterberg, 8 July 1891, quoted in James William Anderson, "'The Worst Kind of Melancholy': William James in 1869," *Harvard Library Bulletin* 30 (1982): 369.

2. Attempts at textualizing James's life are not unusual, though the crucial metaphors must differ. For a psychologically probing evaluation of James, wherein he is

seen to be writing the autobiography of his depression through a modern textualization of the Puritan conversion narrative, see John Owen King, *The Iron of Melancholy: Structures of Spiritual Conversion in America from the Puritan Conscience to Victorian Neurosis* (Middletown, Conn.: Wesleyan Univ. Press, 1983), 141–97.

3. Josiah Royce, "William James and the Philosophy of Life," in *William James and Other Essays on the Philosophy of Life* (New York: Macmillan, 1911), 29; and George Santayana to William James, 6 December 1905, *The Letters of George Santayana*, ed. Daniel Cory (New York: Charles Scribner's Sons, 1955), 82.

4. Josiah Royce, *The Philosophy of Loyalty* (New York: Macmillan Co., 1908), 187–88.

5. These points are perceptively discussed in Lawrence W. Levine, "William Shakespeare and the American People: A Study in Cultural Transformation," *American Historical Review* 89 (February 1984): esp. 53–54.

6. The crisis of autonomy in American culture in this period is brilliantly analyzed in T. J. Jackson Lears, *No Place of Grace: Antimodernism and the Transformation of American Culture, 1880–1920* (New York: Pantheon Books, 1981), 26–58.

7. Goethe's view of Hamlet is insightfully analyzed in Ned Lukacher, *Primal Scenes: Literature, Philosophy, Psychoanalysis* (Ithaca: Cornell Univ. Press, 1986), 201.

8. Samuel Taylor Coleridge, *Shakespearean Criticism*, 2 vols., ed. Thomas Middleton Raysor (New York: Dutton, 1965), 1:34–36; 2:150–55. The dangers or uselessness of attempting to "fill-in" the blanks of Shakespeare's characterization of Hamlet is persuasively argued by Norman N. Holland, *The Shakespearean Imagination* (New York: Macmillan Co., 1964).

9. Peter Brooks, "The Rest Is Silence: Hamlet as Decadent," in *Jules Laforgue: Essays on a Poet's Life and Work*, ed. Warren Ramsey (Carbondale: Southern Illinois Univ. Press, 1969), 93–110.

10. William James to his sister, Alice, 17 October 1867, *The Letters of William James*, 2 vols., ed. Henry James (Boston: Atlantic Monthly Press, 1920), 1:111.

11. Wilhelm Dilthey, *Poetry and Experience*, ed. Rudolf Makkreel and Frithjof Rodi (Princeton: Princeton Univ. Press, 1985), 5:255–59. Dilthey's discussion, of course, is an early expression of his hermeneutic doctrine of empathy as a way of breaking down the horizons of history formed around particular events and individuals.

12. William James to his brother Henry, 13 April 1869, Ralph Barton Perry, *The Thought and Character of William James*, 2 vols.(Boston: Little, Brown and Co., 1935), 1:271–72.

13. This play, within the text of Goethe's novel, is discussed in Lukacher, *Primal Scenes*, 200–202. See also Johann Wolfgang von Goethe, *Wilhelm Meister's Apprenticeship*, trans. R. Dillon Boylan (London: George Bell and Sons, 1881), 297–305.

14. William James, "Diary," 13 April 1868, James Family Papers, Houghton Library, Harvard University. Hereafter cited as JFP.

15. William James to his brother Henry, 13 April 1868, quoted in Perry, *Thought and Character*, 1:272. James would later evoke Hamlet's cultural resonance twice in the chapter "Will," in *The Principles of Psychology*, 2 vols. (Cambridge: Harvard Univ. Press, 1981), 2:1134, 1163.

16. Sigmund Freud to Wilhelm Fleiss, 15 October 1887, *The Origins of Psychoanalysis: Letters to Wilhelm Fleiss*, trans. Eric Mosbacher and James Strachey, and ed. Marie Bonaparte, Anna Freud, and Ernst Kris (New York: Basic Books, 1977), 223–24.

17. Jacques Lacan, "Desire and the Interpretation of Desire in *Hamlet*," in *Literature and Psychoanalysis. The Question of Reading: Otherwise*, ed. Shoshana Felman (Baltimore: Johns Hopkins Univ. Press, 1982), 11–52.

18. Howard M. Feinstein, *Becoming William James* (Ithaca: Cornell Univ. Press, 1984), 103–45.

19. William James, "Great Men and Their Environment," in *The Will to Believe* (Cambridge: Harvard Univ. Press, 1979), 171.

20. William James to his brother Henry, [10] October 1872, JFP.

21. Sigmund Freud, "Mourning and Melancholia," in *The Standard Edition of the Complete Psychological Works of Sigmund Freud*, ed. James Strachey et al., 24 vols. (London: Hogarth Press and the Institute of Psycho-Analysis, 1953–1974), 14:243–58.

22. William James, "Notebook V" (1862), JFP.

23. William James to his daughter, Peg [Mary Margaret], 26 August 1900, *Letters of William James*, 2:130–32.

24. William James to his mother, [c. September 1863,] *Letters of William James*, 1:46.

25. William James to his sister, Alice, 19 November 1867 and 23 June 1868, JFP. On James's interest in women, see Anderson, "'Worst Kind of Melancholy,'" 375–80.

26. See the James and Holmes correspondence in Perry, *Thought and Character*, 1:504–20.

27. William James to Thomas W. Ward, 27 March 1866, *Letters of William James*, 1:76. James's problems were accentuated in 1870 by the tragic death from tuberculosis of Minny Temple. For a highly speculative account of both the nature and impact of the James-Temple friendship or love affair, see Alfred Habegger, "New Light on William James and Minny Temple," *New England Quarterly* 60 (March 1987): 28–53.

28. Catherine Drinker Bowen, *Yankee from Olympus: Justice Holmes and His Family* (Boston: Little, Brown and Co., 1944), 223–24.

29. Quoted in Perry, *Thought and Character*, 1:228.

30. The melancholic pattern of James's life is explored in King, *Iron of Melancholy*.

31. William James to his brother Henry, 25 May 1873, JFP; and Feinstein, *Becoming William James*, 206–22.

32. See Perry, *Thought and Character*, 1:233–35.

33. William James to his father, 5 September 1867, *Letters of William James*, 1:98.

34. Quoted in Gay Wilson Allen, *William James: A Biography* (New York: Viking Press, 1967), 142.

35. Howard M. Feinstein, "The Use and Abuse of Illness in the James Family Circle: A View of Neurasthenia as a Social Problem," in *Ourselves/Our Past: Psychological Approaches to American History*, ed. Robert Brugger (Baltimore: Johns Hopkins Univ. Press, 1981), 233–36.

36. William James, "Diary," [1868–1873,] JFP.

37. William James, *The Varieties of Religious Experience* (Cambridge: Harvard Univ. Press, 1985), 134–35.

38. William James to his brother Bob, 27 January 1868, Perry, *Thought and Character*, 1:258–59; and William James to Tom Ward, January 1868, *Letters of William James*, 1:129–32. Thoughts of suicide were part of the famous crisis before he was "saved" by Renouvier's doctrine of belief. Prior to his new-found faith in free will and freedom, James considered suicide to be the "most manly way" to deal with his problems. See James, "Diary," [1868–1873,] JFP.

39. This is the thesis of Feinstein, *Becoming William James;* see my review essay "Fathers and Sons, Texts and Contexts: Henry James, Sr., and William James," *American Quarterly* 36 (Winter 1984): 719–24.

40. Lacan, "Desire and Interpretation," 20. On the social aspects of Hamlet's madness, see Terence Eagleton, *Shakespeare and Society: Critical Studies in Shakespearean Drama* (New York: Schocken Books, 1967), 53.

41. Perry refers to this period as one of "doubt and discouragement" in *Thought and Character*, 1:243.

42. William A. Clebsch, "The Human Religiousness of William James," in *American Religious Thought: A History* (Chicago: Univ. of Chicago Press, 1973), 142.

43. James, *Varieties of Religious Experience*, 123. The term *anhedonia* is used in Henry Samuel Levinson, *The Religious Investigations of William James* (Chapel Hill: Univ. of North Carolina Press, 1981), 43–45.

44. James, *The Principles of Psychology*, 2:1152–55. *Abulia* is imaginatively applied to James's depression in Anderson, "'Worst Kind of Melancholy,'" 376–78.

45. James, *The Will to Believe*, 117.

46. Ibid., 115.

47. William James to Tom Ward, March [?] 1869, *Letters of William James*, 1:152–53.

48. Bruce Kuklick, *The Rise of American Philosophy: Cambridge, Massachusetts, 1860–1930* (New Haven: Yale Univ. Press, 1977), 160–61. James is quoted in Perry, *Thought and Character*, 1:722.

49. On the vogue of Herbert Spencer, see Richard Hofstadter, *Social Darwinism in American Thought* (Boston: Beacon Press, 1962), 31–50; and E. L. Youmans, ed., *Herbert Spencer on the Americans and the Americans on Herbert Spencer* (New York: D. Appleton and Co., 1883). A judicious account of the limitations of Spencerianism in American thought is Robert C. Bannister, *Social Darwinism: Science and Myth in Anglo-American Social Thought* (Philadelphia: Temple Univ. Press, 1979).

50. Quoted in Gerald E. Myers, *William James: Life and Thought* (New Haven: Yale Univ. Press, 1986), 43.

51. Although James was famous for his opposition to Spencerian and Hegelian monism, one recent critic finds James to have been a closet-Hegelian, someone who actually hoped for a theoretic reconciliation of contrasting motives and experiences, a higher unity that would preserve the singularity of experience while bringing all experience into a vision of higher unity. See Myers, *William James*, 396.

52. See William James, "Bain and Renouvier," 325, and "German Pessimism," 310–14, both in *Essays, Comments, and Reviews* (Cambridge: Harvard Univ. Press, 1987).

53. William James, "Diary," 4 April 1873, JFP.

54. William James, "The Dilemma of Determinism," in *The Will to Believe*, 136.

55. Thomas Davidson, Review of "Is Life Worth Living?" *International Journal of Ethics* 6 (January 1896): 233.

56. William James, "Diary," 4 April 1873, JFP.

57. Friedrich Nietzsche, *Ecce Homo*, ed. and trans. Walter Kaufmann (New York: Vintage Books, 1969), 246.

58. William James, *"Genie und Entartung"* (Genius and Degeneration), in *Essays, Comments, and Reviews*, 513.

59. William James, "Is Life Worth Living?" in *The Will to Believe*, 34–56.

60. William James to his brother Henry, 5 April 1868, Perry, *Thought and Character*, 1:269.

61. William James to his brother Henry, 13 April 1868, Perry, *Thought and Character*, 1:272.

62. Ibid. This Hamletian view of the universe was supplemented by James's reading of Schopenhauer in this period. Although put off by his pessimism, James found that Schopenhauer had a similar conception of a chaotic universe. James later noted that Schopenhauer spoke "the concrete truth about the ills of life." But after James had recovered from his depression and the implications of his view of the universe as an

"abyss of horrors," he rarely had anything positive to remember about Schopenhauer's work. Although he usually granted his philosophical opponents some degree of praise, James excoriated Schopenhauer for his "loud-mouthed pessimism" and described him as "a dog who would rather see the world ten times worse than it is, than lose his chance of barking at it." James would come to maintain that one might avert Schopenhauerian pessimism only by throwing oneself into the flux of experience. James weakly praises Schopenhauer in *Some Problems of Philosophy* (Cambridge: Harvard Univ. Press, 1979), 19. James's diatribe against him, which was occasioned by a request for support for a monument to Schopenhauer to be erected in Frankfort, is in Perry, *Thought and Character*, 1:724.

63. S. P. Fullinwider, "William James's 'Spiritual Crisis,'" *Historian* 38 (November 1975): 55.

64. Robert J. Richards, *Darwin and the Emergence of Evolutionary Theories of Mind and Behavior* (Chicago: Univ. of Chicago Press, 1987), 415n.

65. Feinstein, *Becoming William James*, 242. While agreeing that the confluent textual descriptions of the breakdowns is significant, John Owen King attempts to go beyond the family circle into the realm of myth. In his interpretation, William's panic fear is a modern secularized version of the Puritan conversion narrative turned into the language of Victorian neurosis. James's panic fear was not, in King's estimation, a response to any particular neurosis. It was instead a "struggle reflecting the division" within James's soul caused by the crisis of vocation as well as the contradictions of his culture. King, *Iron of Melancholy*, 159–64.

66. James, *Varieties of Religious Experience*, 134–35.

67. King, *Iron of Melancholy*, 201; and John Clendenning, *The Life and Thought of Josiah Royce* (Madison: Univ. of Wisconsin Press, 1985), 168–75.

68. Sandra M. Gilbert and Susan Gubar, *The Madwoman in the Attic: The Woman Writer and the Nineteenth-Century Literary Imagination* (New Haven: Yale Univ. Press, 1979). On the naturalist writers and their Darwinian flair, see Cynthia Eagle Russett, *Darwin in America: The Intellectual Response, 1865–1912* (San Francisco: W. H. Freeman and Co., 1976), 173–202.

69. The best evaluation of Darwin's influence upon James's emotional and intellectual life is Robert J. Richards, "The Personal Equation in Science: William James's Psychological and Moral Uses of Darwinian Theory," *Harvard Library Bulletin* 30 (1982): 387–425.

70. For the contours of this position in James's thought, see John J. McDermott, "The Promethean Self and Community in the Philosophy of William James," in *Streams of Experience: Reflections on the History and Philosophy of American Culture* (Amherst: Univ. of Massachusetts Press, 1986), 44–58.

71. For the importance of James's vocational security, see Feinstein, *Becoming William James*, 316–29. The significance of Alice Gibbens to James's recovery is stressed in R.W.B. Lewis, "The Courtship of William James," *Yale Review* 73 (Winter 1984): 177–98; Mark Schwehn, "Making the World: William James and the Life of the Mind," *Harvard Library Bulletin* 30 (1982): esp. 439f.; and Marian C. Madden and Edward H. Madden, "The Psychosomatic Illnesses of William James," *Thought* 54 (December 1979): 391.

72. Perry, *Thought and Character*, 1:336–59.

73. Ibid., 1:323.

74. On Renouvier, see the intelligent discussion in Richards, "Personal Equation in Science," esp. 394–98.

75. Perry, *Thought and Character*, 1:323.

76. William James, "Notebook" (c. 1870), JFP; and *Letters of William James,* 1:147–48.

77. Perry, *Thought and Character,* 1:343.

78. James, *The Principles of Psychology,* 1:126. Hereafter volume and page numbers for citations in this book will be cited in the text.

79. Gordon Allport, "The Productive Paradoxes of William James," *Psychological Review* 50 (1943): esp. 96–97.

80. Jacques Barzun, *A Stroll with William James* (New York: Harper and Row, 1983), 34.

81. In his typically ironic style, James, at the point of completing his manuscript, begged to differ with this assessment. Writing to Henry Holt on 9 May 1890, James announced that "no one could be more disgusted than I at the sight of the book. *No* subject is worth being treated of in 1000 pages! . . . as it stands it is this or nothing—a loathsome, distended, tumefied, bloated, dropsical mass, testifying to nothing but two facts: *1st,* that there is no such thing as a *science* of psychology, and *2nd,* that WJ is an incapable." Quoted in F. O. Matthiessen, *The James Family: A Group Biography* (New York: Alfred A. Knopf, 1947), 371.

82. William James, "What the Will Effects," in *Essays in Psychology* (Cambridge: Harvard Univ. Press, 1983), 218–19.

83. Richards, *Darwin,* 445–47.

84. Although in *The Principles of Psychology* James states that this situation contained "in miniature form the data for an entire psychology of volition" (2:1133), he recognized that it was not sufficient for allowing certain desires or ideas to prevail. This thesis might be speculatively applied to James's own recovery from depression. Perhaps the outside stimulus and attention given by college teaching and marriage were sufficient to allow a lapse of consciousness that cleared the space for more responsible ideas to prevail, in the process ending his habits of inactivity and doubt.

85. Myers, *William James,* 199.

86. Quoted in Perry, *Thought and Character,* 2:90.

87. Quoted in Feinstein, *Becoming William James,* 309.

88. Francis Bowen, *The Principles of Metaphysical and Ethical Science Applied to the Evidence of Religion* (Boston: Hickling, Swan and Brown, 1855), 308; and Houghton, *Victorian Frame of Mind,* 20–21.

89. On Bain and James, see the classic essay by Max H. Fisch, "Alexander Bain and the Genealogy of Pragmatism," *Journal of the History of Ideas* 15 (June 1954): 413–44; Feinstein, *Becoming William James,* 308–13; and King, *Iron of Melancholy,* 172–75.

90. William James, *Talks to Teachers on Psychology* (Cambridge: Harvard Univ. Press, 1983), 53.

CHAPTER FOUR
Tedium Vitae

1. Quoted in Ralph Barton Perry, *The Thought and Character of William James,* 2 vols. (Boston: Little, Brown and Co., 1935), 1:343.

2. On the origins of pragmatism, see Dickinson S. Miller, "Some of the Tendencies of Professor James's Work," *Journal of Philosophy* 7 (24 November 1910): 643

3. *The Diary of Alice James,* ed. Leon Edel (New York: Penguin Books, 1982), 67–68.

4. Gay Wilson Allen, *William James: A Biography* (New York: Viking Press, 1967), 341–42.

5. Clifford Geertz, *The Interpretation of Cultures* (New York: Basic Books, 1973), 14.

6. Peter Conn, *The Divided Mind: Ideology and Imagination in America, 1898–1917* (Cambridge: Cambridge Univ. Press, 1983); and Neil Harris, ed., *The Land of Contrasts: 1880–1901* (New York: George Braziller, 1970), 6.

7. Max Nordau, *Degeneration* (1895, New York: Howard Fertig, 1968), 7, 15 passim. The metaphor of weightlessness is from Nietzsche. A full discussion of the term as it applies to American culture is in T. J. Jackson Lears, *No Place of Grace: Antimodernism and the Transformation of American Culture, 1880–1920* (New York: Pantheon Books, 1981), 32–47. Lears's entire volume is an excellent reference point for the cultural conflicts of this era.

8. Alan Trachtenberg, *The Incorporation of America: Culture and Society in the Gilded Age* (New York: Hill and Wang, 1982), 141.

9. Henry Adams, *The Education of Henry Adams: An Autobiography* (Boston and New York: Houghton, Mifflin Co., 1918), 379–90.

10. There is massive literature on neurasthenia's iron grip upon the American elite in this period. The classic text is George M. Beard, *American Nervousness: Its Causes and Consequences* (1881; reprint, New York: Arno Press, 1972). See also James B. Gilbert, *Work without Salvation: America's Intellectuals and Industrial Alienation, 1880–1910* (Baltimore: Johns Hopkins Univ. Press, 1977), esp. 31–43; Barbara Sicherman, "The Paradox of Prudence: Mental Health in the Gilded Age," *Journal of American History* 62 (March 1976): 890–912; and Charles E. Rosenberg, "George M. Beard and American Nervousness," in *No Other Gods: On Science and American Social Thought* (Baltimore: Johns Hopkins Univ. Press, 1978), 98–108.

11. William James, "Vacations" (1873), in *Essays, Comments, and Reviews* (Cambridge: Harvard Univ. Press, 1987), 3–4.

12. *Herbert Spencer on the Americans and the Americans on Herbert Spencer* (New York: D. Appleton and Co., 1883), 30–31, 35; and William James, "The Gospel of Relaxation," in *Talks to Teachers on Psychology* (Cambridge: Harvard Univ. Press, 1983), 152.

13. Adams, *Education*, 238–41.

14. Henry Adams to Charles Milne Gaskell, 2 August 1910, *Letters of Henry Adams (1892–1918)*, 2 vols., ed. Worthington Chauncey Ford (Boston and New York: Houghton, Mifflin Co., 1938), 2:546.

15. There is a vast literature on the bureaucratization of American life. See, most usefully, Lears, *No Place of Grace*, 83–91; Gilbert, *Work without Salvation*, 31–66; and Daniel T. Rodgers, *The Work Ethic in Industrial America, 1850–1920* (Chicago: Univ. of Chicago Press, 1978), 65–93. On Taylor, see the impressive work by Harry Braverman, *Labor and Monopoly Capital: The Degradation of Work in the Twentieth Century* (New York and London: Monthly Review Press, 1974), 85–138.

16. The determinism of much of this fiction is discussed in Lee Clark Mitchell, "Naturalism and the Languages of Determinism," in *Columbia Literary History of the United States*, ed. Emory Elliott et al. (New York: Columbia Univ. Press, 1988), 525–45.

17. Charles E. Rosenberg, *The Trial of the Assassin Guiteau: Psychiatry and Law in the Gilded Age* (Chicago: Univ. of Chicago Press, 1968).

18. William Graham Sumner, "The Absurd Effort to Make the World Over," in *Social Darwinism: Selected Essays of William Graham Sumner* (Englewood Cliffs, N.J.: Prentice-Hall, 1963), 179–80.

19. On Spencer, see Richard Hofstadter, *Social Darwinism in American Thought* (Boston: Beacon Press, 1962), 31–50; and Robert C. Bannister, *Social Darwinism:*

Science and Myth in Anglo-American Social Thought (Philadelphia: Temple Univ. Press, 1979).

20. See the oftentimes brilliant, if sometimes rash, presentation in James Turner, *Without God, without Creed: The Origins of Unbelief in America* (Baltimore: Johns Hopkins Univ. Press, 1985).

21. Lears, *No Place of Grace,* 17–18; and Walter Houghton, *The Victorian Frame of Mind* (New Haven: Yale Univ. Press, 1957), 421–22.

22. William James to George H. Howison, 17 July 1895, *The Letters of William James,* 2 vols., ed. Henry James (Boston: Atlantic Monthly Press, 1924), 2:22–23.

23. John E. Smith, *The Spirit of American Philosophy* (London: Oxford Univ. Press, 1968), 41.

24. Perry, *The Thought and Character of William James,* 2:674.

25. Stuart Hampshire, "William James," in *Modern Writers and Other Essays* (New York: Alfred A. Knopf, 1970), 106. This contention is open to debate. Some would argue that Descartes fully wrote his own autobiography into the text of his philosophy. See Jonathan Rees, *Philosophical Tales: An Essay on Philosophy and Literature* (London and New York: Metheun, 1987), 5–30.

26. William James, "Preface," in *The Will to Believe* (Cambridge: Harvard Univ. Press, 1979), 7. James delineates the limitations of his intended audience in a letter to Dickinson Miller, 30 August 1896, *Letters of William James,* 2:49–50.

27. William James to L. T. Hobhouse, 12 August 1904, *Letters of William James,* 2:207–8.

28. William Johnson, "Pragmatism, Humanism, and Religion," *Princeton Theological Review* 6 (1908): 546.

29. William James, "Is Life Worth Living?" in *The Will to Believe,* 39–40. James described one of the audiences for his "Will to Believe" message as "listless" and unable to comprehend or unwilling to deal with the crux of his argument. William James to Sarah Whitman, 24 April 1896, James Family Papers, Houghton Library, Harvard University. Hereafter cited as JFP.

30. William James, "Preface," in *The Will to Believe,* 7.

31. Williams James, *The Principles of Psychology,* 2 vols. (Cambridge: Harvard Univ. Press, 1981), 1:6.

32. The cultural and scientific edge of pragmatism, as developed by James as well as by Dewey, is brilliantly discussed in David A. Hollinger, "The Problem of Pragmatism in American History," in *In the American Province: Studies in the History and Historiography of Ideas* (Bloomington: Indiana Univ. Press, 1985), 23–43.

33. William James, "Review" of William Clifford, *Lectures and Essays* and *Sensing and Thinking* (1879), in *Essays, Comments, and Reviews,* 356, 360.

34. William James, "The Will to Believe," in *The Will to Believe,* 27. Hereafter essays in this volume will be cited in the text.

35. Some would argue that James had a "prudential" rather than a moral sense of obligation in his "Will to Believe." However, when James was presented with a moral challenge, he presented "a foolish-not-to-believe and -not-immoral-to-believe" argument. See James C. S. Wernham, *James's Will-to-Believe Doctrine: A Heretical View* (Kingston and Montreal: McGill-Queen's Univ. Press, 1987), 3–4.

36. See, typically, Vernon Lee, "The Need to Believe: An Agnostic's Notes on Professor Wm. James," *Fortnightly* 72 (1 November 1899): 838.

37. Rosenberg, *No Other Gods,* 12.

38. William James, "Herbert Spencer, Dead" (1903), in *Essays in Philosophy* (Cambridge: Harvard Univ. Press, 1978), 99.

39. Ibid., 96.

40. Science's coaptation of religion is discussed in Turner, *Without God, without Creed*. The response of Protestant theologians to the intellectual challenge of Darwinism is brilliantly considered in James R. Moore, *The Post-Darwinian Controversies: A Study of the Protestant Struggle to Come to Terms with Darwin in Great Britain and America, 1870–1900* (Cambridge: Cambridge Univ. Press, 1979); see especially his discussion of George Frederick Wright as a "Christian Darwinian," 280–98. The contours of liberal Protestantism around the turn of the century are elucidated in William R. Hutchinson, *The Modernist Impulse in American Protestantism* (Cambridge: Harvard Univ. Press, 1976). A good discussion of Beecher's theology and import is Clifford E. Clark, Jr., *Henry Ward Beecher: Spokesman for Middle-Class America* (Urbana: Univ. of Illinois Press, 1978).

41. An excellent discussion of James's case in "The Dilemma of Determinism" is in Gerald E. Myers, *William James: His Life and Thought* (New Haven: Yale Univ. Press, 1986), 394–95. See also Patrick Kiaran Dooley, *Pragmatism as Humanism: The Philosophy of William James* (Chicago: Nelson-Hall, 1974), 65–68.

42. The reasons for choosing one vision of the universe over the other, which resided in a law of parsimony as much as need and consistency, is presented in William James, "The Sentiment of Rationality" (1879), in *The Will to Believe*, 57–60.

43. John E. Smith, *Purpose and Thought: The Meaning of Pragmatism* (Chicago: Univ. of Chicago Press, 1984), 23; and Dooley, *Pragmatism as Humanism*, 77.

44. Smith, *The Spirit of American Philosophy*, 46.

45. William James to Jane Addams, 12 February 1907, *William James: Selected Unpublished Correspondence, 1885–1910*, ed. Frederick J. Down Scott (Columbus: Ohio State Univ. Press, 1986), 433–34.

46. William James to Henry Holt, 22 November 1878, in Perry, *Thought and Character*, 2:35. James also discusses and condemns Spencerian determinism in *The Varieties of Religious Experience* (Cambridge: Harvard Univ. Press, 1985), 298–99.

47. Grant Allen, "Hellas and Civilisation," *Gentleman's Quarterly* 245 (August 1878): 166–67; and Allen, "Nation-Making: A Theory of National Character," *Gentleman's Magazine* 245 (November 1878): 580–91. This controversy between James and Allen is discussed in Gilbert, *Work without Salvation*, 19–20.

48. Myers, *William James: His Life and Thought*, 412.

49. John Fiske, "Sociology and Hero-Worship: An Evolutionist's Reply to Dr. James," *Atlantic Monthly* 47 (January 1881): 75–84.

50. Grant Allen, "The Genesis of Genius," *Atlantic Monthly* 47 (March 1881): 377.

51. Grant Allen to William James, 18 March [1881?], JFP.

52. William James, "The Importance of Individuals," in *The Will to Believe*, 191–93. James used the carpenters statement again in "The Gospel of Relaxation," in *Talks to Teachers on Psychology*, 122–23.

53. Turner, *Without God, without Creed*, 208.

54. Houghton, *The Victorian Frame of Mind*, 73.

55. Quoted in Lewis Feuer, "The East Side Philosophers: William James and Thomas Davidson," *American Jewish History* 76 (March 1987): 294.

56. William James discussed his own wrestling with suicide in a letter to his friend Tom Ward, January 1868, *Letters of William James*, 1:129–32.

57. Walter Benjamin, *Charles Baudelaire: Lyric Poet in the Era of High Capitalism* (London: New Left Books, 1973), 74–80. An excellent analysis of Benjamin and the crisis of modernity is in David Frisby, *Fragments of Modernity: Theories of Modernity in the Work of Simmel, Kracauer, and Benjamin* (Cambridge: MIT Press, 1986), 187–265.

58. William James to Benjamin Paul Blood, 20 June 1896, *Letters of William James,* 2:38–40.

59. Myers, *William James: His Life and Thought,* 407–8.

60. James, *Varieties of Religious Experience,* 120.

61. Not all readers found the Jamesian imperative to moral struggle a sufficient argument against the appeal of suicide. Thomas Davidson remarked that in the face of a set of "dim, chaotic *maybes* of the formless unknown," young people needed more than "a mere game of hazard, in which, no matter how well you play, you are as likely to lose as to win." Davidson feared that this Jamesian conclusion would be "injurious, especially to reflective young men, such as those for whom Professor James's paper was originally written." Davidson, Review of "Is Life Worth Living?" *International Journal of Ethics* 6 (January 1896): 233.

62. Lionel Trilling, "William Dean Howells and the Roots of Modern Taste," in *The Opposing Self* (New York and London: Harcourt Brace Jovanovich, 1978), 67–91. Howells is quoted in Thomas Bender, *New York Intellect: A History of Intellectual Life in New York City, from 1750 to the Beginnings of Our Own Time* (New York: Alfred A. Knopf, 1987; Baltimore: Johns Hopkins Univ. Press, 1988), 192.

63. William James to his wife, Alice, 29 August 1900, JFP.

64. William James to H. G. Wells, 11 September 1906, *Letters of William James,* 2:259–60.

65. James, *Varieties of Religious Experience,* 293–94.

66. Ibid., 294. James read Thorstein Veblen at the same time as he composed these lines. His only reaction to Veblen's *The Theory of the Leisure Class* (1899) was to find it "awfully jolly in spots, & telling much truth." See William James to Grace Norton, 21 October 1900, *William James: Selected Unpublished Correspondence,* 241–42.

67. James, "What Makes a Life Significant," in *Talks to Teachers on Psychology,* 150–67. For information on the publishing history of that text, see 243. Hereafter quotes from this essay will be cited in the text. The essay is treated at some length by Trachtenberg, *Incorporation of America,* 140–44.

68. Harold Frederic, *The Damnation of Theron Ware, or Illumination* (Lincoln: Univ. of Nebraska Press, 1985), 237.

69. William James to his wife, Alice, 26 July 1896, *Letters of William James,* 2:43–44.

70. James, "The Dilemma of Determinism," 130.

71. William James, "The Powers of Men" (1907), in *Essays in Religion and Morality* (Cambridge: Harvard Univ. Press, 1982), 151.

72. William James, "The Moral Philosopher and the Moral Life," in *The Will to Believe,* 153, 155.

CHAPTER FIVE
The Discourse of Heroism

1. On Saltus and the American *fin-de-siècle,* see Howard Mumford Jones, *The Age of Energy: Varieties of the American Experience, 1865–1915* (New York: Viking Press, 1973), 347–48; and Claire Sprague, *Edgar Saltus* (New York: Twayne Publishers, 1968).

2. John Higham, "The Reorientation of American Culture in the 1890s," in *Writing American History: Essays in Modern Scholarship* (Bloomington: Indiana Univ. Press, 1970), 73–102.

3. Lew Wallace, *Ben Hur: A Tale of the Christ* (New York: Heritage Press, 1960), 318.

4. Henry Nash Smith, *Virgin Land: The American West as Symbol and Myth* (Cambridge: Harvard Univ. Press, 1970), 100.

5. Walter Houghton, *The Victorian Frame of Mind* (New Haven: Yale Univ. Press, 1957), 305–6, 312–16.

6. T. J. Jackson Lears, *No Place of Grace: Antimodernism and the Transformation of American Culture, 1880–1920* (New York: Pantheon Books, 1981).

7. For a sustained and insightful discussion of Eakins as a painter of the heroic in modern life, see Elizabeth Johns, *Thomas Eakins: The Heroism of Modern Life* (Princeton: Princeton Univ. Press, 1983).

8. Lears, *No Place of Grace*, 118.

9. H. Stuart Hughes, *Consciousness and Society: The Reorientation of European Social Thought, 1890–1930* (New York: Alfred A. Knopf, 1958); Carl Schorske, *Fin-de-Siècle Vienna: Politics and Culture* (New York: Alfred A. Knopf, 1980); and Eugen Weber, *France: Fin de Siècle* (Cambridge: Harvard Univ. Press, 1986).

10. Theodore Roosevelt, "The Strenuous Life," in *The Strenuous Life: Essays and Addresses* (New York: Century Co., 1901), 1–24. Roosevelt had been a student in James's psychology class at Harvard. There is nothing to indicate that he learned much in it. On this score, see Gay Wilson Allen, *William James* (New York: Viking Press, 1967), 169.

11. Henry Adams, *The Education of Henry Adams* (Boston and New York: Houghton, Mifflin Co., 1918), 417.

12. On social reform in this period, see Robert M. Crunden, *Ministers of Reform: The Progressives' Achievement in American Civilization, 1889–1920* (New York: Basic Books, 1982). This is not to suggest that the reform ethos of the Progressive era had a sobering effect upon female reform activism. The cases of Florence Kelly and Jane Addams belie this.

13. Robert Dallek, *The American Style of Foreign Policy: Cultural Politics and Foreign Affairs* (New York: New American Library, 1983), 43–44. Roosevelt's "belligerent nationalism" is seen as a reaction against the flabbiness of American culture in John M. Cooper, *The Warrior and the Priest: Woodrow Wilson and Theodore Roosevelt* (Cambridge: Belknap Press of Harvard Univ. Press, 1983), 36.

14. Personal issues also may have contributed to Roosevelt's imperial impulse. Cooper persuasively argues that Roosevelt's jingoism may have been a form of compensation, an attempt to right what he perceived as the sole blot upon the otherwise spotless record of his father's life—a failure to participate in the Civil War. See Cooper, *Warrior and the Priest*, 12–13. Cloaked as it was in the heroic, James's fierce anti-imperialism was perhaps another method for settling old scores with nonparticipation in the Civil War.

15. I do not intend to suggest that a doctrine of the heroic, predicated upon a traditional vision of the individual and heroic will, might not serve some custodians of culture and power as a hegemonic device during a period of intense class conflict. Certainly the Gramscian formula or social-control thesis proceeds in a reasonable, if somewhat predictable, direction when it contends that workers who had exercised free will and individualism would be less likely to embrace socialism and consequently would not pose as great a threat to the health of the capitalist state. The espousal or assimilation of ideals of individual autonomy and energetic action would translate into a more docile working class. Here the worker might blame himself or herself for deficiencies in status or success. Or the worker, at least one submitting to the logic of this cultural ideal, would work with greater vigor upon the assumption that directed labor existed as both its own reward and as a necessary means toward success.

But it appears that the ideal of the heroic life, while it might have eventuated in a diminution of radicalism, at least in the manner in which T. J. Jackson Lears has formulated the issue, need not have resulted in this exact scenario. Workers also developed their own forms of the heroic and found little difficulty incorporating them into their own ideological superstructure; the rhetoric of the Industrial Workers of the World is a case in point. However, Lears is correct in positing consumerism and nationalism as powerful hegemonic tools in the corruption of working-class radicalism. More importantly, James's discourse of heroism was primarily directed at elite Americans—not to energize them to control better those beneath them in the social structure, but rather to enable them to escape both numbing tedium and religious doubts. This agenda had currency within the context of James's own life as well as his intellectual and cultural concerns. Although the implications of his ideas are wide-ranging, they can hardly be deemed hegemonic. Jamesian relativism might have undermined, rather than supported, the complacent assumptions of capitalism. For the argument on hegemony by Lears, see his essay "The Concept of Cultural Hegemony: Problems and Possibilities," *American Historical Review* 90 (June 1985): 567–93.

16. Jacques Barzun, *Classic, Romantic and Modern* (New York: Anchor Books, 1961), 14.

17. Quoted in Gerald E. Myers, *William James: His Life and Thought* (New Haven: Yale Univ. Press, 1986), 317. The Promethean theme, as it applies to James's life and thought, is fully developed in John J. McDermott, *Streams of Experience: Reflections on the History and Philosophy of American Culture* (Amherst: Univ. of Massachusetts Press, 1986), 52.

18. William James, *Pragmatism* (Cambridge: Harvard Univ. Press, 1975), 10.

19. Spencer's view is quoted and discussed in J.D.Y. Peel, *Herbert Spencer: The Evolution of a Sociologist* (New York: Basic Books, 1971), 137.

20. William James, "The Thing and Its Relations" (1905), in *Essays in Radical Empiricism* (Cambridge: Harvard Univ. Press, 1976), 46.

21. William James, "Remarks on Spencer's Definition of Mind as Correspondence" (1878), in *Essays in Philosophy* (Cambridge: Harvard Univ. Press, 1978), 21.

22. The teleological imperative in James's philosophy and psychology is succinctly presented in Marcus Peter Ford, *William James's Philosophy: A New Perspective* (Amherst: Univ. of Massachusetts Press, 1982), 59–74.

23. William James, *A Pluralistic Universe* (Cambridge: Harvard Univ. Press, 1977), 117–18.

24. William James, "A World of Pure Experience" (1904), in *Radical Empiricism*, 42.

25. William James, "Humanism and Truth" (1904), in *The Meaning of Truth* (Cambridge: Harvard Univ. Press, 1975), 9.

26. William James, *Pragmatism* (Cambridge: Harvard Univ. Press, 1975), 142.

27. Ralph Barton Perry, *The Thought and Character of William James*, 2 vols. (Boston: Little, Brown and Co., 1935), 2:674.

28. Howard M. Feinstein, *Becoming William James* (Ithaca: Cornell Univ. Press, 1984), 156.

29. George M. Fredrickson, *The Inner Civil War: Northern Intellectuals and the Crisis of Union* (New York: Harper Torchbooks, 1968), 232.

30. Chauncey Wright to Miss Grace Norton, 18 July 1875, *Letters of Chauncey Wright*, ed. James Bradley Thayer (Cambridge: John Wilson and Son, 1878), 342–43.

31. William James, "The Importance of Individuals" (1890), *The Will to Believe* (Cambridge: Harvard Univ. Press, 1979), 191.

32. William James to Wincenty Lutoslawski, n.d., quoted in Perry, *Thought and Character*, 2:271–72.

33. William James, "Is Life Worth Living?" (1895), in *Will to Believe*, 39–40.

34. William James, *The Varieties of Religious Experience* (Cambridge: Harvard Univ. Press, 1985), 291.

35. Recent discussions of the various shadings of James's will to believe doctrine are succinctly and controversially analyzed in James C. S. Wernham, *James's Will-to-Believe Doctrine: A Heretical View* (Kingston and Montreal: McGill-Queens Univ. Press, 1987).

36. Much of my discussion of *Varieties* has profited from the excellent analysis of Henry Samuel Levinson, *The Religious Investigations of William James* (Chapel Hill: Univ. of North Carolina Press, 1981). Also helpful is Don Browning, "William James's Philosophy of the Person: The Concept of the Strenuous Life," *Zygon* 10 (June 1975): 162–74.

37. Quoted in Perry, *Thought and Character*, 2:383.

38. James, *Varieties*, 290–91; and James, "The Moral Philosopher and the Moral Life," in *The Will to Believe* (Cambridge: Harvard Univ. Press, 1979), 160–61.

39. On James's moral philosophy, see Bernard P. Brennan, *The Ethics of William James* (New York: Bookman Associates, 1961); and John K. Roth, *Freedom and Fate: The Ethics of William James* (Philadelphia: Westminster Press, 1969). The best study of the connections between James's ethics and epistemology is Ellen Kappy Suckiel, *The Pragmatic Philosophy of William James* (Notre Dame, Ind.: Univ. of Notre Dame Press, 1982).

40. James, "Moral Philosopher," in *Will to Believe*, 161.

41. James, *Varieties*, 407.

42. Ibid., 406–7. See also William James, *Some Problems of Philosophy* (Cambridge: Harvard Univ. Press, 1979), 407. Wittgenstein, who was an admirer of *Varieties*, essentially agreed with James. "For a truly religious man," Wittgenstein contended, "nothing is tragic." Quoted in *Ludwig Wittgenstein: Personal Recollections*, ed. Rush Rees (Totowa, N.J.: Rowman and Littlefield, 1981), 122.

43. Lionel Trilling, *Sincerity and Authenticity* (Cambridge: Harvard Univ. Press, 1972), 95–96.

44. The account of James's panic fear is in *Varieties*, 134–35.

45. Ibid., 134–35. See also William James to Thomas Davidson, 8 January 1882, quoted in Perry, *Thought and Character*, 1:737–38.

46. William James, "Response to Questionnaire on Religious Views" (1904), in *Letters of William James*, 2 vols., ed. Henry James (Boston: Atlantic Monthly Press, 1920), 2:212–13.

47. William R. Hutchinson, *The Modernist Impulse in American Protestantism* (New York: Oxford Univ. Press, 1982), esp. 76–110, 145–84.

48. James, *Varieties*, 407. Hereafter citations of this book will be cited in the text.

49. For a very strong reading of James's religious views in the light of his Darwinian understanding of the saintly type, see Levinson, *Religious Investigations*, 130–31.

50. William James, *Talks to Teachers on Psychology* (Cambridge: Harvard Univ. Press, 1983), 97.

51. William James, "The Will to Believe," in *The Will to Believe*, 33.

52. Quoted in Myers, *William James*, 460.

53. William H. Mallock asked the same question, "Is Life Worth Living?" He answered "yes," if one believed in moral necessity and God's existence. Mallock sought traditional religious grounds upon which to formulate moral action. He recommended that modern men and women place their trust in the doctrines of Catholicism. Only through such devotion and faith would modern individuals find the ultimate and enduring truths necessary to live. James read Mallock's work and probably formulated

his title and response from this reading. See Mallock, *Is Life Worth Living?* (New York: G. P. Putnam's Sons, 1879), 260, 303, 318–20. The James quote is in his essay "Is Life Worth Living?" in *Will to Believe*, 56.

54. Philip Rieff, *The Triumph of the Therapeutic: Uses of Faith after Freud* (New York: Harper, 1968), 11.

55. George Santayana to Corliss Lamont, 8 June 1950, *The Letters of George Santayana*, ed. Daniel Cory (New York: Charles Scribner's Sons, 1955), 394.

56. This genre of literature is briefly yet insightfully discussed in Daniel T. Rodgers, *The Work Ethic in Industrial America, 1850–1920* (Chicago: Univ. of Chicago Press, 1974), 74–75, 258. A typical example of this intense interest is Walter A. Wyckoff, *The Workers: An Experiment in Reality*, 2 vols. (New York: Charles Scribner's Sons, 1897–98).

57. This theme is fully discussed in Lears, *No Place of Grace*, esp. xiii, 5.

58. William James to his brother Henry, 15 August 1895, JFP.

59. William James, "What Makes a Life Significant," in *Talks to Teachers on Psychology*, 154–56.

60. Ibid., 155.

61. Ibid.

62. William James to his daughter, Mary [Mary Margaret], 6 May 1903, *Letters of William James*, 2:192–93; and to his son Henry, 14 August 1899, JFP. For James's thoughts on nature and primitivism, see William Leverette, "Simple Living and the Patrician Academic: The Case of William James," *Journal of American Culture* 6 (Winter 1983): 36–43. On the general phenomenon of the "rediscovery" of nature in the years after the decline of the romantic movement, see David E. Shi, *The Simple Life: Plain Living and High Thinking in American Culture* (New York: Oxford Univ. Press, 1986), 154–74.

63. James, "What Makes a Life Significant," 162–63. He offered the same critique of miners, finding that they "spend everything instead of saving." William James to his brother Henry, 15 August 1895, JFP.

64. William James, "The Energies of Men," in *Essays in Religion and Morality* (Cambridge: Harvard Univ. Press, 1982), 132.

65. James did, of course, announce that "overtension and jerkiness and breathlessness and intensity and agony of expression" led to neurasthenia. Yet he also noted that the lack of adequate stimulation—the apparent failure of Americans to find a "theatre for heroism"—contributed to the weak qualities of many individuals. See William James, "The Gospel of Relaxation," in *Talks to Teachers on Psychology*, 122–23.

66. William James to Thomas Ward, 27 March 1866, *Letters of William James*, 1:78.

67. An excellent discussion of the connection between James and positive thinking, emphasizing the moralism and traditional imperatives to discipline in the mind-cure movement, is Donald Meyer, *The Positive Thinkers: Religion as Pop Psychology from Mary Baker Eddy to Oral Roberts* (New York: Pantheon Books, 1980), 315–24.

68. James, "The Gospel of Relaxation," 117–18; and James, "The Energies of Men," 141.

69. William James, "*Review* of Human Personality" (1903), in *Essays in Psychical Research* (Cambridge: Harvard Univ. Press, 1986), 207. On his general views of the promise and problems of psychic research, see James, "The Confidences of a 'Psychical Researcher'" (1909), in ibid., 361–75. The best analysis of the relationship between spiritualism and reformist impulses in American society is R. Laurence Moore, *In Search of White Crows: Spiritualism, Parapsychology, and American Culture* (New York: Oxford Univ. Press, 1977). On how the question of immortality might be con-

nected with psychic research and human freedom, see Eugene Fontinell, *Self, God, and Immortality: A Jamesian Investigation* (Philadelphia: Temple Univ. Press, 1986).

70. On James and mind cure, see Meyer, *Positive Thinkers*, 315–24. Less impressive, but still useful, is Gail Thain Parker, *Mind Cure in New England: From the Civil War to World War I* (Hanover, N.H.: Univ. Press of New England, 1973), 151–68.

71. James, *Varieties*, 94.

72. James, "Energies of Men," 139.

73. Ibid., 139–41; William James to Wincenty Lutoslawski, 6 May 1906, *Letters of William James*, 2:252–55.

74. James, "Energies of Men," 134.

75. William James, "The Feeling of Effort," in *Essays in Psychology* (Cambridge: Harvard Univ. Press, 1983), 120.

76. James, *Principles of Psychology*, 2:1181–82.

77. This view of Royce's call for a fight against evil is developed in R. Jackson Wilson, *In Quest of Community: Social Philosophy in the United States, 1860–1920* (New York: Oxford Univ. Press, 1970), 144, 158.

78. Bruce Kuklick, *The Rise of American Philosophy: Cambridge, Massachusetts, 1860–1930* (New Haven: Yale Univ. Press, 1977), 259. Kuklick discusses the problem of evil in Royce's philosophy more fully in *Josiah Royce: An Intellectual Biography* (Indianapolis: Hackett Publishing Co., 1985), 62–65 passim.

79. Edward H. Madden, "Introduction," in *Will to Believe*, xxvi–xxxii. For an earlier critique of James's propensity to sanction the presence of evil, see the riveting review by Vernon Lee, "The Need to Believe: An Agnostic's Notes on Professor James," *Fortnightly* 72 (1 November 1899): 838–39. On Lee, see Stephen Donadio, *Nietzsche, Henry James, and the Artistic Will* (New York: Oxford Univ. Press, 1978), 22–31.

80. James, "The Will to Believe," in *The Will to Believe*, 130

81. On the contours of James's conception of a finite God, see Madden, "Introduction," xxxvi.

82. James, *Varieties*, 48.

83. The essay "On Some Mental Effects of the Earthquake" is in *Essays in Psychology*, 331–38. I discuss this essay in "William James and the 'Weightless' Nature of Modern Existence," *San Jose Studies* 12 (Spring 1986): 7–19.

84. On these lectures and their preparation, see James to his wife, Alice, 10 January 1906; and to his brother Henry, 1 February 1906, both in JFP. See also William James's notes for the Stanford University course Philosophy 1A and "Syllabus Used in Philosophy 1A," JFP.

85. Fredrich Paulsen, *Introduction to Philosophy*, trans. Frank Thilly, with a preface by William James (New York: Henry Holt and Co., 1895), 158–80.

86. William James to Tom Ward, March [?] 1869, *Letters of William James*, 1:152.

87. For James's problems with the argument from design, using the Mont Pelée example, see *Pragmatism*, 56–59.

88. James, *Varieties*, 346n.7.

89. William James to Miss Frances R. Morse, 12 April 1906, *Letters of William James*, 2:247–50; and to his brother Henry, 22 April 1906, JFP.

90. James, "Some Mental Effects," 332.

91. A full account of James's trip into San Francisco is in a draft letter from Dr. William Freeman Snow to Henry James, 9 May 1920, and in James's "Diary for 1906," both in JFP.

92. James, "Some Mental Effects," 336–37.

93. James, "Energies of Men," 134.

94. James, "Some Mental Effects," 338; and Perry, *Thought and Character,* 2:273.
95. James, "Some Mental Effects," 336–38.
96. Dr. William Freeman Snow to Henry James, 9 May 1920, JFP.
97. Ibid., 338.

CHAPTER SIX
The Imperial Imperative

1. William James to Maxwell J. Savage, 4 January 1910, quoted in *William James: Selected Unpublished Correspondence, 1885–1910,* ed. Frederick J. Down Scott (Columbus: Ohio State Univ. Press, 1986), 534.

2. The best and most recent examinations of William James's technical philosophy are Gerald E. Myers, *William James: His Life and Thought* (New Haven: Yale Univ. Press, 1986); John J. McDermott, *Streams of Consciousness: Reflections on the History and Philosophy of American Culture* (Amherst: Univ. of Massachusetts Press, 1986), esp. 44–58; 107; John E. Smith, *Purpose and Thought: The Meaning of Pragmatism* (Chicago: Univ. of Chicago Press, 1978); H. S. Thayer, *Meaning and Action: A Critical History of Pragmatism* (Indianapolis: Bobbs-Merrill Co., 1968), 133–64; Ellen Kappy Suckiel, *The Pragmatic Philosophy of William James* (Notre Dame, Ind.: Univ. of Notre Dame Press, 1982); and Marcus Peter Ford, *William James's Philosophy: A New Perspective* (Amherst: Univ. of Massachusetts Press, 1982).

3. William James, *A Pluralistic Universe* (Cambridge: Harvard Univ. Press, 1977), 10–11.

4. *The Diary of Alice James,* ed. Leon Edel (New York: Penguin Books, 1964), 68.

5. William James to William Dean Howells, Nov. 16, 1900, Howells Papers, Houghton Library, Harvard University. William James to Sarah Whitman, 3 March 1898, James Family Papers, Houghton Library, Harvard University. Hereafter cited as JFP. Ralph Barton Perry, *The Thought and Character of William James,* 2 vols. (Boston: Little, Brown and Co., 1924), 2:303–4.

6. Typical expressions of his illnesses appear in letters from the period of 1892 to 1902. See, for example, William James to his wife, Alice, 1 or 2 August 1892; to his brother Henry, 17 December 1893; 15 September 1894; and to his wife, 9 September 1900, all in JFP. See also James to George H. Howison, 17 July 1895, *The Letters of William James,* 2 vols., ed. Henry James (Boston: Atlantic Monthly Press, 1920), 2:22–23. Perry, *Thought and Character of William James,* 2:208. The most sustained rendering of James's illnesses during this period is Daniel W. Bjork, *William James: The Center of His Vision* (New York: Columbia Univ. Press, 1988), 228–39.

7. William James to Miss Rosina H. Emmet, 9 September 1898, *Letters of William James,* 2:84.

8. Private postscript to letter from William James to Hugo Munsterberg, 17 November 1899, *Selected Unpublished Correspondence,* 207.

9. "Although the stream of his interests was never confined to any narrow channel, the last decades can be clearly distinguished by their emphasis: in the '80s on general psychology, in the '90s on ethics and religion, and between 1900 and 1910 on systematic philosophy. Instead of devoting his last years to faith, practice, and sermonizing, he gave them to the technicalities of theoretical inquiry." Perry, *Thought and Character,* 2:363. The division between technical and public philosophy was never as exact as Perry suggests.

10. William James to Carl Stumpf, 6 August 1901, quoted in Perry, *Thought and Character,* 2:199–200. In this letter, James announced his desire to elaborate "a more systematic *Weltanschauung*" in the time remaining in his life. It appears that at this

time he did not consider the elaboration of his philosophical system to be inconsistent with his roles as a public philosopher and political activist. In an earlier letter to Stumpf, James had expressed his movement away from psychology and toward "becoming exclusively a moralist and metaphysician." James suggested that the "proper occupation for one's latter years" was the contemplation of "the widest view of life." James to Stumpf, 10 September 1899, quoted in Perry, *Thought and Character*, 2:195. James reiterated his desire to return to America and to captain its destiny through his role as an intellectual in a letter to Frances R. Morse, 17 September 1899, *Letters of William James*, 2:102–3.

11. Christopher Lasch, "The Anti-Imperialists, the Philippines, and the Inequality of Man," in *The World of Nations: Reflections on American History, Politics and Culture* (New York: Vintage, 1974), 70–79.

12. Robert L. Beisner, *Twelve against Empire: The Anti-Imperialists, 1898–1900* (New York: McGraw-Hill Book Co., 1974), 18–34.

13. Ibid., 76; William M. Armstrong, *E. L. Godkin: A Biography* (Albany: SUNY Press, 1978), esp. 180–92; and Armstrong, *E. L. Godkin and American Foreign Policy, 1865–1900* (New York: Bookman Associates, 1957), 185–99. See also Kermit Vanderbilt, *Charles Eliot Norton: Apostle of Culture in a Democracy* (Cambridge: Harvard Univ. Press, 1959).

14. Patrick Brantlinger, *Bread and Circuses: Theories of Mass Culture as Social Decay* (Ithaca: Cornell Univ. Press, 1983), 17–52. The discourse of heroism linked James to the imperialists more than did any discourse of racism. And, more than the Mugwumps, James was attracted to and fascinated by the phenomenon of the mob. But James was not totally without connections to the Mugwump ideology.

15. Henry Steele Commager, *The American Mind: An Interpretation of American Thought and Character since the 1880's* (New Haven: Yale Univ. Press, 1950), 318. Commager also listed a Mugwump preference for all things English. Yet he did admit that not all Mugwumps were either superficial or doctrinaire.

16. William James to E. L. Godkin, 15 April 1889, and to Henry L. Higginson, 8 February 1903, both in *Letters of William James*, respectively, 1:284; 2:182.

17. William James, "Great Men and Their Environment," in *The Will to Believe* (Cambridge: Harvard Univ. Press, 1979), 182–83.

18. William James, "Robert Gould Shaw: Oration by Professor William James" (1897), in *Essays in Religion and Morality* (Cambridge: Harvard Univ. Press, 1982), 72.

19. William James to his brother Henry, 5 June 1897, *Letters of William James*, 2:60–61.

20. William James, "The Gospel of Relaxation," in *Talks to Teachers on Psychology* (Cambridge: Harvard Univ. Press, 1983), 120. See also William James to F.W.H. Myers, 5 February 1896, *Letters of William James*, 2:32–33.

21. See the compilation of James's weaknesses in George R. Garrison and Edward H. Madden, "William James—Warts and All," *American Quarterly* 29 (Summer 1977): 207–21, esp. 215–17.

22. William James to E. L. Godkin, 15 April 1889, *Letters of William James*, 1:284. Although James rejected anti-Semitism and promised to boycott the hotel, he carefully added that Thomas Davidson should be certain that a room at another hotel might first be secured. See William James to Davidson, 2 May 1899, JFP.

23. See William James to his brother Henry, 9 May 1886, *Letters of William James*, 1:252.

24. For E. L. Godkin's views, see Godkin to Charles Eliot Norton, 29 November [1908], *The Gilded Age Letters of E. L. Godkin*, ed. William Armstrong (Albany:

SUNY Press, 1974), 515. Said Godkin: "Morals in this community . . . are entirely gone. I fancy that the press has had a good deal to do with this awful decline—the greatest in human history. But then the people make the press."

25. William James to Hugo Munsterberg, 2 September 1896, quoted in Perry, *Thought and Character,* 2:146.

26. William James to his wife, Alice, 27 August 1896; 1 November 1908, JFP. See also James to C. W. Eliot, 24 December 1900, quoted in Perry, *Thought and Character,* 1:434.

27. Beisner, *Twelve against Empire,* ix; and Geoffrey Blodgett, "The Mugwump Reputation, 1870 to the Present," *Journal of American History* 66 (March 1980): 867–86. William James certainly joined the Mugwumps in urging that structure—or "socialist equilibrium," as he once called it—be brought to bear upon the unruly American economy. James was cognizant that the 1890s, a period of severe economic depression, social dislocation, and class conflict, represented a watershed for Americans.

28. William James to Mrs. Charles Russell Lowell, 6 December 1903, *Selected Unpublished Correspondence,* 324.

29. Walter LaFeber presents a detailed evaluation and discussion of the events surrounding the Venezuelan controversy, but one always influenced by his "economic" reading and his desire to find commercial interests at the center of American foreign policy. Thus, in good New Left fashion, he downplays the psychic motivations that may have also entered into the culture of imperialism. LaFeber, *The New Empire: An Interpretation of American Expansion, 1860–1898* (Ithaca: Cornell Univ. Press, 1963), esp. 280–81; 242–83. A less detailed but still useful account is Armstrong, *E. L. Godkin and American Foreign Policy,* 179–84.

30. William James to E. L. Godkin, Christmas Eve [1895], Godkin Papers, Houghton Library, Harvard University. Portions of this letter are in *Letters of William James,* 2:28.

31. William James, "Answer to Roosevelt on the Venezuelan Crisis" (1896), in *Essays, Comments, and Reviews* (Cambridge: Harvard Univ. Press, 1987), 152–53.

32. William James to E. L. Godkin, Christmas Eve [1895], *Letters of William James,* 2:28.

33. Lewis Wurgaft, *The Imperialist Imagination: Magic and Myth in Kipling's India* (Middletown, Conn.: Wesleyan Univ. Press, 1983), xi–xx.

34. William James, "The True Harvard," in *Essays, Comments, and Reviews,* 76.

35. William James, "The Social Value of the College-Bred," in *Essays, Comments, and Reviews,* 109; and James to his brother Henry, 26 January 1896, JFP.

36. William James to William Salter, 8 April 1898, JFP. James also saw the war resulting in new responsibilities for, and maturity of, the nation. James to his brother Henry, 12 June 1898, JFP.

37. William James to his brother Henry, 3 May 1898, JFP.

38. William James to William Salter, 21 April 1898, JFP.

39. William James to his brother Henry, 10 April 1899, JFP.

40. William James to Théodore Flournoy, 17 June 1898, *The Letters of William James and Théodore Flournoy,* ed. Robert C. LeClair (Madison: Univ. of Wisconsin Press, 1966), 72–73; and James to his brother Henry, 20 February 1899, JFP.

41. William James, "Review of Gustave LeBon, *The Crowd*" (1897), in *Essays, Comments, and Reviews,* 533–35.

42. For the negative aspects of the crowd, see the analysis of James Mark Baldwin's work in R. Jackson Wilson, *In Quest of Community: Social Philosophy in the United States, 1860–1920* (London: Oxford Univ. Press, 1968), 73–74.

43. William James, *The Principles of Psychology* (Cambridge: Harvard Univ. Press, 1981), 2:1045.

44. William James to Théodore Flournoy, 27 January 1903, *Letters of William James and Théodore Flournoy*, 136.

45. James's concern with the crowd phenomenon reached its highest point when he wrote letters to the editor protesting the lynching craze in the South. See "A Strong Note of Warning Regarding the Lynching Epidemic" (1903) and "Epidemic of Lynching" (1903), both in *Essays, Comments, and Reviews*, 170–76.

46. William James to François Pillon, 15 June 1898, *Letters of William James*, 2:73–75.

47. William James to Carl Stumpf, 10 July 1901, quoted in Perry, *Thought and Character*, 2:199.

48. John Murray Cuddihy, *The Ordeal of Civility: Freud, Marx, Lévi-Strauss, and the Jewish Struggle with Modernity* (New York: Delta Books, 1974). Cuddihy limits his hypothesis to Jewish thinkers but also argues that a key to understanding them was their impassioned theoretical attempt to break down the barriers separating the elite from outsiders. To a degree, James was involved in the same enterprise.

49. William James to his brother Henry, 21 June 1899, JFP.

50. William James to Théodore Flournoy, 17 June 1898, *Letters of William James and Théodore Flournoy*, 72–73.

51. There is sharp debate about the degree of James's involvement in anti-imperialist agitation. The strongest condemnation of James's activism as peripheral is by George R. Garrison and Edward H. Madden. They contend that James's anti-imperialism was naïve and minimal, confined to letters to editors. See their essay "William James—Warts and All," 207–9. A similar critique of the limitations of James's anti-imperialism is in Stuart Creighton Miller, *The American Conquest of the Philippines, 1899–1903* (New Haven: Yale Univ. Press, 1982), 110. The opposite position, which contends that, compared to other university professors of his era, James was a strong advocate of anti-imperialism, is in Myers, *William James*, 429–30. I believe that it is not crucial to assess or to judge the correctness of James's political positions, difficult though they are to avoid. Instead, my analysis primarily attempts to connect his concepts of imperialism to his other ideas and to the context of his life and culture. Once this is accomplished, the importance of anti-imperialism to James's life and thought becomes apparent.

52. This was not to prove an easy task. Beisner charts the shift from optimism to abject pessimism in James's view of American foreign policy. See Beisner, *Twelve against Empire*, 42–45.

53. James, *A Pluralistic Universe*, 7.

54. For James's responses to Tolstoy, see James to his wife, Alice, 24 July 1896; to Théodore Flournoy, 30 August 1896, both in *Letters of William James*, 40 and 41, respectively; to his brother Henry, 28 September 1896; and to his wife, Alice, 28 March 1903, both in JFP.

55. William James to his wife, Alice, 24 July 1896, *Letters of William James*, 2:41. The extent of James's ethnic pluralist sentiments is demonstrated in Larry C. Miller, "William James and Twentieth-Century Ethnic Thought," *American Quarterly* 31 (Fall 1979): 533–55.

56. H. Fielding [Harold Fielding-Hall], *The Soul of a People* (London: Richard Bentley and Son, 1898), 3, 17, 362–63.

57. William James to his wife, Alice, [17 April] 1899, JFP.

58. William James, "The Philippines Again" (1899), Letter to the Editor of the Evening Post, 161; and "The Philippine Question" (1899), Letter to the Editor of the

Boston Evening Transcript, both in William James, *Essays, Comments, and Reviews,* 159–62.

59. William James, "On Some Hegelisms," in *The Will to Believe,* esp. 207.

60. William James, "Notebook O" (c. 1905), JFP.

61. William James, "The Philippine Tangle," in *Essays, Comments, and Reviews,* 157.

62. The complete text of the talk is in James, *Talks to Teachers on Psychology,* 132–49. Hereafter references to this lecture will be cited in the text. On the importance of this essay to James, see the editorial comments appended to *Talks to Teachers on Psychology,* 244. See also William James to Dr. G. C. Ferrari, 13 October 1902, Typescript, Special Collection on Educators, Stanford University Library; and Perry, *Thought and Character,* 2:265–66.

63. I discuss Emerson, James, and public philosophy in my essay "Ralph Waldo Emerson and William James as Public Philosophers," *Historian* 49 (November 1986): 49–63. See also Mary Kupiec Cayton, "The Making of an American Prophet: Emerson, His Audiences, and the Rise of the Culture Industry in Nineteenth-Century America," *American Historical Review* 92 (June 1987): 597–620.

64. William James to Mrs. Henry Whitman, 7 June 1899, *Letters of William James,* 2:90.

65. William James to William Dean Howells, 16 November 1900, Howells Papers, Houghton Library, Harvard University.

66. James, *Principles,* 2:924.

67. William James, "The Experience of Activity" (1905), in *Essays in Radical Empiricism* (Cambridge: Harvard Univ. Press, 1976), 81.

68. James, *A Pluralistic Universe,* 27.

69. Ibid., 19.

70. James, *Essays in Religion and Morality,* 62.

71. William James to Wincenty Lutoslawski, 2 September 1896, *Selected Unpublished Correspondence, 1885–1910,* 147. The expansive message of "On a Certain Blindness" reappears in its companion piece, "What Makes a Life Significant" (c. 1898). The latter piece juxtaposes the tedium of the Chautauquans with the explosive energy of the working class. He damns modern-business civilization for "crowding out all other qualities." Business threatens heroism: "The higher heroisms and the old rare flavors are passing out of life." In a footnote adorning this ubiquitous lament for the heroic, James notes that readers might either interpret this complaint as a call to arms or logically reason that the Spanish-American War solved the need for heroism. This was not the case, for James explained in a footnote to the essay that recent "outbursts of the passion of mastery" exhibited in the war represented nothing more than "episodes in a social process which in the long run seems everywhere tending towards the Chautauquan ideals." Thus did James part company with the war policy of Roosevelt, while agreeing with him about the inherent validity and usefulness of a strenuous existence. See James, "What Makes a Life Significant," in *Talks to Teachers on Psychology,* 154. James never totally rejected Roosevelt and thought him a viable candidate for president of Harvard University. James admitted in 1909 that "I believe his [Roosevelt's] influence on our public life and on our people's feelings about public life has been of enormous value." See William James to Henry Lee Higginson, in *Life and Letters of Henry Lee Higginson,* ed. Bliss Perry (Boston: Atlantic Monthly Press, 1921), 361–62.

72. William James, "Remarks at the Peace Banquet," in *Essays in Religion and Morality,* 120.

73. William James to Ernest Howard Crosby, 8 November 1901, *Selected Unpublished Correspondence,* 268–69.

74. William James to his wife, Alice, 4 January 1895 and 16 May 1899, JFP; and William James to Mrs. E. L. Godkin, 14 March 1902, quoted in Perry, *Thought and Character,* 2:293–94. See also William James, "Address to the Anti-Imperialist League, Nov. 28, 1903," in *Report of the Fifth Meeting of the New England Anti-Imperialist League* (Boston: New England Anti-Imperialist League, 1903), 25.

75. James's plans to study the military mind are mentioned in Daniel B. Schirmer, "William James and the New Age," *Science and Society* 33 (Fall-Winter 1969): 441. See also Henry James's comments in *Letters of William James,* 2:284.

76. William James, *The Varieties of Religious Experience* (Cambridge: Harvard Univ. Press, 1985), 289–91.

77. Ibid., 292.

78. Ibid.

79. See the coverage of William James's speech "The Psychology of the War Spirit" —delivered at Stanford University on 21 February 1906, as reported in the *Daily Palo Alto*—in the textual comments in James, *Essays in Religion and Morality,* 251–52.

80. See James's discussion of these ideas in *Principles,* 2:1028–29. His strongest presentation of the case for war as a means of overcoming boredom is in "Remarks at the Peace Banquet," 122.

81. James, "Remarks at the Peace Banquet," 122. The Darwinian flavor in James's argument in favor of certain aspects of the military spirit is discussed in Julius S. Bixler, "Two Questions Raised by 'The Moral Equivalent of War,'" in *In Commemoration of William James, 1842–1942* (New York: Columbia Univ. Press, 1942), 58–71.

82. The publishing history of "The Moral Equivalent of War" is discussed in the editorial notes to *Essays in Religion and Morality,* 250–64. Hereafter references to this essay will be cited in the text.

83. It is interesting to speculate on how James's ideas jibe, in their bare outlines, with those of Edward Bellamy's *Looking Backward,* which James read. Whereas Bellamy's civic armies bring groans of boredom and images of totalitarianism, James's vision avoids these implications, but only at the cost of stressing the military passions and by avoiding a full and realistic vision of this futuristic utopia. James's ideas on "The Moral Equivalent of War," with an analysis of Bellamy's concepts, are in George M. Fredrickson, *The Inner Civil War: Northern Intellectuals and the Crisis of Union* (New York: Harper and Row, 1965), 217–38. On the totalitarian implications of Bellamy's utopia, see Arthur Lipow, *Authoritarian Socialism in America: Edward Bellamy and the Nationalist Movement* (Berkeley and Los Angeles: Univ. of California Press, 1982).

84. For a critique from a feminist perspective of James's thesis on the domination of nature, see Jane Roland Martin, "Martial Virtues or Capital Vices? William James's Moral Equivalent of War Revisited," *Journal of Thought* 22 (Fall 1987): 32–44.

85. Myers, *William James,* 602n.151.

86. As James explained this concept to H. G. Wells, "I myself believe that a compulsory blood-tax paid in mines, on freight-trains, winter cod fishermen, and dish washing . . . will have eventually to take the place of the military blood-tax, and will make the race more manly." James to Wells, 15 April 1908, JFP. John Dewey found "Moral Equivalent" one of James's weakest works. Dewey contended that James failed to understand fully the labor problem. Why, Dewey wondered, would working-class people need any artificial stimulus to hardihood when their daily lives were filled with all the strenuosity anyone might reasonably require? Quoted in Myers, *William James,* 602n.151.

87. Sigmund Freud, *An Outline of Psycho-Analysis* (New York: W. W. Norton and Co., 1969), 42.

88. Bertrand Russell, "Pragmatism," *Edinburgh Review* 209 (1909): 363–68.

CHAPTER SEVEN
The Politics of Pragmatism

1. William James, "The Function of Cognition," in *The Meaning of Truth* (Cambridge: Harvard Univ. Press, 1975), 32n.

2. William James, "Philosophical Conceptions and Practical Results" (1898), in *Pragmatism* (Cambridge: Harvard Univ. Press, 1975), 264–65. Hereafter references to both "Philosophical Conceptions" and *Pragmatism* will be cited in the text.

3. William James to his daughter, Margaret [Mary Margaret], 27 April 1907; James to Théodore Flournoy, 26 March 1907, both in James Family Papers, Houghton Library, Harvard University. Hereafter cited as JFP. William James to his brother Henry, 4 May 1907, *The Letters of William James*, 2 vols., ed. Henry James (Boston: Atlantic Monthly Press, 1920), 2:279.

4. For critiques of James's *Pragmatism* by James's contemporaries, see Arthur O. Lovejoy, "The Thirteen Pragmatisms," *Journal of Philosophy, Psychology, and Scientific Methods* 5 (January-February 1908): 5–12, 29–39; F. H. Bradley, "On the Ambiguity of Pragmatism," *Mind* 17 (April 1908): 226–37; G. E. Moore, "Professor James' 'Pragmatism,'" *Proceedings of the Aristotelian Society for the Study of Philosophy* 8 (1907–8): 33–77; Bertrand Russell, "Pragmatism," *Edinburgh Review* 209 (1909): 363–87; and Russell, "Transatlantic 'Truth,'" *Albany Review* 2 (January 1908): 393–410.

5. The fullest discussion, especially good on the controversy surrounding James's meaning and claims for *Pragmatism*, is Gerald E. Myers, *William James: His Life and Thought* (New Haven: Yale Univ. Press, 1986), 292–306.

6. James T. Kloppenberg, *Uncertain Victory: Social Democracy and Progressivism in European and American Social Thought, 1870–1920* (New York: Oxford Univ. Press, 1986), 145; and Brand Blanshard, "Metaphysics and Social Attitudes," *Social Frontier* 4 (December 1937): 79–81.

7. Albert William Levi, *Philosophy as Social Expression* (Chicago: Univ. of Chicago Press, 1974), 27.

8. Russell, "Pragmatism," 363; and Taylor, "Some Side Lights on Pragmatism," *University Magazine* (McGill University) 3 (April 1904): 45. Many commentators favorably or unfavorably stressed pragmatism's "Americanism." Some saw James's doctrine as expressive of the worst aspects of the American capitalist ethos. This was the position expressed most forcefully by James G. Huneker, James's contemporary. A more favorable view of the Americanism in *Pragmatism* expressed a hearty individualism, a frontier spirit; it captured the era's democratic ethos. Thus did William Caldwell, Professor of Moral Philosophy at McGill University, exclaim: "It may well be that the common reason of mankind has as much to learn from Americanism in the department of theory as it has already been obliged to learn from this same quarter in the realm of practice." James's philosophical protagonist Josiah Royce also recognized, not disapprovingly, an American spirit of strenuosity, ethical behavior, and openness to diverse perspectives within James's philosophy.

Emphasis upon the American nature of pragmatism, especially in light of the wildly diverse readings of exactly what constituted that character, does not take one far in terms of understanding the social expression of *Pragmatism*. The very generality of the descriptive term *American* confounds, and the vast multiplicity of possible readings endures too hardily without illumination. However, many commentators were also quite emphatic and exact in seeing the epistemology of James's text as leading to, or supportive of, a political position of imperialism. Although they were, no doubt, aware of his impassioned and sustained antagonism to the imperial stance, analysts of Jamesian pragmatism uncovered a subtext within the philosophical argument, one that unerringly pointed in the direction of an imperial, rapacious will.

On these issues, see James G. Huneker, "A Philosophy for Philistines," in *The Pathos of Distance* (New York: Charles Scribner's Sons, 1913), 251–52; and William Caldwell, "Pragmatism as Americanism," in *Pragmatism and Idealism* (London: Adam and Charles Black, 1913), 169. See also Josiah Royce, "William James and the Philosophy of Life," in *William James and Other Essays in the Philosophy of Life* (New York: Macmillan, 1911), 36. Evaluations of the connection between Americanism and pragmatism are H. S. Thayer, *Meaning and Action: A Critical History of Pragmatism* (Indianapolis: Bobbs-Merrill Co., 1968), 432–47; David A. Hollinger, "The Problem of Pragmatism in American History," in *In the American Province: Studies in the History and Historiography of Ideas* (Bloomington: Indiana Univ. Press, 1985), 26; and Henry Steele Commager, *The American Mind: An Interpretation of American Thought and Character since the 1880s* (New Haven: Yale Univ. Press, 1950), 91–98.

9. Literary critic Frank Lentricchia has made a daring attempt to connect James's pragmatism with his anti-imperialism. But Lentricchia posits too simple and direct a relationship, often brushing aside the complexity of James's arguments in both philosophy and politics. See his "The Return of William James," *Cultural Critique*, no. 4 (Fall 1986): 5–31. A version of this essay is in "On the Ideologies of Poetic Modernism, 1890–1913: The Example of William James," in *Reconstructing American Literary History*, ed. Sacvan Bercovitch (Cambridge: Harvard Univ. Press, 1986), 220–49.

10. William James to David Starr Jordan, 10 July 1899, David Starr Jordan Papers, Stanford University Archives; and James to his brother Henry, 12 June 1898, 4 July 1898, JFP. See also James to William M. Salter, 8 April 1898, JFP. On the passion of the crowd, see James to Théodore Flournoy, 17 June 1898, *The Letters of William James and Théodore Flournoy*, ed. Robert C. LeClair (Madison: Univ. of Wisconsin Press, 1966), 72–73.

11. George Howison to Thomas Davidson, 26 September 1898, Howison Papers, Bancroft Library, University of California, Berkeley; James was well aware of the controversy that his blasts against Kant caused. See William James to his wife, Alice, 28 August 1898, JFP. See also Howison to James, 18 November 1898, JFP. James's comments are interesting in light of how contemporary analysts of James see him as working in an explicitly neo-Kantian framework. For the best in this vein, see Murray G. Murphey, "Kant's Children: The Cambridge Pragmatists," *Transactions of the Charles S. Peirce Society* 4 (Winter 1968): 3–33; and Bruce Kuklick, *The Rise of American Philosophy: Cambridge, Massachusetts, 1860–1930* (New Haven: Yale Univ. Press, 1977), 272–74, 316–19. On Kant's use of the pragmatic idea, see Philip P. Wiener, *Evolution and the Founders of Pragmatism* (Philadelphia: Univ. of Pennsylvania Press, 1972), 23. James did not cease his attacks on Kant. In 1905 he declared human experience as pluralistic, in contrast to neo-Kantian systems of thought, which approach experience *"through the whole."* William James to Walter Taylor Marvin, 6 June 1905, *William James: Selected Unpublished Correspondence*, ed. Frederick J. Down Scott (Columbus: Ohio State Univ. Press, 1986), 376–77.

12. William James, "Humanism and Truth," in *Meaning of Truth*, 49n.4.

13. Russell, "Pragmatism," 384–85, 388. Russell's volatile critique of Jamesian pragmatism was hardly singular. Edwin E. Slosson, a popular-science writer, after

finding much to commend in pragmatism's scientific spirit, nonetheless fretted that "the pragmatic method is like the invention of gunpowder. This new controversial weapon carries further and can be used by anybody . . . in careless hands it may lead to intellectual anarchy." Slosson, "Pragmatism," *Independent* 62 (23 February 1907): 424.

The force of these criticisms has not been lessened by the passage of time. In the 1930s, critics' debates over the relationship between metaphysics and morals commonly suggested a close affinity between James's pragmatic doctrines and Benito Mussolini's fascism. In perhaps the most concise and damning assertion of the Bismarckian edge of pragmatism, Marxist Harry K. Wells denounced pragmatism as "the philosophy of imperialism." The charge of fascist affinity to pragmatism was voiced in Blanshard, "Metaphysics and Social Attitudes," 80. This assertion was strongly condemned in Horace M. Kallen, "Mussolini, William James, and the Rationalists," *Social Frontier* 4 (May 1938): 253–56. For Blanshard's reassertion of this thesis, see "Metaphysics and Social Attitudes: A Rejoinder," *Social Frontier* 4 (April 1938): 221. The Marxist emphasis upon pragmatism as an argument for capitalism and imperialism is in Harry K. Wells, *Pragmatism: Philosophy of Imperialism* (New York: Books for Libraries Press, 1954); R. Jeffrey Lustig, *Corporate Liberalism: The Origins of Modern American Political Theory, 1890–1920* (Berkeley and Los Angeles: Univ. of California Press, 1982); Victor J. Jerome, "Accident and History," *Philologica Pragensia* 6 (1963): 337–42; and Thelma Herman, "Pragmatism: A Study in Middle Class Ideology," *Social Forces* 22 (May 1944): 405–10.

14. William James to his brother Henry, 8 September 1908, JFP.

15. For a discussion of the "cash-value" metaphor in James's work, see my essay "William James and the Cash-Value Metaphor," *ETC: A Review of General Semantics* 42 (Spring 1985): 37–46.

16. Myers, *William James*, 302.

17. William James, *Essays in Radical Empiricism* (Cambridge: Harvard Univ. Press, 1976), 24, 43.

18. Richard Rorty, "Pragmatism, Relativism, and Irrationalism," in *The Consequences of Pragmatism* (Minneapolis: Univ. of Minnesota Press, 1982): 160–62.

19. John E. Russell, "Solipsism: The Logical Issue of Radical Empiricism," *Philosophical Review* 15 (November 1906): 606. See also Walter Pitkin, "A Problem of Evidence in Radical Empiricism," *Journal of Philosophy, Psychology, and Scientific Methods* 3 (22 November 1906): 645–50.

20. Moore, "Professor James' 'Pragmatism,'" 61–63.

21. James, *Meaning of Truth*, 5.

22. Julius Bixler, "Two Questions Raised by 'The Moral Equivalent of War,'" in *In Commemoration of William James: 1842–1942* (New York: AMS Press, 1967), 67; and David A. Hollinger, "William James and the Culture of Inquiry," in *In the American Province*, 9.

23. William James, *On Some Problems of Philosophy* (Cambridge: Harvard Univ. Press, 1979), 55.

24. William James, "The Pragmatist Account of Truth and Its Misunderstanders" (1907), in *Meaning of Truth*, 104.

25. Ibid., 113–15. James's definition of his philosophical position is in his letter to Dickinson L. Miller, 5 August 1907, *Letters of William James*, 2:295.

26. The importance of a scientific way of thinking to pragmatism is discussed in Hollinger, "William James and the Culture of Inquiry," 4–22; see also Morton White, *Social Thought in America: The Revolt against Formalism* (Boston: Beacon Press, 1957).

27. William James, "Notebook O" (c. 1905), "Notes for Wellesley Talk," both in JFP.

28. James, "Humanism and Truth," in *Meaning of Truth,* 47.

29. Moore, "Professor James' 'Pragmatism.'" A compelling account of the credits and debits of James's conception of truth is in Ellen Kappy Suckiel, *The Pragmatic Philosophy of William James* (Notre Dame, Ind.: Univ. of Notre Dame Press, 1982), 91–121.

30. William James to W. Cameron Forbes, 11 June 1907, *Letters of William James,* 2:289–90. James used almost the same terms as early as 1899; how amazing, James then wrote, that America "will puke up its own historical soul in five minutes, at a feather's touch." James to David Starr Jordan, 10 July 1899, David Starr Jordan Papers, Stanford University Archives.

31. James offered such sentiments quite often. See, typically, William James to E. L. Godkin, Christmas Eve [1895], *Letters of William James,* 2:28.

32. William James to William M. Salter, 11 September 1899, *Letters of William James,* 2:100–101.

33. William James to Miss Frances R. Morse, 17 September 1899; and James to William M. Salter, 11 September 1899, both in *Letters of William James,* 2:102–3, 101, respectively. The argument for the importance of local traditions in an age when the idols of certitude have been crushed is provocatively raised in Thomas L. Haskell, "The Curious Persistence of Rights Talk in the 'Age of Interpretation,'" *Journal of American History* 74 (December 1987): 984–1012.

34. Quoted in Myers, *William James,* 439–40.

35. William James, "Robert Gould Shaw: Oration by Professor William James," in *Essays in Religion and Morality* (Cambridge: Harvard Univ. Press, 1982), 72–74.

36. William James, *A Pluralistic Universe* (Cambridge: Harvard Univ. Press, 1977), 99.

37. On James's ethics, with stress on the responsibility of the individual, see James Campbell, "William James and the Ethics of Fulfillment," *Transactions of the Charles S. Peirce Society* 17 (Summer 1986): 224–40.

38. William James, "The Absolute and the Strenuous Life," in *Meaning of Truth,* 124.

39. William James to Charles A. Strong, 9 April 1907, *Letters of William James,* 2:270.

40. James, "The Absolute and the Strenuous Life," 123.

41. Myers, *William James,* 414.

42. John J. McDermott uses Promethean imagery to describe James's vision of human striving in his essay "The Promethean Self and Community in the Philosophy of William James," in *Streams of Experience: Reflections on the History and Philosophy of American Culture* (Amherst: Univ. of Massachusetts Press, 1986), 44–58.

43. Kuklick, *Rise of American Philosophy,* 309–12.

44. Kloppenberg, *Uncertain Victory,* 173–74.

45. *The Autobiography of W.E.B. DuBois* (New York: International Publishers, 1969), 133; Robert E. Park, *Race and Culture* (Glencoe, Ill.: Free Press, 1950), vi–vii; and Walter Lippmann, "An Open Mind: William James," *Everybody's Magazine* 23 (December 1910): 801.

46. George Santayana, *Character and Opinion in the United States: With Reminiscences of William James and Josiah Royce and Academic Life in America* (London: Constable and Co., 1920), 91.

47. William James, "The Social Value of the College-Bred," in *Essays, Reviews, and Comments* (Cambridge: Harvard Univ. Press, 1987), 106–12.

48. Ibid., 109.

49. William James, "What Makes a Life Significant," in *Talks to Teachers on Psychology* (Cambridge: Harvard Univ. Press, 1983), 166.

50. William James, "The Moral Equivalent of War," in *Essays in Religion and Morality*, 170. See also Ralph Barton Perry, *The Thought and Character of William James*, 2 vols. (Boston: Little, Brown and Co., 1935), 2:288–89.

51. James, "Moral Equivalent of War," 169.

52. William James to William Dean Howells, 13 November 1907, Howells Papers, Houghton Library, Harvard University.

53. William James to Jane Addams, 13 December 1909 and 12 February 1907, *William James: Selected Unpublished Correspondence: 1885–1910*, 528, 433–34, respectively.

54. William James, "Herbert Spencer" (1904), in *Essays in Philosophy* (Cambridge: Harvard Univ. Press, 1978), 107–22; and James to Ernest Howard Crosby, 23 October 1901, in *Selected Unpublished Correspondence*, 266.

55. William James to William Dean Howells, 16 November 1900, Howells Papers, Houghton Library, Harvard University.

56. William James to Howard Crosby, 8 November 1901, *Selected Unpublished Correspondence*, 268–69.

57. William James to Mrs. Henry Whitman, 7 June 1899, *Letters of William James*, 2:90.

58. William James to Wincenty Lutoslawski, 2 September 1896, *Selected Unpublished Correspondence*, 147.

59. James's success in this endeavor must remain uncertain, for readers as sophisticated as Russell and as politically reactionary as Mussolini have seen in James's epistemology and metaphysics a brief for the imperial will. This interpretation obviously was not James's intent. See Perry, *Thought and Character*, 2:575–78.

60. William James to F.C.S. Schiller, 1 February 1904, *Selected Unpublished Correspondence*, 335–36.

Index

WILLIAM JAMES, PUBLIC PHILOSOPHER

Designed by Ann Walston

Composed by
The Composing Room of Michigan, Inc.,
in Sabon text and display

Printed by BookCrafters
on 50-lb. Booktext Natural
and bound in Holliston Aqualite